HER MAJESTY VICTORIA.

Queen of Great Britain and Ireland, Empress of India

CANADA'S SONS
ON KOPJE AND VELDT

A HISTORICAL ACCOUNT OF THE
CANADIAN CONTINGENTS

Based on the official despatches of Lieutenant-Colonel W. D. Otter and the other Commanding Officers at the front; on the letters and despatches of such War Correspondents as C. Frederick Hamilton, S. C. Simonski, Stanley McKeown Brown, John Ewan and W. Richmond Smith.

BY

T. G. MARQUIS, B.A.

AUTHOR OF STORIES OF NEW FRANCE; STORIES FROM CANADIAN HISTORY; MARGUERITE DE ROBERVAL

WITH AN INTRODUCTORY CHAPTER
BY
GEORGE MUNRO GRANT, L.L.D

PRINCIPAL QUEEN'S UNIVERSITY

RICHLY ILLUSTRATED

The Naval & Military Press Ltd

Published by
The Naval & Military Press Ltd
Unit 10 Ridgewood Industrial Park,
Uckfield, East Sussex,
TN22 5QE England
Tel: +44 (0) 1825 749494
Fax: +44 (0) 1825 765701
www.naval-military-press.com
www.military-genealogy.com
www.militarymaproom.com

In reprinting in facsimile from the original, any imperfections are inevitably reproduced and the quality may fall short of modern type and cartographic standards.

AUTHOR'S PREFACE.

In the preparation of this story of the three Canadian Contingents that have been so heroically fighting the Empire's battles in South Africa, the utmost care has been taken to get only the most reliable information. It has been my aim to make a readable book, and at the same time one that will be an authentic history of the part played by Canada in the fierce war just terminated, the fiercest and most disastrous struggle that England has endured since the Crimea, and one that will doubtless cost her, before South Africa is in a safe and settled condition, vastly larger sums than any other war in her history.

Through the kindness of the Minister of Militia, the Honorable F. W. Borden, I have had access to the official reports of the officers commanding the various contingents, and have in this way been enabled to give with historical accuracy the events that have been reported and misreported in the despatches from the front. I have likewise examined with the greatest care the fine work done by such able Canadian correspondents as C. Frederick Hamilton and John Ewan, of the Globe; Stanley McKeown Brown, of the Mail and Empire; S. C. Von Tuger Simonski, of the Montreal Herald; W. Richmond Smith, of the Montreal Star, and others.

But what has been of greater value to me in grasping for myself the story of Canada's Sons at the front has been the hundreds of letters—honest, straightforward, soldierly letters—from sons and brothers and husbands in the contingents. Many letters written "between shots," with the smell of the powder still on the hand that wrote them; written by feverish trembling hands in the field hospital; written when the limbs were aching from the long march, with gnawing hunger and devouring thirst making the spirit long for Canada and home. Manly letters these! No boasting; all showing that the soldiers realized the awfulness of war but with no thought of leaving the field till the work they had volunteered to do was accomplished.

Part I of this book, "From Quebec to Bloemfontein," deals entirely with the work done by the First Contingent; Part II, "From Bloemfontein to Canada via Pretoria," describes not only the work of the First Contingent, but that of the Second and of the Strathcona's Horse as well. It has been thought proper to add an appendix giving the names of all the officers and men of the Royal Canadian Regiment of Infantry, the Canadian Mounted Rifles, the Royal Canadian Artillery, and the Strathcona's Horse. An honor roll of those who have died on the field of battle and in the hospital has likewise been given. The Spartan boy it is said, had to learn the names of the heroes of his native city who fell at Thermopylæ; it would be well if Canadians could at least turn when occasion demanded it to the names of those who died in the first war in which Canada showed herself an active, vital part of the Empire.

Principal Grant's preparatory chapter will be found of exceptional interest. No man in the Dominion is better fitted than he by his scholarship, his patriotism, and his loyalty to speak with authority on Canada and its relation to the Empire.

T. G. MARQUIS.

TABLE OF CONTENTS.

PART ONE.
FROM QUEBEC TO BLOEMFONTEIN.

INTRODUCTORY CHAPTER.

IMPERIAL SIGNIFICANCE OF THE CANADIAN CONTINGENTS
BY
GEORGE MONRO GRANT, LL.D.

                                                                  PAGE

John Morley's Attitude Towards Imperial Federation.—The Australasians in England's Hour of Need.—Canada's Attitude.—The World Surprised.—The Strength of the Imperial Tie.—A Living Unity Stronger Than Compacts or Statutes.—The United States' Law-Makers Unwittingly Help Imperial Unity.—Canada Her Own Treaty-Maker.—The Ultimatum and Its Effect.—Hon. Mr. Tarte and the Duke of Devonshire on Canada and the Empire.—No Startling Constitutional Change Expected.—Loyalty to Canada Demands Increased Military Force.............. 1

CHAPTER I.
RUMOURS OF WAR.

Rumours of War.—Canadian Sympathy With Uitlanders.—The Boer Underestimation of England's Strength.—The War-Cloud Thickens.—War Still Thought Improbable.—Kruger Stubborn, Chamberlain Determined.—Sir W. Laurier on the Situation.—Parliament Passes Sympathy Resolution.—Sir Charles Tupper Would Aid England.—Hon. Geo. E. Foster's Eloquent Address.—Canada Committed.—Uitlanders Appreciate Canada's Action.—War Inevitable.—The "Bitter Cry" of the Uitlander.—The Boer and Slavery.—England Waking Up.—The Ultimatum Launched.. 11

CHAPTER II.

WAR.

The Horrors of Modern War.—M. Bloch's "The War of the Future."—The Boers Prepared for War.—The Forts of Pretoria.—England's Difficulties.—Effects of Ultimatum on the Empire.—Kruger's Folly.—Dr. Leyds and the Hollander Clique.—Goldwin Smith and the War.—Gladstone's Magnanimity of 1881.—" Remember Majuba!"—Canada With England.—The People Demand Action on Part of Government.—First Shot Fired.—Canada's Offer of Troops Accepted by England............................ 29

CHAPTER III.

MOBILIZING THE TROOPS.

Recruiting Begun.—A Ready Response in Every Province.—The Patriotic Fund.—Her Majesty's Message.—Col. Otter's Farewell Words in Toronto.—The Commandant's Career.—Lieutenant-Colonel Buchan's Career.—The Troops Reach Quebec.—Conan Doyle and the Children of the Empire.—The Character of the Recruits.—Canadians Already in the Field.—England's Need of Canada's Aid.—A Foretaste of War.—The Minister of Militia Addresses the Troops.—Lord Wolseley on the Canadian Voyageurs.—Lord Minto's and General Hutton's Farewell Words.—On Board the Sardinian.. 47

CHAPTER IV.

ON THE SARDINIAN.

The Sardinian Leaves Canada.—Organizing the Overcrowded Ship.—Heavy Weather.—A Death on Board.—Drill Commenced.—Tropical Weather.—Bath Drill.—Passing the Time.—Kipling's Influence.—Sea Sights.—A Strange Visitor.—Passing Cape Verde Islands.—Preparations for Battle.—In the Tropics.—"A Sail!"—Letters Despatched Home.—Bad News From the Front.—Crossing the Line.—Band Concerts.—Maxim Gun and Revolver Practice.—" Land!"... 71

CHAPTER V.

AT CAPE TOWN.

Approaching Cape Town.—Table Mountain.—The Anchor Dropped.—The Scene in Table Bay.—The Sardinian Welcomed.—Bird's Eye View of Cape Town.—Sir A. Milner's Aide-de-Camp.—The Progress of the War.—Welcomed Ashore.—Preparations to Leave the Ship.—Off for Green Point Camp.—Sight Seeing.—The Pro-Boer Party in South Africa.—The Contingent Leaves for the Front.—Sir Alfred Milner's Personality.—The Imperial Problem Solved.. 91

CHAPTER VI.

ON THE ROAD TO THE FRONT.

Climbing the Karroo.—G. W. Steevens' on the Desert's Charm.—The Tedious Journey.—At De Aar.—A Dust Storm.—A Three Days' Sojourn in the Wilderness.—Off for Orange River.—Going Into Camp With the Regulars.—The Longing for a Green Field.—A Rain Storm.—Sleeping in Battle Array.—A Soldier Shot by a Picket.—The Chill of the African Night.—Building Sidings and Platforms.—Meeting Lieut.-Col. Girouard.—The Flash-Light of Kimberley.—Visiting the Hospital.—At the Grave of Captain Wood of the R. M. C.—A Step Nearer the Front.. 109

CHAPTER VII.

LEARNING THE GAME OF WAR.

At Belmont.—A Famous Battlefield.—In the Vicinity of Boer Forces.—The Regiment in Camp.—An Oasis in the Desert.—Outpost duty.—Camping on the Battle Field.—Doing Patrol Work.—Ghastly Memorials of the Fight.—Digging Trenches.—The New Drill.—Bullet-Scarred—Belmont Village.—A Call to Arms.—News of the Calamity at Magersfontein.—Cars Loaded With Wounded.—A Death in the Regiment.—The Men Being Disciplined.—Scarcity of Water.—Officers Not Distinguishable From the Men.—Julian Ralph on Officers Uniforms.—C. Fred. Hamilton Describes the New Drill.—Rifle Practice.—Christmas and Still at Belmont.. 127

CHAPTER VIII.

CHRISTMAS WEEK.

The Sabbath Calm.—Peace and Good-Will to Men.—The World Busy With Wars.—Preparations for Christmas.—A Call to Arms.—The Arrival of the Fowl.—A Dust-Devil.—Major Buchan Addresses the Men.—Christmas Dinner.—A Christmas Poem by One of the Contingent.—The Officers Dinner.—The Queen's Health.—The Queen the Centre of Imperial Life.—Christmas Sports.—An Impromptu Entertainment.—Colonel Pilcher in Command at Belmont.—The Regiment Tested.—More Troops in Camp.—A Blinding Dust Blizzard.—The Old Year Ending and War Still Distant.. 143

CHAPTER IX.

UNDER FIRE.

The Bandits of Douglas.—Marching to the Rebels Stronghold.—The Eve of Battle.—Approaching the Boer Laager.—The Enemy Sighted.—The Shrapnel Finds the Foe.—The Canadians Await the Advance.—In the Fire Zone.—Occupying Kopjes.—Beating Down the Enemy's Fire.—Agonizing Thirst.—Water Under Fire.—The Boers Trapped.—The Stronghold Seized at Bayonet's Point.—With the Wounded and Prisoners.—The Loot of the Camp.—The Importance of this Miniature Battle.—Burying a Comrade.—Occupying Douglas.—The March to Belmont 161

CHAPTER X.

THE CONTINGENT AT PLAY.

The Welcome to the Victors.—The Pastimes of the Regiment.—Target Practice.—Cricket in the Desert.—Tackling Ostriches.—The Ostrich Described.—A Difficult Bird.—Athletic Sports.—C Company Wins the Tent-Pitching.—The Tug-of-War.—The Australians as Athletes.—The Kaffir Boys' Race.—Looting.—Association Football With the Gordons.—Rugby at Bloemfontein.—Influence of Games on Imperial Unity...................... 181

CHAPTER XI.

A WEARY MONTH.

Hope Deferred.—Men Grow Lax in Their Duties.—An Expedition Into the Orange Free State.—The March.—At Commandant Lubbe's.—Looting the Farm.—A Close Call.—The Bivouac.—Back to Belmont.—Roberts and Kitchener at Cape Town.—Buller as a General.—His Place in This War.—Roberts Waiting Time.—The Campaign Hard on Horses.—A Third Expedition.—Enteric in the Regiment.—The Queen's Chocolate.—More Like War.—Major Denison Appointed to Lord Roberts' Staff.—Part of Regiment March to Graspan.—Roberts and Kitchener in Camp.—The Field-Marshal and His Chief-of-Staff Contrasted.—Canadians Brigaded with 19th Brigade under Colonel Smith-Dorrien 193

CHAPTER XII.

THE MARCH TO PAARDEBERG.

The Forward Movement Begins.—Three Companies at Graspan.—Marched Back to Belmont.—Forward in Earnest.—Bivouacking as Graspan.—Trying March to Ramdam.—On to Watervaal Drift.—Dragging Naval Guns Across the Riet.—Roberts Praises the Regiment.—At Wegdraal Drift.—Cronje Leaves Magersfontein.—Boers Outwitted by Roberts' Advance.—The Trenches at Magersfontein.—Kimberley Relieved.—The Canadians at Jacobsdal.—Cronje's Masterly Retreat.—General Kelly-Kenny and "Fighting Mac" in pursuit.—The Search-Light of Kimberley.—Boers Capture British Transports.—A night March.—Battle Ahead.—Fording the Modder 213

CHAPTER XIII.

THE FIRST BATTLE.

Through Dangerous Waters.—Cronje Entrapped.—The Canadians advance to Battle.—Under Fire.—The First Victim—Lying on the Plain.—The Scorching Sun.—Cronje's Men.—Firing on the Foe.—The Pluck of the Canadians.—Plan of Attack.—Heroism of Correspondents and Chaplains.—Father O'Leary's Narrow Escape.—

Captain Bell's Gallant Maxim-Gun Work.—Surgeon-Captain Fiset's Bravery.—The Fearless Ammunition Men.—Conduct of Officers.—Incidents of the Battle.—A Blessed Thunder-Storm.—Exhausted Men Asleep in Firing Line.—The Fatal Charge.—"The Men of Paardeberg."—Destructive Work of the British Guns...................... 233

CHAPTER XIV.

A WEEK OF WAR AND DEATH.

Battle Sights and Sounds.—Retreat in the Darkness.—Lost Comrades.—Bringing in the Wounded.—Boers Fire on Ambulance Men.—Ghastly Sights in the Moonlight.—Cronje Retreats up the Modder.—Clearing Field of the Dead.—A Fierce Bombardment.—Cronje's Position.—Canadians Again Under Fire.—The Terrifying "Pom-Pom."—Destruction of Boer Laager.—Bivouac in the Open.—Cronje's Resistance Aids Boer Cause.—English Admiration of Cronje.—Canadians as Outposts of the Army.—Weary Nights of Rain.—Cronje Requests Armistice.—Roberts Refuses.—The Modder a Sink of Death.—Week of War Thins Canadians' Ranks.—Rest Before the Final Blow.... 253

CHAPTER XV.

THE SURRENDER OF CRONJE.

Cronje Looking for Relief.—His Dauntless Courage.—The Boers Growing Desperate.—Majuba Day Recalled.—"Fighting Mac's" Part in Battle of Majuba Hill.—Fitz-Patrick's Description of the Fight.—Roberts Determines to Avenge Majuba Hill.—The Canadians in the Trenches.—The Canadians Advance through the Darkness.—A Deadly Fire Sweeps the Ranks.—The Fatal Order to Retire.—G and H Companies Hold Their Ground.—The Boers Raise White Flag.—"The Dawn of Majuba Day."—The Formal Surrender.—Roberts' Report of Canadian Gallantry.—The Beginning of the End.—Burying the Canadian Dead 273

CONTENTS. xi

CHAPTER XVI.
REST AFTER BATTLE.

Cronje's Troops.—Four Generations in the Boer Army.—
Cronje's Wife.—Hale's Picture of the Boers.—"Tommies"
Disgusted with the Ragged Rabble.—A Canadian Soldier's
Opinion of South Africa.—Boers Marched to Modder.—
Cronje's Stolid Silence.—The Canadians in the Boer
Laager.—The Fine Trenches.—The Loot of the Camp.—
Rest After Nine Days Fighting.—Away From Filthy
Paardeberg.—At Osfontein.—Laurier's Message Received.—British Authorities Congratulate Canada.—Looking Toward Bloemfontein................................ 293

CHAPTER XVII.
WITH THE SICK AND WOUNDED.

The Darker Side of War.—The Wounded on the Battlefield.—The Surgeons and Stretcher-Bearers.—The
Operating Tent.—Captain-Surgeon Fiset.—Many Canadians
in Hospital.—Trekking the Wounded From Paardeberg.—
On the Ambulance Train.—At Wynberg.—Hardships Endured by Sick.—Lieut. E. W. Morrison's Gloomy Picture
of Hospitals.—The Bloemfontein Experiences.—Lieut.-
Colonel Ryerson's Good Work at Kimberley.—Praised by
Methuen and Roberts.—Kipling and Conan Doyle with
the Canadian Sick.—Back to the Front or to England...... 307

CHAPTER XVIII.
TO BLOEMFONTEIN.

Forward Toward Bloemfontein.—The Enemy Make a
Stand.—The Artillery Duel at Poplar Grove.—The Trying
Forced March.—The Boer Reserves.—The Presidents'
Message.—Salisbury's Reply.—Canadians Outmarch
British Regiments.—The Battle of Abraham's Kraal.—
Desolation in Path of Army.—Nearing Bloemfontein.—
French's Good Work.—The Surrender of Bloemfontein.—
The Hoisting of the Union Jack.—Kruger and Steyn in
Flight.—Lord Roberts' Despatch to War Office.—Condition
of Canadians After a Month of Fighting.—Resting at
Bloemfontein.. 314

TABLE OF CONTENTS.

PART TWO.

FROM BLOEMFONTEIN TO CANADA VIA PRETORIA.

CHAPTER I.

A SECOND CALL TO ARMS.

                                                                                 PAGE

In October Canadians Thought the War Insignificant.—Boer Successes Change Public Opinion.—England Accepts Canada's Offer of a Second Contingent.—Mounted Infantry and Artillery Needed.—Canada Enrolls Four Squadrons of Mounted Rifles and Three Batteries.—Lieut.-Col. Lessard Chosen to Command 1st Batt. of Rifles.—Commissioner Herchmer in Command of 2nd Batt., and Lieut.-Col. Drury of the Artillery.—Guidons Presented to Rifles at Ottawa.—Lord Minto's Farewell Words.—E and D Batteries Leave Halifax.—Col. Herchmer's Men Sail on Pomeranian.—C Battery and 2nd Batt. of Rifles Sail on Milwaukee.—Lord Strathcona's Generous Offer.—The Strathcona Horse.—Lieut.-Col. Steele in Command.—The Strathcona's Sail on Monterey 331

CHAPTER II.

THE ARTILLERY, MOUNTED RIFLES AND STRATHCONA'S ON THE DEEP.

The Laurentian Delayed by Storm.—The "Rolling Polly."—Mortality Among the Horses.—In the Harbour of San Vincent.—Passing the Time on Board Ship.—Good News on Reaching Cape Town.—The Canadians as Athletes.—

CONTENTS.

PAGE
Cape Town Citizens Generous.—The Pomeranian and Milwaukee Reach Table Bay.—The Monterey at Sea.—Pneumonia Among the Horses.—Crossing the Line.—Ship on Fire.—War Still Being Vigorously Waged When Monterey Reaches Cape Town.................................... 342

CHAPTER III.

THE "REBEL CHASERS FROM AMERICA."

Work for the Rifles and Artillery.—The Rebels of Prieska and Kenhart.—The Canadians to Join Suppression Column.—On the March to Carnarvon.—Rumours of Boer Forces at Van Wyk's Vlei.—Loyalists of Carnarvon.—Stormy Weather.—Through Muddy Roads and Swollen Streams —Kenhart Re-Annexed to Cape Colony.—The Rains a Blessing.—The "Rebel Chasers From America."—Ordered to De Aar.—Mounted Rifles to be Sent to the Front.—D and E Batteries Left to Guard Line of Communication.—After the Rebels of Douglas.—E Battery Under Fire.—The Fight at Faber's Farm.—E Battery Saves the Day.—Burying the Dead.—Gallant Conduct of Col. Sam Hughes.—D and E Batteries Stay at De Aar.......... 350

CHAPTER IV.

THE FIRST AND SECOND CONTINGENTS JOIN HANDS AT BLOEMFONTEIN.

Life at Bloemfontein no Paradise.—Hardships of the Bivouac. —The Boers Quiet.—Botha and DeWet to the Front.—A Fight at Karree Siding.—The Disaster of Sannas Post.—Q Battery's Heroic Work.—The Canadians as Rear Guard to 9th Division.—First Contingent Badly Used Up.—A Second Disaster at Reddersburg.—Tents After Fifty-Three Days in the Open.—B Squadron at Bloemfontein.—First and Second Contingents Join Hands.—Part of B Squadron Entrapped.—Rescued By Their Comrades.—Calm Under Fire.—A Squadron at Fischer's Farm.—Waiting for the General Advance.. 367

CHAPTER V.

FIGHTING NORTHWARD.

The "Fighting Nineteenth" After the Boers.—The Battle of Israel's Poort.—Colonel Otter Wounded.—Bravery of Captain Burstall.—The Way Cleared to Thaba N'Chu.—Fatiguing Work.—The Fight at Taba Mountain.—The Luck of the Canadians.—The Death of Harry Cotton.—A Trying Night.—The "Ocean Cavalry" Rout the Boers.—The Vet is Reached.—The March into Winburg.—The Regiment Greatly Weakened.—A Rest Near Winburg..... 378

CHAPTER VI.

THE SCOUTS OF AN ARMY.

Lord Roberts' Army Leaves Bloemfontein.—Lieut. Col. Evans in Command of 2nd Batt. C. M. R.—The C. M. R. Scout in Advance of Main Army.—Under a Fierce Fire.—The Column Reaches Brandfort.—The Advance Continues.—The C. M. R. Under Shell-Fire.—A Bird's-Eye View of the Main Army.—The Fight at the Vet.—A Gallant Feat.—The Boers Driven From the Vet............ 394

CHAPTER VII.

CROSSING THE ZAND.

The Boers in Flight.—The Enemy Strongly Entrenched at the Zand.—The C. M. R. in a Perilous Position.—The "Fighting Nineteenth" Reach the Zand.—On the Eve of Battle.—The Battle of the Zand.—The Wounding of Stanley M. Brown.—The Mounted Forces Turn the Boers' Flank.—The Flight to Kroonstad.—A Treacherous Deed.—A Ghastly Bivouac................................. 409

CHAPTER VIII.

OCCUPYING KROONSTAD.

The Pursuit of the Boers.—A Rear Guard Action.—The Fall of Kroonstad.—Roberts' Enthusiastically Received by the Citizens.—The First Contingent a Skeleton of its Former Self.—The C. M. R. do Gallant Work Without Loss.—A Man-Hunt.—The Winburg Column Advance Towards the Vaal 421

CHAPTER IX.

CROSSING THE VAAL.

A White Flag Incident.—Lindley Entered.—DeWet at Work Again.—Heilbron Entered by Ian Hamilton.—A Part of Boer Convoy Captured.—Captain-Surgeon Fiset Left Behind at Heilbron.—Celebrating the Queen's Birthday.- Colonel Otter Rejoins the Regiment.—The The R. C's First of Lord Roberts' Infantry to Cross the Vaal.—The C. M. R. Leave Kroonstad.—A Trying Night March.—The Vaal Crossed at Lindeque Drift.............. 431

CHAPTER X.

INTO THE GOLD CITY.

The Boers in a Strong Position.—The Klipriversberg Fight.—The Fine Work of the C. M. R.—Flanking the Enemy.—Within Sight of Johannesburg.—Lieut. Borden's Gallant Adventure.—The R. C's Distinguish Themselves in the Battle of Doornkop.—The Way Cleared to Johannesburg.—The Union Jack Hoisted in Johannesburg.—The City of the Uitlander............... 444

CHAPTER XI.

ON TO PRETORIA.

A Delay Near Johannesburg.—The C. M. R's and the R. C's Advance on Pretoria.—Marching Through a Rough District.—The Mounted Men Under Fire.—The "Deed that Staggered Humanity."—Pretoria Surrenders.—General Botha Escapes with Guns.—The "Fighting Nineteenth" Broken up.—Their Good Work............................ 452

CHAPTER XII.

WINDING UP THE WAR.

C Battery Sent to the Relief of Mafeking.—At Beira.—On to Buluwayo.—They Join Hands with Col's. Plumer and Mahon.—Attacking the Besiegers.—Mafeking Relieved.—D and E Batteries at the Front.—The Strathcona's given a Difficult Task.—With Buller's Force.—The Scouts of an Army.—Winning a Victoria Cross.—Guerilla Warfare.— The First Contingent Homeward Bound.—Gallant Work of the C. M. R.—Canada Proud of Her Sons............... 459

LIST OF ILLUSTRATIONS.

	PAGE
Her Majesty Victoria	Frontispiece
Lord Strathcona and Mount Royal	xix
The Very Rev. G. M. Grant, D.D.	xx
Lieut.-General Lord Kitchener	15
Field Marshall Lord Roberts, V.C.	16
The Marquis of Salisbury, K.G.	25
Lieut.-Col. W. D. Otter	26
The Hon. Sir Richard J. Cartwright	35
The Right Hon. Sir Wilfrid Laurier, G.C.M.G.	36
Lieut.-Col. S. B. Steele	45
Lieut.-General R. S. S. Baden-Powell	46
The Right Hon. Joseph Chamberlain, M.P.	55
Hon. Sir Charles Tupper, Bart., G.C.M.G.	56
Major-General E. T. H. Hutton	65
Major-General Ivor J. S. Herbert	66
The Canadian Contingent Leaving Quebec for the Cape	75
Manitoba Volunteers Being Addressed by the Mayor	76
On the "Sardinian"—A Group of Canadian Officers	85
On the "Sardinian"—A Group of Canadian Officers	86
Toronto Men Sharpening Bayonets on the Sardinian	95
Group of Officers of Canadian Mounted Rifles (North West Squadron)	96
Departure of the Canadians from Cape Town	105
The Canadian Contingent Passing up Adderley Street, Cape Town	106
Lieuts. Mason and Temple Going on Picket Duty	115
The New Brunswick Quota of the Second Contingent, C.M.R.	116
Right Hon. Cecil J. Rhodes, P.C., M.L.A.	125
Francis William Reitz	126
Marthinus Theunis Steyn	135
The Hon. Jan. Hendrick Hofmeyr	136
Lieut.-Col. Sir Fred. Middleton, K.C.M.G., C.B.	145
Major-General Richard G. A. Luard	146
Queen Victoria on the Morning of Her Accession	155
Colonel Sir Casimir S. Gzowski, K.C.M.G.	156
The Toronto Company's Baptism of Fire	165
Smart Colonial Officers of the Canadian Contingent at the Front	166
Colonel Pilcher's Expedition to Douglas	175
Fording a River	176
Lieut.-Col. C. W. Drury and Lieut.-Col. F. L. Lessard	185
Major S. Denison and Lieut.-Col. Buchan	186
Major General Thomas Bland Strange	195
Colonel Walker Powell	196
Lieut.-Col. Henry Cassady Rogers	205
Major George Stewart	206
Lieut.-Col. Charles Edward Montizambert	215

LIST OF ILLUSTRATIONS.

	PAGE
Major J. C. McCorkill, B.C.L.	216
Major John Daley	225
Major Alexander George Hesslein	226
The Canadians Crossing Paardeberg Drift on the Modder	235
Physician and Story-Teller	236
The Rev. P. M. O'Leary	245
The Cornwalls Assisted by the Canadians Driving the Boers from the River Bank	246
Surgeon-Captain Fiset	255
Lieut.-Col. John Macpherson	256
Canadians at Cape Town	265
Second Canadian Contingent	266
Major Robert Cartwright	275
Capt. F. L. Cartwright	276
Lieut.-Col. Charles John MacDonald	285
Lieut.-Col. Alexander William Anstruther	286
Lieut.-Col. J. Bell Forsyth	295
Lieut.-Col. Leon P. Vohl	296
George Sterling Ryerson, M.D., C.M.	305
Major Henri Beaufort Vidal	306
The First Contingent Departing from Quebec	315
North-West Mounted Police	316
Major George William Ryan	325
Lieut.Col. Robert Thompson Banting	326
No. 4, Troop D Squadron, C.M.R.	335
No. 3, Troop D Squadron, C.M.R.	336
The Canadian Contingent Ready to Embark	345
Dr. Borden, Minister of Militia, on Board the S. S. "Monterey"	346
Officers of Strathcona's Horse	355
The Flag of Strathcona's Horse	356
Major Sam Hughes, M.P.	365
Major John Strathearn Hendrie	366
Group of Officers	375
Departure of the Canadian Transvaal Contingent	376
The British Columbia Contingent	385
The Departure of Lord Strathcona's Horse from Ottawa	386
Strathcona's Horse, Presentation of Guidons at Ottawa	395
Strathcona's Horse, Ottawa	396
Lieut. H. C. Borden	405
Canadians Leaving Cape Town for the Front	406
Lieut.-Col. Thomas Page Butler, D.C.L., Q.C.	415
Lieut.-Col. Alphonse D. Aubry, M.D.	416
The Occupation of Kroonstad	425
Greater Britain to the Succour of the Mother Country	426
Lieut.-Col. Julien Brosseau	435
Lieut.-Col. A. Denis	436
Major Donald Cameron Forster Bliss	441
Major Hiram Bender	442

DONALD A. SMITH.
1st Lord Strathcona and Mount Royal.

THE VERY REV. G. M. GRANT, D.D.

CANADA'S SONS ON KOPJE AND VELDT.

INTRODUCTORY CHAPTER.

By George Monro Grant, LL.D.

IMPERIAL SIGNIFICANCE OF THE CANADIAN CONTINGENTS.

Not very many years ago, John Morley—last and greatest representative of the Manchester school—proved to his own satisfaction that Imperial Federation was a delusion, by assuming that Canada or Australasia would refuse sympathy, money or men, in case of a war which for instance involved the Empire in South Africa. Never has the irony of events more directly confounded the argument of the philosopher. War commenced in South Africa. Just at that point British Supremacy was threatened.

As Cape Town is the half way house between the Mother Country and Australasia, in the not unlikely event of the Suez Canal being blocked, in time of war, the people of New Zealand and Australasia, whose chief market is Great Britain, felt that their interests were threatened, but Canada was directly concerned little more than if war had broken out in

Saturn. But what happened? An electric current flashed across the Continent, from Halifax to Victoria, thrilling all English-speaking hearts at any rate, and a cry went up that the war was Canada's as well as England's. Parliament was not in session and there was no constitutional way of taking action. The Prime Minister, as a French-Canadian, knew well that there could be no enthusiasm for such a war among his compatriots, and therefore he very naturally took his stand on the Constitution and our previous practice of allowing the Mother Country do the fighting, at her own cost and charges, while we did the singing of "God Save the Queen."

But the people would take no denial. A contingent must be sent; and when reverses came, a second was called for, and the Government would have gained votes had they then sent five or ten thousand instead of fifteen hundred more men. Canadians were ready to make any sacrifices; and they spoke, read and thought of nothing but the war. Their enthusiasm "took England by surprise," said the Prince of Wales, at a great assembly in London on the 7th of April. It took the world at large much more by surprise, added Lord Salisbury on the same occasion. "They fancied that the Great British Empire, which looks so large on the map, was so separated by distant seas that its practical utility for co-operation was entirely destroyed, but they have learned their mistake." And, it may be added, it took ourselves, the few foes among us as well as the many friends of Imperial Unity, by surprise. We did not know that what some consciously valued was unconsciously cherished, with all the force of a native instinct or elemental passion, in the hearts of millions. But the lightning has flashed. The revelation has been made. And now it is not amiss to ask, what were the causes which led to so startling a manifestation and what are the political or other consequences likely to result.

The underlying cause, it seems to me, is to be found in the fact that the British Empire is a living unity, though not formally bound together by a constitution. This fact has been ignored by people to whom written statutes and compacts are everything, but not by those who with Emerson regard law as simply a memorandum. The United Kingdom has managed to get along for a thousand years since Alfred without a written constitution. It, however, has a Parliament whose supremacy is unquestioned; while there is no Parliament for the Empire, for admittedly the august body which sits at Westminster would never dream of coercing Canada or Australasia. But there is something antecedent to and more vital than a Parliament. Unity of race, of history, of traditions, of aims and moral ideas constitutes a vital unity. As long as the outlying portions of the Empire had matters to attend to of overwhelming importance which absorbed their whole thought, they could take only a sentimental interest in foreign affairs. They were not selfish. When New Brunswick was threatened with invasion by the State of Maine, its sister Province of Nova Scotia sprang to arms as one man in its defense. When Riel murdered Scott, Ontario went wild. When, subsequently to his being amnestied by the Governor of Manitoba, he broke into rebellion on the banks of the Saskatchewan, the other provinces sent their sons in mid-winter to restore peace to the North-West. Up to that time, as regards foreign affairs, Canada was willing to accept the trustee-ship of the Imperial Parliament. Our national life was weak, and we had undertaken to administer half a continent.

But the making of the nation went on apace. Our neighbors unwittingly helped on the process. A succession of tariff measures culminating in the McKinley and Dingley Bills, forced us to widen our horizon beyond the continent to which we belonged. Everywhere the flag meant open markets, the protection of life and all that makes life valuable. Increasingly attractive, as the symbol and bond of union, became the personality of the Queen. The Jubilee of 1887, followed by the Great Jubilee of 1897, awakened feelings which had long been dormant in some breasts and had been chilled in others by the "so loyal is too costly" cry, flippantly expressed by press and politicians in London. The menace of President Cleveland's Venezuela message revealed the depth of the political gulf which separates the Dominion from the Republic. The Imperial Commission, consisting of four Canadians and one representative of Great Britain, appointed to settle all disputes that threatened friendly relations with the United States, was a public notice that—so far as this continent is concerned—Canada would make and the Imperial Government would sign any treaty that might be made. That put us on our honor, and it showed that we were partners and not dependents. While political status was so generously recognized and extended we felt more strongly than ever that the Empire meant freedom, equality for all white men, the independence of judges, and everything else which the British Constitution is popularly supposed to mean.

Then came the ultimatum, the invasion of sister

colonies, and the forcible annexation of districts to the Dutch Republics of South Africa. Those who had pleaded the cause of the Boers, who had shown the provocations they smarted under, and who had urged patience with them were silenced. Kruger and Steyn had abandoned moral for military ground, and there was nothing for it but war to a finish. Is it wonderful that Canada resented the insult, appreciated the common danger, and felt that she must now act up to the motto of "Each for all, and all for each."

When we come to speak of probable results, a tone of moderation is becoming. The issue of every election is uncertain; and if King Demos keeps his secret when nothing is at stake but Party Supremacy, he is infinitely more reserved when the reconstruction of the Empire is involved. He is not sure what to-morrow, or the day after may bring forth, and he is not sure how far changed circumstances might change the case and change his point of view. Some wise observers predict a recoil from the passion of nine, six, or three months ago. Cold fits succeed hot fits. Others declare that the foundation of an Imperial Constitution has been laid and that the blood of our soldiers has sealed the compact. The Hon. Mr. Tarte and the Duke of Devonshire are, racially and by mental build and habit, opposites; yet both declared recently at the same meeting in London that "the time is not far distant when the Canadian will be as full-fledged a citizen of the Empire as the Englishman," and "that nothing but criminal neglect or apathy on our part can prevent the influences tending to unity from resulting at no distant date in the political as well as the social Federation and Unity of the Empire."

French-Canadians are expected to oppose. On the contrary they are more likely to take the lead in movements tending in that direction. The thinkers and writers who are the factors in moulding the opinions of their countrymen—men like Laurier, Frechette, Sulte and others—hold that we have been marching to Imperialism of necessity, ever since the Responsible Government, which guaranteed the liberty and the characteristics of Quebec, was placed beyond question.

For my own part, I do not look for any startling Constitutional change or any paper scheme for re-organizing the Empire. That is not the way of the British. They build after the fashion of the insects that construct coral reefs, atolls, and fair islands in the Southern seas. They do the duty of to-day, and that becomes precedent, and so "freedom slowly broadens down," based not on theories but on necessities. Has our new departure then to have no more significance than any other of the events which have been shaping our course for the past fifty years to those who had eyes to see? Yes; it has revealed the mind, the heart, and the settled determination of the Canadian people in such fashion that no one will hereafter venture to cross it any more than the boldest will offer to swim Niagara. More, the larger patriotism, which has now taken possession of Canadians, cannot possibly vanish. It may become more critical, but it will abide and grow. We are henceforth a nation, and as every great statesman of the American Republic from Washington to Cleveland, always urged on their fellow-countrymen, "the nation that cannot resist aggression is constantly exposed to it," so, we

INTRODUCTORY CHAPTER.

must make our militia force a reality; must organize a naval reserve; must defend our coasts; must attract Newfoundland into our confederation; and must do these things at once. The party that does not understand the necessity for action is not loyal to Canada, or it is blind to the signs of the times.

PART ONE.

FROM QUEBEC TO BLOEMFONTEIN.

PART ONE.

CHAPTER I.

RUMOURS OF WAR.

ALL through the Summer of last year rumours of war came ticking across the wires from South Africa, but Canadians were so accustomed to the annual Eastern War Cloud and the occasional mutual shaking of fists at each other of France and England that at first but little attention was paid to these rumours. Russia and France knew England's resources and would think twice before precipitating a war with an empire of almost inexhaustible resources; of precipitating a war in which, be they victors or vanquished, the struggle would cost tens of thousands of men, and must leave them on the verge of bankruptcy. Surely, thought Canadians, the sturdy, stubborn little Republic of South Africa would not have the temerity to attempt what France and Russia with their hate and their experience; their skill, their wealth, and their hordes, would not dare attempt!

But Canadians living in a land of responsible institutions, in a land where the humblest toiler has a voice in the affairs of the nation, and as a result an interest in and a knowledge of the affairs of other nations, could not realize the ignorance and stubbornness that prevailed in the Transvaal. The

Boer was totally unlike the great Powers that are forever warring with words with England. Their character, their language, their situation, have all shut them off from the rest of mankind, and while they have accepted through the Uitlanders, who have made their homes among them, many of the mechanical marks of civilization, in language, in religion, in social and political ideas they have remained children of the eighteenth century. In their ignorance, too, such a victory as their splendidly planned and executed fight at Majuba Hill in 1881, over a handful of British soldiers made them think that if they went out in force with all their modern weapons of war and their fine marksmen they would soon be able to drive the British into the sea. In their folly they judged of England's strength by her standing army; and even such a brave, humane, and astute soldier as the late, universally respected General Joubert, had no conception of the vast army of volunteers which England could transport across six thousand miles of ocean in a few weeks.

Canadians did not realize the character of the people England had to deal with, and so when in the early summer threat and counter-threat flashed between England and South Africa but little attention was paid to them in Canada. Our people thought that little more than words would come of it, and that, while the stubborn Boer would no doubt make a vigorous opposition to England's demands, in the end concessions would be made that would leave the Uitlander as free as the citizens of Cape Colony, Natal, and the Orange Free State.

But in July things began to look very black indeed. Ultimatums, or messages very like ultimatums, began to pass between the President of the Transvaal and the Secretary of State for the Colonies; a stir made itself felt in the War Office, and what was then considered a large army was made ready to go to Africa at a moment's notice. At the same time the Volksraad offered concessions to the Uitlanders; and while they held in one hand a message of peace, with the other they bought more arms and ammunition. At Johannesburg but little faith was placed in the subtly-worded Franchise concessions, and it was universally believed that Kruger and his confederates were dallying to gain time.

Still Canada could not deem war possible, and when in July Queensland offered the Home Government two hundred and fifty mounted infantry with a machine gun if necessary, their offer was appreciated in this country, but it was thought merely a bit of Imperial enthusiasm. War was impossible! Still Canadians realized that battalion after battalion was being sent to South Africa; that big guns and small guns, Howitzers, Maxims, and machine guns, were being bought and painted khaki color; that the Hollander clique with Dr. Leyds at its head was at work; that, while the British dailies kept repeating that peace was probable, on the two great questions that finally made the war, the Franchise and the matter of Suzerainty, no advance was being made. It was only the reiterated assurances of that Napoleon of finance and enterprise, Cecil Rhodes, that there was not the slightest chance of war, that kept Canadians from believing each day that on the morrow war would break out. So the war barometer rose and fell; to-day the Uitlanders were denouncing the Franchise Law as wholly inadequate; to-morrow the Volksraad pretended to make further concessions. But through it all President Kruger stubbornly held to his original ground, the Transvaal for the Boer; and Joseph Chamberlain, as determined, made no retreat from the stand he had taken on the Franchise, and what irritated the Boers more, on the much debated question of the Suzerainty. He spoke with no uncertain voice when towards the end of July he said: "We have undertaken the cause of the Uitlanders and are bound to see it through."

Between England and Canada since the Diamond Jubilee, while the Imperial idea had taken no definite shape, the feeling of Imperial unity had been growing stronger and stronger; and it seemed a fitting thing that in an empire of so many diverse people a French-Canadian should have been chosen to cement by his tact and wisdom this Imperial bond. He saw, and his ministers saw, that a word in season might strengthen England's hands; not that she needed it so far as the Transvaal was concerned, but in case of war it would be well to let the foreign powers, ever ready to take advantage of England's danger, see that the Mother Country did not stand alone; that her children were willing and able to help her with sympathy, with men, and with money. The Canadian ministers knew the people they were governing and they unhesitatingly made ready to introduce the South African difficulty to the House of Commons, knowing that there would be no opposition within the walls of Parliament, and that their action would receive the applause, the approval of the whole of Canada.

A livelier interest was therefore aroused in the minds of the Canadian public with regard to the

LIEUT.-GENERAL LORD KITCHENER.

FIELD MARSHAL LORD ROBERTS, V.C.
In his tent while on the way to Bloemfontein.

situation when, on July 31 the Prime Minister rose in the House and addressing Mr. Speaker said :—

"I beg to interrupt the regular course of the business, in order to offer certain resolutions which I believe the state of things now existing in a distant country under the Suzerainty of Her Majesty seems to render appropriate. . . . Some eighty thousand of Her Majesty's subjects have been allowed to become residents of that country, to purchase lands there, to open mines, to develop trade, to establish industries, and to build up cities, yet are denied almost every kind of participation in its administration. They are subjected to discriminating and heavy taxation, and yet are denied any kind of representation, and although forced to bear their full share of citizenship are denied the rights and privileges and liberties of citizens.

"If I be asked: What is the reason of this expression of sympathy, what object would it serve, what result would it effect? I simply answer: The object to be sought is that we should extend to our fellow-countrymen in South Africa the right hand of good fellowship, that we should assure them that our heart is with them and that in our judgment they are in the right; the object would be to assure the Imperial authorities, who have taken in hand the cause of the Uitlanders, that on that question we are at one with them, and that they are also in the right—and perhaps the effect might be also that this mark of sympathy, extending from continent to continent and encircling the globe might cause wider and more humane counsels to prevail in the Transvaal and possibly avert the awful arbitrament of war. Animated by these reasons, and speaking,

I believe, the sentiments of all men in Canada, not only of one class but of all classes, not only of one race but of all races, I beg to move, seconded by Mr. Foster, the following resolution:—

1. Resolved, That this House has viewed with regret the complications which have arisen in the Transvaal Republic, of which Her Majesty is Suzerain, from the refusal to accord to Her Majesty's subjects now settled in that region any adequate participation in its government;

2. Resolved, That this House has learned with still greater regret that the condition of things there existing has resulted in intolerable oppression, and has produced great and dangerous excitement among several classes of Her Majesty's subjects in Her South African possessions;

3. Resolved, That this House, representing a people which has largely succeeded by the adoption of the principle of conceding equal political rights to every portion of the population in harmonizing estrangements and in producing general content with the existing system of the government, desires to express its sympathy with the efforts of Her Majesty's Imperial authorities to obtain for the subjects of Her Majesty who have taken up their abode in the Transvaal such measure of justice and political recognition as may be found necessary to secure them in the full possession of their rights and liberties."

Sir Wilfrid had conferred on the subject with the venerable leader of the Opposition, Sir Charles Tupper, and had communicated this resolution to him and he was to have seconded it, but was unfortunately unable to attend the House on July 31. However he could not be silent in such a critical moment in his country's history, so he sent a note to the Premier saying: "I think we are bound to give all the aid in our power to Her Majesty's Government in the present crisis."

"All the aid in our power." These words were significant; he would give not merely sympathy and moral support, but if necessary men and treasure as well; he would have Canada become an active part of the Empire.

The resolution was seconded by Mr. George E. Foster, who in the course of an eloquent address said:—

"These men may be Outlanders so far as the Dutch Republic is concerned; but we extend to them to-day as has been done from almost every quarter of the British world that hand grasp which will make the eighty thousand British subjects there feel that though Outlanders so far as the Transvaal Republic is concerned, they are Inlanders taken warmly to the great heart of the British Empire."

When Sir Wilfrid moved: "That a copy of this resolution be transmitted to Her Majesty's Secretary of State for the Colonies by the Speaker of the House," there was no dissenting voice. The enthusiasm was unbounded. Every member rose to his feet, and all made the House of Commons ring with the National Anthem. The people in the galleries caught the enthusiasm and rising in a body joined in the demostration of patriotism to Canada and loyalty to England.

Canada was committed by her representatives. She had made Britain's difficulty her difficulty. Come what would, be it peace, be it war, she had cast in her lot with the Motherland. There could be no turning back now: after such a resolution her sons must be ready for the call to arms.

When on the morrow the action of the peoples' representatives of both parties became known, the whole country said, "Well done!" It is true there were dissenting voices here and there, but they were drowned in the clamor of approval.

Still there was but little thought of war. The people of Canada were convinced that the Transvaalers could never be guilty of stubbornly causing a war with the British Empire; and they hoped, as no doubt the Premier had hoped when he moved the resolution, that the action of what is practically a Republic, the freest and best governed on earth, might have some weight with President Kruger and the Volksraad.

At any rate it was to England a most significant step, and the leading English journals declared it to have a "moral weight impossible to ignore," and that "it would be difficult to overrate its moral significance." England knew now beyond a doubt that her greatest colony was with her, and that if she should be plunged into war her strongest child would be ready to spring to arms in her behalf. At this time she had no dream that she would need such help, but in case of European complications it would be well to know just where her children stood.

If it strengthened the hands of England it was a still greater boon to the Uitlander, and especially to the many hardy Canadians among them, who had risked fortune and life in far Africa. They read with delight the strong resolution of the Canadian Government and sent the following note and resolution, which had been passed by the Canadian Society of Johannesburg on August 10, to the Right Honorable Sir Wilfrid Laurier, Premier of Canada :—

"Resolved, That this meeting of Canadians res - dent at Johannesburg and on the Rand, desires to express its unbounded satisfaction and gratitude to the Canadian Parliament for its unanimous resolution of moral sympathy, and if necessary practical support to the Imperial Government, in its efforts to obtain for the Uitlanders their just demands for equal rights for all white men, without distinction, in this country.

"It further wishes to place on record the important fact that the Uitlanders are justly entitled to these rights, not only as British subjects and white men, but in fulfilment of the solemn promises made by President Kruger and the Boer Government when Great Britain granted this country its right to Internal Government and without which promises this privilege would never have been granted."

This resolution did much to bring home to the people of Canada the state of affairs in South Africa. Canadians were there, our fellow countrymen were living under a system of government that would not be tolerated for one hour in this country. The liveliest interest had now been stirred up on the question, and people, educated and uneducated, simple and gentle, began to make an effort to find out what the grievances were, and the vague terms Oligarchy, Suzerainty, Oppression, Franchise, Monopoly, as applied to the Transvaal, began to have some meaning. The intolerant Boer began to loom up before them as did the Family Compact Party in the early days of this century; and as blood was then shed before the wrongs were redressed so it might have to be again.

But if Sir Wilfrid deemed that his resolution would have any weight with the Volksraad he was much mistaken. Scarcely had this resolution had time to cross the water when word was brought back that the Pretoria forts were being strengthened and that oxen for the transport waggons were being purchased on a large scale in Bechuanaland. The Uitlanders, too, had lost heart and the trains from the Transvaal were taxed to their utmost capacity with refugees. But for the optimistic attitude of Cecil Rhodes, who declared publicly, "There would be no blood shed; President Kruger like a sensible man will climb down"—but for this man's attitude war seemed inevitable.

In the meantime the Transvaal Government was distributing Mausers, getting their splendid artillery into efficient shape, and buying up vast stores of food and war materials. The British Government had recalled Major-General Sir William Francis Butler, Commander of the Forces in South Africa, probably on account of his pro-Boer sympathies, and had sent out Sir Frederick Forestier-Walker to replace him. An army of twenty thousand men was ready, proposal and counter-proposal flashed across the cables; and so closed August with the gloomy prognostication from President Kruger that war was inevitable.

Ever since the passing of the resolution of sympathy with the Uitlander the Canadian people had been working to get an intelligent view of the war situation; and while many were in doubt as to England's right to interfere in the internal affairs of the South African Republic, all detested the stubborn tyrrany of the little oligarchy of Boers and Hollanders at Pretoria. The "Bitter Cry" of the

Uitlander had reached them across the broad Atlantic.

"We," they declared in the manifesto of the Transvaal National Union, "are the vast majority in this state. We own more than half the land, and, taken in the aggregate, we own at least nine tenths of the property in this country; yet in all matters effecting our lives, our liberties and our properties, we have absolutely no voice. Dealing now first with the Legislature, we find taxation is imposed upon us without any representation whatever, that taxation is wholly inequitable, (a) because a much greater amount is levied from the people than is required for the needs of Government; (b) because it is either class taxation pure and simple or by the selection of the subjects, though nominally universal, it is made to fall upon our shoulders; and (c) because the necessaries of life are unduly burdened."

Everything that Canadians, living under responsible government, hated prevailed in the Transvaal; everything they cherished was denied their fellow-countrymen residing in this dark corner of Darkest Africa; so that while some doubted the legal right of England to interfere, all were antagonistic to the Oligarchy who by treachery had got capitalists to invest money in their domains, and who by promises they never intended to keep had done much to lure a large population to their Republic. Republic it was only in name; oligarchy and tyranny of the worst type it was in reality. The many had no voice in the affairs of the State; public money disappeared, no one seemed to know whither, although the revelations of the last eight months have made it evident that it was going to Europe with Dr. Leyds for secret service purposes, and was being expended at home to make the Transvaal an arsenal, to make it so strong that only an army of the vastest dimensions could bring the stubborn burghers to their knees. They little deemed, poor, ignorant people, that England had such an army, that in a few weeks she could transport across six thousand miles of water the largest force ever sent out of any country in modern times, and the vastest equipment that has been seen since war began.

Unjust taxation, bribery, monopolies, the abuse of railway concessions, an iniquitous educational system, oppressive franchise were not the only things detestable in the Transvaal. Such things are found to a greater or less degree in every country, and patience and time are sure to redress them. Slavery, a thing abhorred by Canadians, was favored by the Boers. In their narrowness, their bigotry, they looked upon the children of Ham as only suited to be beasts of burden to them, and the well-authenticated stories of their evasion of the anti-slavery clauses of the conventions of 1881 and 1884, their excessive cruelty to the blacks in their so-called employment, created in Canadians a feeling that the Boer needed chastisement to bring him to his senses.

Still it was not believed that war would come. At the last moment it was felt that President Kruger would see that it was only right to grant, in a modified form no doubt, the demands of the Uitlanders, and what utter folly it would be to challenge England to war.

September opened gloomily, the Boers vigorously denied the English right of suzerainty and would now make no further concessions to the Uitlander, saying that: "The Government, both the Raads

THE MARQUIS OF SALISBURY, K.G.
Prime Minister of Great Britain.

LIEUT.-COL. W. D OTTER.

and the Burghers, feel that they have offered all they intend to offer, and they are now resolved to stand or fall by this decision."

To prove that they meant what they said the Burghers throughout the length and breadth of the Republic were notified to be ready at a moment's notice and the Transvaal artillery, their main stay, was called out. The English War-Office now seemed to wake up; the stubborn and defiant attitude of President Kruger was met by increased preparation on the part of England. Indian troops were warned to be in readiness; hospital outfits were prepared on an extensive scale; and it was generally understood that in case of war Sir Redvers Buller, at that time the idol of the British public, would rush to Cape Town to take command of the army in South Africa.

Thicker grew the war cloud, and when it was announced that the Orange Free State, " Come what may will stand by the Transvaal," not even the hopeful words of Sir Alfred Milner and Cecil Rhodes that there would be no war, prevented Canadians from feeling that they would be called upon to give more than sympathy to the Uitlanders. Ever since rumours of war were in the air, the roads to Durban and Cape Town had been crowded with refugees and Johannesburg was like a plague-smitten city; troops were massing on the Natal border; looting was reported from Lichtenburg and elsewhere; armoured trains were being rushed to Ladysmith and Kimberley; and the entire railway system of the South African Republic was placed under military control.

Through it all our Government was calm. Even while New Zealand and Australia were making offers to the Home Government no action was taken, but Canadians knew that action was intended and when the definite need would arise they would act and act quickly. They had not long to wait; on the 9th of October President Kruger issued his astounding Ultimatum, and England was at war; and for the first time in Canada's history, she, by the action of her Government on July 31, had to take her part in a war of the Empire. Gladly did she face her duty. War, War! echoed throughout the Dominion, and in every city, town, hamlet, from Victoria to Charlottetown, young men, the flower of country, cried "We are ready!"

CHAPTER II.

WAR.

ALTHOUGH the sky had been black with war clouds for many weeks, the thunder stroke of this ultimatum was none the less appalling. War, modern war, seemed a horrible thing to contemplate. It is true the destructive bayonet now plays but a minor part in battle, it is true that but a small percentage of the wounded die; still the words lyddite, melinite, cordite; the "Pom-Pom," Howitzer, Maxim-Nordenfelt, and Creusot, made a people unfamiliar with war terms wonder what would be the result of a war in which such destructive weapons were used.

M. Bloch had just issued the final volume of his great work, "The War of the Future." Canada was now called upon to face the horrors of a war such as the great Russian military authority had described. Would her sons be willing to volunteer for a war in which the modern rifle would be used, a rifle "capable of sending its deadly projectile almost point-blank for six hundred and sixty yards, capable of killing at from two to two and a half miles; with power to pass through half a dozen men in succession"; only the strongest fortifications could resist its progress and whence it came the soldier could not know as the smokeless powder sending it on its mission of death gave no hint of where the enemy lay concealed. If the rifle fire was horrible to anticipate still more terrifying was the thought of the shell fire. "On the average shells burst into two hundred and forty pieces, instead of nineteen to thirty, as was the case in 1870. The schrapnel employed in 1870 burst into thirty-seven pieces, now it gives as many as three hundred and forty. An iron bomb weighing eighty-two pounds which with the old powder gave forty-two fragments, filled with peroxylene gives twelve hundred and four pieces. Splinters and bullets bring death and destruction not only as in 1870, to those in the vicinity of the explosion, but at a distance of two hundred and twenty yards away, and this though fired at a distance of three thousand three hundred yards."

War was no longer war; strength of arm, keenness of weapon had lost their former significance. Chemistry, mathematics, and trenches had taken the place of swordsmanship, judgment, and the heroic charge.

In a London despatch of October 6, we have these words with regard to M. Bloch's book:—

"M. Bloch quotes a description of a battle of the future under these conditions, penned by a French officer of great scientific distinction. It is a thrilling and yet horrible picture. At six thousand six hundred yards the artillery duel will begin. Shells tear up the soil and burst, raining down hundreds of fragments and bullets. Men and horses are overwhelmed by this rain of lead and iron. Guns destroy one another, batteries are mutually annihilated. In the midst of this fire the battalions will advance. At two thousand two hundred yards the rifle bullets whistle around and kill, each one not only finding a victim, but penetrating files ricochetting and striking again. Volley succeeds volley; bullets in great handfuls, constant as hail and swift as lightning, deluge the field of battle. Melinite bombs will turn farm houses, villages and hamlets to dust, destroying everything that might be used as cover, obstacle or refuge. The moment will approach when half the combatants will be mowed down; dead and wounded will lie in parallel rows, separated one from the other by that belt of a thousand paces swept by a cross fire of shells which no living being can pass. This impossible zone of deadly fire is the problem of future warfare. It cannot be crossed."

In the face of this marshalling of facts, in the face of these tragic forebodings, would our sons be willing to join in a modern war? We would soon see.

But surely a little Republic such as the Transvaal could not for a moment stand against the armies of England! The death and destruction foreboded in M. Bloch's book would surely be one-sided. An ignorant, illiterate people living so far from the great centres of commerce and invention could not surely have the weapons and military skill to compete with the wealthiest Empire the world has ever seen. The march from Cape Town to Pretoria would be but a continuous triumph, if the Boer cause did not collapse as soon as it was seen that England was determined to fight to a finish, and that there would be no more "Majuba Days."

The Anglo-Saxon world, however had had plenty of warning that a fierce struggle was impending, and that, though England must win in the end by mere mass, for a time at least the horrors of a modern war would be experienced.

Just before the breaking out of hostilities, and while the air was charged with the electricity of war, "Oom Paul's People" by Howard C. Hillegas, an American journalist, appeared. The book was not without prejudice, but any one perusing it must have seen that England's march to Pretoria would be accompanied more often by the music of screaming bullets and shrieking shells than by the pipe and drum. Ever since the Jameson raid, and before it, the Boers had been preparing for the inevitable fray, as they considered it. Their country, by nature the strongest and most easily defended of any inland country in the world, had been carefully studied, the plan of resistance mapped out, and the method of attack conceived. Able German, French, and American military experts had been engaged. An efficient artillery corps was established, and every man and boy and probably many of the women, were taught how to use their Mausers to the best advantage. "Several million pounds were annually spent in Europe in the purchase of the armament required by the plans formulated by the experts, and the whole country was placed on a war-footing. Every important strategic position was made as impregnable as modern skill and arms could make it, and every farmer's cottage was supplied with arms and ammunition, so that the volunteer army might be mobilized in a day."

"Pretoria," says Hillegas, "being the Capital, and naturally the chief point of attack by the enemy, has been prepared to resist the onslaught of any number of men, and is in a condition to withstand a siege of three years. The city lies in the centre of a square, and at each corner of it is a lofty hill surmounted by a strong fort, which commands the valleys and the surrounding country. Each of the four forts has four heavy cannon, four French guns of fifteen miles range, and thirty heavy Gatling guns. Besides this extraordinary protection, the city has fifty light Gatling guns which can be drawn by mules to any point on the hills where an attack may be made. Three large warehouses are filled with ammunition, and the large armory is packed to the eaves with Mauser, Martini-Henry, and Wesley-Richards rifles. Two extensive refrigerators with a capacity of two thousand oxen each, are ample provision against a siege of many months."

A people making such preparations as here described could mean but one thing—war, and probably war to a finish. An easy victory they could not have anticipated, and a protracted siege they were ready for.

Would Canadians be willing to make the arduous journey across seven thousand miles of ocean, to face a people so well prepared for war and apparently so determined, so stubborn, to fight to the bitter end. But few of our men had ever handled a rifle, whereas to the people they were contemplating going against the rifle was a constant companion; at once "the young Boer's primer" and "the grandfather's testament." They had relied on it in the Great Trek, and it had proved their unerring friend at Majuba Hill. Were they the same people as of old? If so, England would have no easy task; win she would but only by vastly superior numbers; only after hundreds, perhaps thousands, had stepped in to fill up the gaps made in the ranks of the advance army. Would Canadians be found when the hour of trial came ready to fill the gaps made by the Creusot guns and the Mauser rifles?

The public were not long kept in suspense. On the 9th of October President Kruger issued his astounding ultimatum and on the 10th it was published in full in every paper in this country. The effect was immediate. When Canadians read the surprising demands it contained—demands such as no nation great or small had ever before made of England—there was but one cry—War be it! Thus it is written, and thus when the South African Republics are no more; when their rule, their language even is but a memory among men, it will stand written; and to the world it will ever be known as Kruger's Folly:—

"Her Majesty's unlawful intervention in the internal affairs of this Republic in conflict with the London Convention of 1884, by the extraordinary strengthening of her troops in the neighborhood of this Republic, has caused an intolerable condition of things to arise, to which this Government feels itself obliged, in the interest not only of this Republic, but also of all South Africa, to make an end as soon as possible; and this Government feels itself called on and obliged to press earnestly, and with emphasis for an immediate termination of this state of things, and to request Her Majesty's Government to give assurances upon the following four demands:

"First, that all points of mutual difference be regulated by friendly recourse to arbitration or by whatever amicable way may be agreed upon by this Government and Her Majesty's Government.

"Second, that all troops on the borders of this Republic shall be instantly withdrawn.

"Third, that all reinforcements of troops which

THE HON. SIR RICHARD J. CARTWRIGHT.

THE RIGHT HON. SIR WILFRID LAURIER, G.C.M.G.

have arrived in South Africa since June 1, 1899, shall be removed from South Africa within a reasonable length of time, to be agreed upon with this Government, and with the mutual assurance and guarantee on the part of this Government that no attack upon or hostilities against any portion of the possession of the British Government shall be made by this Republic during the further negotiations within a period of time to be subsequently agreed upon between the Governments; and this Government will on compliance therewith, be prepared to withdraw the armed burghers of this Republic from the borders.

"Fourth, that Her Majesty's troops which are now on the high seas, shall not be landed in any part of South Africa.

"This Government presses for an immediate affirmative answer to these four questions, and earnestly requests Her Majesty's Government to return an answer before or upon Wednesday, October 11, 1899, not later than 5 o'clock P.M.

"It desires further to add that in the unexpected event of an answer not satisfactory being received by it within the interval, it will with great regret be compelled to regard the action of Her Majesty's Government as a formal declaration of war and will not hold itself responsible for the consequences thereof, and that, in the event of any further movement of troops occurring within the above mentioned time in a nearer direction to our borders, this Government will be compelled to regard that also as a formal declaration of war."

It could not be said that this ultimatum fell like a bolt from the blue. The current of events for a month had made the world expect war, while common-sense said there would be no war; and so when it did come in the form of these astonishing demands for a moment all were stunned. But only for a moment. Kruger might be mad, but the Volksraad was at his back in this action. His burghers, too, were clamoring for war, and war they would get.

It is true that many people in Canada and England felt that much could be said in their behalf up to this stage; that there might be, in the event of the stock-jobbers getting control of the Transvaal, as they surely would if all the Uitlanders were at once enfranchised, a harder if more refined tyranny established than that of the selfish Oligarchy which was apparently swayed by the Hollander clique with Dr. Leyds as the moving spirit. But this ultimatum so far as Canada was concerned put an end to openly expressed sympathy with the Republics; from the 10th of October there was not left in Canada a pro-Boer of any standing, excepting perhaps Mr. Goldwin Smith; and his attitude can be accounted for largely by his anti-Imperial point of view, and his very praise-worthy cry against war. Peace at any price may be very good, but the price demanded is often war.

Gladstone was no doubt right from a Christian point of view when he made terms with the Boers after the disastrous fight at Majuba Hill—especially when he could not forecast the future prosperity of the Transvaal—but from an international point of view he acted, as time proved, very unwisely indeed. If a man or a nation enters upon a fight the struggle should be finished, and either utter defeat accepted and terms accepted with defeat, or magnanimity shown to a vanquished foe. To stop in the middle of a struggle and practically accept the demands of the enemy will never be taken to mean that the error of the course pursued has been recognized, but that fear of defeat has dictated the action. So it was in 1881; Gladstone's magnanimity was laughed at by his enemies; England was in the eyes of the Boers a weak nation, and Englishmen afraid to meet their superb markmanship.

So when this ultimatum was launched there was but one cry in England—an unreasoning cry perhaps, but one that had been in the heart of the nation for nineteen years—Avenge Majuba Hill! and the cry was re-echoed around the world, every colony accepting with the Motherland this challenge to war,—for such it was.

On the 10th of October the New South Wales Lancers departed from London for South Africa, and in the farewell given them the English people showed the world at large and their own Government where they stood. The city went wild. The streets along the line of march were packed and amidst the rejoicing that a child of the Empire was about to take part in the Empire's war there was the fierce cry of that pent up spirit of nineteen years,—"Remember Majuba!"

God help the Republics! There would be no turning back this time. Kopje, spruit, donga, desert, would be no deterrance, and they would match markmanship with markmanship. The crowd in the street not only shouted farewells, but they clamored to go to the front themselves, or at least to be permitted to send their sons.

With the news of this rejoicing at the breaking out of war came the message to Canada that she would be asked to contribute four units of one hundred and twenty-five men each, and the only regret was that ten times the number had not been asked. Scarcely was it known that Canada would take her part in England's war when telegram after telegram began to pour in to the Militia Department from every part of the Dominion, from every State in the Union, and even from the far distant City of Mexico.

In many ways our young men had been prepared for the call. Sir Charles Tupper, who was in at the making of the Great Dominion, now saw, in his eightieth year, a splendid opportunity of having another life's dream realized—his dream of Imperial Federation. If Canada did but once strike a blow in defence of the Empire, her voice might soon be heard in the councils of that same Empire. With this feeling, in season and out of season, he had been urging on the people and the Government the need of taking prompt action, of at least doing as much as Australia and New Zealand were doing. Major Hughes, too, had at once rushed to the fore, and as early as July had been endeavoring to raise a force something after the manner of "Teddy" Roosevelt's Rough Riders; but his course was irregular and the Government interfered. A strong resolution moved by Lieutenant-Colonel Denison and seconded by Lieutenant-Colonel Mason had been passed on October 2, at a representative meeting of Militia officers held in Toronto, urging on the Government that it was Canada's clear duty to stand by the Empire. With the appeals of Sir Charles Tupper, the enthusiasm of Major Hughes, the people of Canada were found to be thoroughly in accord, and while the Government had been discreetly silent, it was known that they would act when the time came for action.

With the message that Canada would be asked

for four units was published the statement that an order had been given to The Sanford Manufacturing Co. for two thousand pairs of Infantry trousers and one thousand tunics. Evidently the Government expected to send more men than they had been asked for. This order meant that they had at least a contingent of one thousand soldiers in view.

At first some of the leaders in the Government thought that Parliament should be called to sanction the raising and equipping of volunteers and transporting them to South Africa at the Government's expense. It would be, they thought, a bad precedent to make such a new departure without first getting the voice of the people's representatives. But there are times when constitutions and constitutional mode of procedure can safely be laid aside; and the time had arrived in Canada's history. So strong was public feeling, so vehemently did the press of both parties cry out for the Government to lose no time, that the life of the Government causing delay would have been in danger.

This was all the astute leader of the Government desired. He had made Imperial pretentions at the time of the Diamond Jubilee, and had been the central Imperial figure at that celebration. He had in July caused the eyes of the English world to turn towards Canada through his strong Imperial resolution and now the time had come to act, and act he did.

Scarcely had the news come that on the 12th of October war had been formally declared by the Republics, and that "The Mosquito," an armoured train had been shelled and wrecked at Kraaipan by the Boers, than he at once called his Cabinet together; and it was officially decided to obey the wishes of the people and send a contingent to South Africa.

The following military order was at once issued by Lieutenant-Colonel Forester, Chief Staff Officer:

"His Excellency the Governor-General in Council having been pleased to approve the despatch of Canadian volunteers, formed into eight companies of infantry for active service in South Africa, it is hereby notified that one thousand volunteers will be accepted."

Recruiting was to begin at once. The one thousand men were to go in eight units of 125 men each. Ontario was to furnish three, Quebec two, the Maritime Provinces two, and Manitoba and British Columbia one.

On the 13th of October the offer of one thousand troops had been sent to England and for answer the following despatch came back:

"Her Majesty's Government have received with much pleasure your telegram of the thirteenth of October, conveying Canada's generous offer of one thousand troops, which they gratefully accept."

CHAMBERLAIN.

In some quarters the Government was censured for not bearing the entire expense of this contingent from the time of the recruiting to the return to Canadian soil. The Government, however, acted with great calmness and wisdom during the heated discussion that followed the issuing of their orders with regard to the equipping, transporting, and paying the men of the contingent.

They had volunteered the men to England, it was for them to do England's bidding; and had England said we accept the contingent on condition that Canada assumes entire responsibility, the Government would no doubt have acceded to their demand, but to do so Parliament would have to be called.

The following were the conditions sent by the English Government and these conditions were at once complied with:

"Troops to be disembarked at the port of landing, South Africa, fully equipped at the cost of the Colonial Government or volunteers, from the date of disembarkation the Imperial Government will provide pay, at the Imperial rates, supplies and ammunition, and will defray the expense of transportation back to Canada, and pay wound pensions and compassionate allowances at Imperial rates.

"Troops to embark not later than the 31st of October, proceeding direct to Cape Town for orders. Inform accordingly all who have offered to raise volunteers."—CHAMBERLAIN.

Two weeks to raise one thousand men, equip them, obtain transport and store the ship for the long sea voyage the whole length and breadth of the Atlantic! This was a heavy undertaking for a peace power such as Canada. Had the Government been at liberty to select the one thousand men from Montreal or Toronto or any other of our centres of population it might have been easy; but this force had to have representatives from every part of the Dominion. No Province would be ignored; all had a host of young men ready, if necessary, to die for England.

The task of the mobilization of the Contingent was not an easy one, but it could be done; and done it was, to the credit of the Hon. F. W. Borden and the Militia Department, without a hitch, in shorter time than the Home Government had stipulated.

LIEUT.-COL. S. B. STEELE.

LIEUT.-GENERAL R. S. S. BADEN POWELL.

CHAPTER III.

MOBILIZING THE TROOPS.

RECRUITING began at once and met with a ready response. M. Bloch's picture of the horrors of modern warfare was no deterrent to Canadian loyalty. Great eagerness was shown in every Province and the thousand men requested might have been recruited ten times over. In such military centres as Toronto, Montreal, Quebec and Halifax enthusiasm was to be expected, but the same eagerness was displayed in every town and village in the English parts of the Dominion, and even the French subjects of Her Majesty, who could not have been expected to show the same readiness, made a willing response. From the fruitful fields of little Prince Edward Island; from the garrison city by the sea, Halifax; from the tree-lined streets of Fredericton, nestling fair and peaceful on the banks of the picturesque St. John; from the shadow of Mount Royal, the throbbing heart of our commercial existence; from Toronto, the fairest city in the Dominion; from the rich plains of Manitoba where the sword has been beaten into the ploughshare; from beyond the mighty Rockies, from the sound of the Great Pacific—came trooping the armed host, all converging on Quebec where a gallant band of patriotic soldiers was awaiting them and making preparations to give them a hearty welcome.

The truth of the words of Sir John Thompson, that

force for good in the Dominion so prematurely cut off, was realized for the first time: "The day has come when friends and foes alike, in considering the strength of the Empire, must take into account the strength of the colonies across the sea."

If volunteers were ready to answer to the call to arms, their fellow-citizens were as ready to wish them God-speed, and to do what they could to make life pleasanter for them while on their arduous journey over seas and on the veldt. A patriotic fund was started and before the war closed over three hundred thousand dollars had been subscribed; but this was a mere tithe of what was contributed, as in every city where volunteers were enrolled, in every town and village where men made ready for the front, purses were raised and gifts showered on the lads who had suddenly become heroes.

This readiness to respond to the Empire's need was much appreciated in England, and the following message served as another link in the chain that was binding Canada to the Motherland:

"Her Majesty the Queen desires to thank Her people of the Dominion of Canada for their striking manifestation of loyalty and patriotism in their voluntary offer to send troops to co-operate with Her Majesty's Imperial forces in maintaining her position and the rights of British subjects in South Africa. She wishes the troops God-speed and a safe return."

In Toronto and Montreal and Halifax, indeed in every centre of importance, the wildest enthusiasm prevailed at the farewells. Whether England had been right or wrong before the ultimatum the people recked not. The ultimatum had left but one course open and a more popular war was never entered

MOBILIZING THE TROOPS.

upon. As on the hearts of the people of England, so on the hearts of Canadians were written the words " Majuba Hill." There would be no peace till the memory of that reverse was wiped out.

At the farewell in the Armouries at Toronto, Colonel Otter who had been appointed to the command of the Contingent, thus addressed the thousands who had come to say their adieus:—

" I cannot refrain from saying just one or two words and as far as possible under the present very exciting circumstances expressing my gratification for the warm, hearty, loyal and kind reception. You all know we appreciate from the bottom of our hearts your kindness to us to-day. I do not think you need fear us not doing our duty. We are Canadians and Britishers, and I am satisfied that I speak for the thousand Canadian soldiers in the Contingent, when I say that this is the proudest day in our lives."

We have reason to know that he has done his duty. These were modest, soldierly words. The man who spoke thus was afterwards to be known as the leader of " The Men of Paardeberg." Under a hot fire at Black Mountain in the battle of Israel's Poort he was to be twice wounded while directing his men to seek cover, and despite his wounds was to remain in the field until the work he had been sent out to accomplish had been performed to the letter of his orders. The Government had made no mistake in choosing the commanding officer; his experience made the men glad to follow him and Canadians willing to entrust their sons to his keeping.

Like many others of the most prominent statesmen, soldiers, and financiers of this province, W. D.

Otter received the most significant part of his early education at Upper Canada College. In 1861 he joined the militia force in Toronto and was promoted to a lieutenancy in 1864. He saw his first service at the Niagara Frontier in 1864 and 1865, and in August of the latter year was appointed Adjutant of the Queen's Own. He passed through the Fenian Raid of 1866, proving himself an enthusiastic soldier in camp and on the march, and a brave one in the action at Ridgeway. So much were his services appreciated that in 1873 he was sent to England as second in Command of the Wimbleton Team. In 1874 he succeeded to the command of the Queen's Own. He was soon to have some slight active service, being called out first during the "Pilgrimage Riots," Toronto, in 1875, and two years later during the Grand Trunk Railway Riots, at Belleville. In 1883 he was appointed to the much coveted position of Commandant of the Wimbleton Team, and while in England he gathered important information with regard to military schools. He was appointed Commandant of the School of Infantry, Toronto, in December 1883, and organized C Company, Royal Canadian Regiment of Infantry.

So far his work had been that of an amateur soldier, but an opportunity was soon to be given him of learning what it meant to command troops under hot fire. In 1869, shortly after Confederation, when the rights of the Hudson Bay Company to Prince Rupert's Land were purchased by the Dominion Government, the Half-Breeds, hardy plainsmen and hunters, ignorant of books and unacquainted with the world beyond the limits of their own prairie province, who did not understand this transfer of their lands and themselves, and imagined that they were being robbed of their property and about to be enslaved by their new rulers, broke into open rebellion. The rising brought to the front a hot-blooded Half-Breed, Louis Riel.

He had been educated for the church and this, combined with his magnetic personality and daring, made the French Half-Breeds or Metis and Indians glad to accept him as their leader. He proclaimed a provisional government, and began his career by murdering in a most cowardly manner a settler named Scott.

Colonel Wolseley, now Commander-in-Chief of the British forces, led an expedition of some 1200 men to Fort Garry and suppressed the rebellion without firing a shot. Unfortunately Riel escaped to the United States. The claims of the Half-Breeds were recognized, and for a time all went well; but like the Boers in Cape Colony when their country was transferred from the Dutch to the English, many irreconcilables among the Half-Breeds trekked, if such a word can be used in connection with the western plains, farther north and west. But civilization pressed upon them, discontent with the Dominion Government spread among them; and the Dominion officials, slow to act and careless, or worse, gave much ground for this discontent, and in 1885 Canada found herself with a costly war on her hands.

As in 1869 the rebels were led by Louis Riel, and his successes when he first took up arms with the Metis attracted to his cause the two able Indian Chiefs "Poundmaker" and "Big Bear."

In the struggle that took place Colonel Otter learned much about the kind of warfare he was afterwards to experience in South Africa. He had command of the Battleford Column which, when it assembled at Swift Current, consisted of 543 men of all ranks. The composition is interesting, and reads very much like one of the flying columns sent from Belmont against the rebels in the Douglas and Sunnyside districts and into the Orange Free State. It was made up of 50 men of the North-West Mounted Police (one gun) under Lieutenant-Colonel Herchmer, afterwards appointed to the command of C and D Squadrons of the Canadian Mounted Rifles for service in South Africa; B Battery Royal Canadian Artillery, with 113 men and two guns under Major Short, since killed in Quebec while gallantly fighting a fierce fire; one-half I. S. C. 49 men under Lieutenant Wadmore; 51 men of the Governor General's Footguards under Captain Todd; 274 men of Queen's Own Rifles under Lieutenant-Colonel Miller, and six scouts.

The region through which Colonel Otter had to march this force, was, in April, not unlike the region he afterwards led the Royal Canadians over on the march from Graspan to Pretoria. It was a "vast unoccupied prairie."

It was in 1885 that this unhappy rising of the Indians and Half-Breeds of the North-West against the Government took place, and Colonel Otter was placed in command of the Battleford column. This was the first real chance he had of proving his soldierly qualities and he began his career with one of the finest forced marches on record. It was 160 miles from Saskatchewan Landing to Battleford, and he commenced his campaign by sweeping his column across the stretch of prairie separating these two places in five

MOBILIZING THE TROOPS. 53

and a half days. His force was pitted against the celebrated Indian Chief "Poundmaker," and he successfully outwitted him; and in the fight at Cut Knife Creek prevented him from joining his forces with "Big Bear," thus preventing them from together marching with their united bands to the assistance of the rebel commander-in-chief Louis Riel. Later he commanded the column sent to capture if possible "Big Bear." In every action he proved himself careful of his men, unsparing on himself, and wherever danger was there he was to be found.

This experience on the battlefield only whetted his desire for greater military knowledge, so in 1895 we find him in England attached to the regular army taking the most careful instruction in cavalry, in infantry, and in artillery. At the close of his course he succeeded in passing an examination entitling him to rank as a lieutenant-colonel in the British army.

From the commencement of his military career in 1861 he seems to have had singleness of aim. To be a great soldier has evidently been his ambition, and although the opportunity of putting military genius into practice in this country has been very remote he has been, in season and out of season, an ardent student of military institutions and tactics. As a result when the hour of need arose he found himself fully equipped for one of the most arduous tasks that ever fell to the lot of a commandant.

His senior Major, Lieutenant-Colonel Buchan, has likewise had a brilliant record. Like Colonel Otter he is a Canadian born and an Upper Canada College boy. He, too, joined the Queen's Own Rifles and served through the North West Rebellion during which he narrowly escaped giving his life for his country at Fish Creek when his horse was shot under him. Since 1874 when he joined the Queen's Own as an ensign he has been an enthusiastic military student, and like his commandant, has taken instructions in England in the three great arms of the service.

Canada was indeed happy in having two such men to lead her contingent. It is to be doubted if any British or other Colonial corp was as well officered for the particular work the Empire had to do. Their experience in the North-West Rebellion was of particular advantage to them. The prairie was not unlike the veldt; and in race characteristics, in mode of life, in tactics, the North-Western crack-marksmen resembled the sharp-shooting Boer.

On October 26th the troops these two distinguished officers were to command, began to arrive at Quebec, and by the 29th the one thousand men, gathered in from every town and city from the far Pacific to the far Atlantic, had reached the historic Citadel of French-Canada without a mishap. Their journey to their point of departure for South Africa had been a continuous triumph. At Montreal, Toronto, and Halifax tens of thousands had crowded their line of march and pressed into the station unheeding the authorities who struggled to keep them back. At every stopping place, too, along their route the inhabitants turned out to wish them God-speed. Books would not contain the number of official addresses from mayors, and reeves, and societies that were delivered on this occasion. Torch-light processions, the music of local bands, the shouting of the crowds, told that in every village and town

THE RIGHT HON. JOSEPH CHAMBERLAIN, M.P.

HON. SIR CHARLES TUPPER, BART. G.C.M.G.

there was the same spirit shown as in the packed streets at Halifax, Montreal, Winnipeg, and Toronto. A peace people had been roused, not for war, but for Empire. The rights or the wrongs of the struggle played but a small part in the minds of the soldiers or their enthusiastic admirers; Queen and Empire were everything. It was England's need that was calling them; it was their joy and honor to answer to the call. It is true that the wrongs of the Uitlanders satisfied their conscience in thus flying to arms; but it must have been evident to all, and it must have been of peculiar pleasure to England, to see that her children had risen to a man at her call. Dr. Conan Doyle, the novelist, who has showed his patriotism by going himself to the front, well expressed in a poem written before the Canadian Contingent had reached Quebec the feeling that animated all hearts:

> "Who's that calling?
> The old sea-mother calls,
> In her pride at the children that she bore.
> 'Oh, noble hearts and true,
> There is work for us to do,
> And we'll do it as we've done it oft before.
> Under the flag,
> Under the flag our fathers bore.
> They died in days gone by for it,
> And we will gladly die for it.
> God save the Red Cross Flag!"

The regiment assembled at Quebec was—and it is said in no spirit of boasting—as fine a lot of men as was ever brought together for war, if not the finest. They were the flower of Canada. It was only necessary to glance the eye over the ranks to see how well set up all were; magnificent physiques for the march or the battlefield. But those more familiar with the young men of Canada knew what fine humanity was here represented. There in the ranks stood the stroke oar of the International Champions of America and the winner of the Junior Single Sculls of the Dominion, and with him were five or six others almost as famous in aquatic sports; there was a celebrated pole-vaulter, a sprinter, a cricketer, a paddler, every sport was represented. Over fifty of those bronzed, strong-limbed lads were familiar names on the foot-ball field, and many of them had just doffed their sweaters in the midst of the season to don the tunic. The mimic war of the "gridiron" had well fitted them for real war with all its hardships and dangers. In the ranks, too, were men of wealth and culture, and not a few University men. So eager were our young men to enlist that many officers had resigned their commissions to beg for a place in the ranks. Taken for all in all it was as fine a body of soldiers as could have been brought together, and the loss of many of these gallant fellows to Canada is irreparable. England now owes us a great debt, a debt which trade can never repay.

And these were not the only Canadians to be found in England's service. Every day was bringing news of officers, who had won their rank at the Royal Military College, Kingston, who were also doing gallant service for the Empire. Girouard, who had so notably distinguished himself in the Campaign against the Khalifa, and had been made Director-General of all the Egyptian Railways, was ordered to the Cape to repeat the splendid work he had done in Egypt. He had made Kitchener's way easy against the Khalifa; he was now to make

"Bobs" path straight to Pretoria. Morris was in Ladysmith, McInnes at Kimberley, and others in every corps—gallant fellows such as Cameron, Wood, and Osborne, who were to give their lives for England. Of one of them the celebrated war-correspondent Bennet Burleigh has said in his late work "The Natal Campaign:" "Faultlessly brave little Captain Hensley with whom I have been often in the armoured train and the field, was killed outright, shot in the head." Individually our sons were giving their genius and their lives for England; they were now about to show what as a body of men one thousand strong they would be able to accomplish.

Although England had called to the Colonies at the beginning of the struggle, she did not realize her real need. It was considered by all, and Mr. Chamberlain had even given expression to the feeling on several occasions, that so far as this trivial war was concerned, England could manage alone; but the Colonial display would be an excellent object-lesson to the world, and a splendid opportunity of taking a step towards Imperial Union. The battles of Glencoe and Elands Laagte, too, at the beginning of the war seemed to point to a speedy termination. It was indeed thought by most Canadians and by many of the members of the contingent itself, that the lads would merely have a pleasant trip to South Africa, and a charming sojourn of a few weeks in that mysterious continent. But a change came over the spirit of the public.

It was found that the British victories had been exaggerated, that while the English had proved themselves worthy sons of the sires who fought and fell at Inkerman and Balaclava, the Boer loss had

not been large, and that instead of being utterly
"routed" they had managed to carry off their guns
and their wounded. Mafeking, too, was in danger;
Kimberley was surrounded, and the garrison cut
off; the British forces on the Natal Border were
being, despite their victories, forced back on Ladysmith. A protracted war was evident; much weary
marching must be gone through, much heavy
fighting endured before the Transvaal border could
be crossed.

On the 29th of October the entire contingent had
assembled at Quebec. On the route some of them
had had for the first time their experience in
military life. Their food was the first hint that they
had now left behind home comforts, home luxuries;
the regulation fare of "plain soup, boiled meat, and
great hunks of bread" was a foretaste of what they
might expect in the field. Quebec, too, was to try
their metal. The weather was cold and grey and
dismal, rain and sleet caused them to shiver as they
made their final preparations for leaving the land
of the Maple Leaf. They heeded it but little, however, and though many had to eat their food in the
open air they took all their discomforts as huge
jokes. Little did they think that for months, food,
scant food at that, would be eaten in the open air,
that for weeks at a time they would have to sleep
with nothing but the blue dome of an African sky
for tent roof and the hard veldt for their couch. If
they had realized it they would still have gone with
the same eagerness to the war.

It was a happy circumstance from a historical
point of view that this contingent was to have as its
point of departure Quebec rather than Halifax.
Here our Canadian life began with Champlain's

colony; everything about the great brown cliffs reminded the young soldiers of the sternness of war. Here Wolfe, that gallant type of a noble soldier, had died in giving Canadians a country; here too the covetous invader had been beaten back when this citadel alone remained to Guy Carleton and his small body of British troops and French citizens; here, too, confederation took place—the Great Dominion, a nation within an Empire, became a fact. Now by bringing together the best blood of our land from every part of Canada this confederation was to be finally realised, was to become a living thing.

In his farewell address Mayor Parent uttered words worthy of such a place and such an occasion:

"No matter how diverse may be our origin, and the languages that we speak, who is there that will dare to affirm that we have not all the qualities necessary for the making of a real nation? Who dare say, upon such an occasion as the present, that we are not all sincerely united and loyal towards the Canadian Dominion and loyal to England, which has given us so complete a measure of liberty? We French-Canadians have loyally accepted the new destinies that Providence provided for us upon the battlefield of 1759. Is it possible that anybody can have forgotten 1775 and 1812? On the summit of this proud rock of Quebec, rendered illustrious by Jacques Cartier and Champlain, behold but a few steps from this place the superb monument erected by an English Governor to the memory of Wolfe and Montcalm.

"Why may we not make it the emblem and the symbol of our national unity? Let us leave to each individual amongst us the privilege to retain as a sweet souvenir worthy of a noble heart, the rose or the thistle, the fleur-de-lis or the shamrock, and even the pot of earth the Irish immigrant brings with him from under distant skies, and let us be united for the great and holy cause that we have in hand, the foundation of a great nation and the development of the boundless resources of a rich and immense country. Our best wishes accompany you in the long journey, at the end of which you will no doubt find glory as well as sufferings, privations and perhaps even—heroic sacrifices."

War is horrible!—and let us pray that the call to war may never again be heard within our borders—but this one has done undeniable good. A country with a noble, fighting past is more firmly based than one that has never known war, and if the West should ever cry for separation from the East the blood of the lads from British Columbia, Quebec, and the Maritime Provinces will cry to us from Kopje and Veldt, and we will be true to our past and remain united.

At Quebec the men were feted and the officers dined. The banquet given to Colonel Otter was a memorable one. The Minister of Militia spoke at some length and well-voiced the feeling of every man present and of every citizen of Canada.

"This is an epoch in the history of the Empire at large. It has been a long time coming, but at last the people of Canada have realized their responsibility and the debt they owe the Empire. Canada has thrown off her swaddling clothes, and stands forth as a full grown member of the family which makes up the Empire. We are now making history very fast in connection with this great Empire. Canada is not alone in sending assistance to the

MOBILIZING THE TROOPS.

Mother Country. She has become, not an Empire with a number of dependencies, but an Empire, with a collection of great nations, of which perhaps Canada is the leading one. It has been a process of development slow in the past, but rapid of late. We have been worried a great deal about the nature of the constitution whereby the parts of the great Empire would form portions of the united Empire. This has been worked out just as the great British constitution has been worked out, by a process of development—just as the British constitution is unwritten, so this work is unwritten, and before we know it we find ourselves taking part in the wars of the Empire. We don't know exactly how it has come about, but somehow it has come about. I rejoice that this is a people's movement, not that of any government or party: it eminates from the whole people of Canada and is being endorsed by them as shown by the words and deeds of the people at all points where the troops started from. For proof look at the bank accounts and the work of noble women. No party or government can say that it has had more to do with this than other people. It is a popular movement, and this fact justifies the Government in taking this action in sending the contingent without calling on Parliament. I believe in Constitutional Government—that Parliament must govern the country—but there is something superior to Parliament, it is the people. The voice of the whole people of Canada is backing up the gallant thousand."

The 30th of October will ever be a noteworthy day in the Dominion. For on that day a large body of men were to start for far Africa in the Empire's war, volunteers it is true, but sent by the people and with the consent and aid of the Government. It must not be forgotten, however, that individual Canadians had long been fighting in England's wars. It is true that that fine company of voyageurs which went on the fruitless expedition after Gordon, had won the admiration of England, but these soldiers fought at a time of no great crisis in England's history. Now a united body went forth when the solidarity of the Empire was threatened. It would, however, be well to have in mind Lord Wolseley's message to Lord Lansdowne after the return of the Nile Contingent to Canada.

"They have," he said, "earned for themselves a high reputation among the troops of the Nile. It was, moreover, a source of much satisfaction to these troops to find the Canadians represented on this expedition and sharing with them their privations and risks, at a time when English, Scotch, and Irish soldiers were employed, the presence with them of Canadians shows in a marked manner the bonds which unite all parts of our great Empire."

That contingent went for Gordon; this one was going for Queen and Empire. From every part of the Dominion thousands flocked to give them a worthy farewell. At early morning the soldiers were paraded and addressed by Lord Minto, who as a soldier, could appreciate the excellent body of men before him and the work done in mobilizing them in so short a time.

"You are going forth," he said, "followed by the good wishes of a united country. You are our representatives. We know your bravery and patriotism, and we doubt not of your success. In the name of Her Majesty The Queen, I wish you farewell and God-speed."

MAJOR-GENERAL E. T. H. HUTTON.

MAJOR-GENERAL IVOR J. S. HERBERT.

General Hutton, who has since done such gallant work in South Africa, too, spoke briefly, but with a force that made a deep impression.

"Bear in mind," he said, "that your honor is our honor, that your renown is our renown, and if at any time the strain and drudgery seem hard to bear, remember that in far off Canada are thousands of men and women who look to you to uphold their honor. French-Canadians and British-Canadians recollect the responsibility that rests on your shoulders. I know that you will acquit yourselves like men and like soldiers."

The noblest words uttered that day, however, was the modest speech of Colonel Otter. He was saving his energy for deeds.

"I make no promises," he said, "but I feel in my heart that you can rely on the regiment to maintain and uphold the honor and glory of Canada and of the Empire."

After inspection at the Esplanade the troops were formed into column and marched to the Sardinian. All along the line of march the streets were packed with a dense crowd, cheering and shouting; and weeping, too, for here and there could be heard a sob from some wife or mother or sister or daughter, who had come to Quebec to say farewell for perhaps the last time to husband, son or brother or father.

Since eight o'clock the soldiers had been without food and in heavy marching order, and they were glad, indeed, when the ship that was to be their home for the next four weeks was reached. Till four o'clock came and the captain made ready to cast off the lines the crowd was not allowed to be heavy of heart; the bands of the Royal Canadian Artillery and the pipers of the Royal Scots kept their spirits up by playing stirring airs; and the soldiers themselves, glowing with pride at the thought of being chosen to represent their country in England's war, burst out frequently into rousing, patriotic airs. And so with sounds of rejoicing the last hours in Canada of this brave body of choice spirits were spent. Through the rejoicing, however, a half-sob could here and there be heard as a prayer went up that some dear one might be saved from the dangers of the deep and the fierce fire of the battlefield.

This embarkation was the most significant thing yet done by Canada. The departure of these volunteers with the consent and co-operation of the Government of the Dominion, and the cheers and prayers of the people showed just where Canada stood in the Empire. It is true that on former occasions Canadians had proved themselves ready to help the Motherland, it is true that individual Canadians had won renown in the British army in Europe, in India, and in Africa; but this was the first time that Canada had acted as a united country solely to aid England.

The 100th Regiment was raised in Canada for Imperial defense in 1858, and afterwards served in England, at Gibraltar, at Malta, and in India; but it was not raised and officered by the Governments of the different provinces then forming Canada, but by the British Government. However the word "Niagara" on its colors reminded the parts of the Empire where it served that there was a child of the Empire in the far West ready to spring to arms in England's hour of need.

In 1884 the body of Canadian *voyageurs* was organized at this same fortress to go to the mysteri-

MOBILIZING THE TROOPS.

ous Nile to assist in rescuing that heroic soldier, General Gordon, from the hands of the barbarous fanatics who held him in Khartoum. This force was on a small scale, and in no way moved the people of Canada; but the shouts that now echoed and re-echoed at the foot of the great fortress that had stood many seiges, and had yielded only to British Arms, found an echo in every heart in the Great Dominion: and that grim stronghold scarred with many fights was the one spot in America worthy of such a crowd and such an occasion.

At that hour of parting, on ground hallowed by the death of Wolfe, and made glorious by the stubborn and successful resistance of Guy Carleton against the rebels under Montgomery and Arnold, if the Government had called for another contingent of 1000 men they could have been recruited on the spot.

Never before were Canadians stirred as on that day. In 1812 the national spirit was feebly burning and in places was dim indeed; at the time of the Fenian Raid the insignificance of the force of maurauders made them too contemptible for excessive national feeling. But on this day from Victoria to Halifax the feeling that focused at Quebec, the unselfish loyalty of a child for a parent, filled people of all creeds and nationalities living under the flag of the Dominion with joy at the great opportunity given them to prove that their loyalty was of the kind which is glad to make sacrifices.

CHAPTER IV.

ON THE SARDINIAN.

The lines were cast off at 4 o'clock and the good old Sardinian with the most precious freight—the pick of a nation's sinew and brain—she had ever carried, began to steam down the St. Lawrence, shrilly screaming her farewells to the shouting multitude.

Fully fifty thousand people had come together to bid God-speed to the thousand heroes, for such they had become. The wharfs were black with surging figures, the terraces along the citadel's front were lined with a sea of faces, indeed every point of vantage on the high cliffs, had some one on it waving and cheering; and the cheering and waving did not cease till their voices could be heard no longer by the soldiers on the crowded decks and in the rigging.

A fleet of steam yachts followed the Sardinian down the broadening river wishing her *bon voyage*. For an hour they accompanied the steamer past the Beauport shore, past the tall cliffs where Montmorenci leaps sheer to the stream below, past the beautiful Island of Orleans, picturesque even in its bareness; until darkness was falling they followed her and then with farewell shrieks from their whistles, they sped back to the now silent city.

It was a splendid leave taking; and to make it

all the more impressive the sun which had been hidden for several days before the departure came out in all its glory. To know how beautiful sunset can make the earth it is necessary to visit Quebec and to see the gorgeous evening light playing among the purple hills. On this November evening the earth was bathed in a garment of color,—purple, and azure, and crimson, and golden glowed on the horizon and melted on the hills and faded from the heavens as the Sardinian and her consorts sped oceanwards ; then darkness fell.

The difficulties now began for the officers in command of the Contingent. The ship was ridiculously small for the number of men on board, and they were literally falling over each other at every turn. The galleys were not large enough, or perhaps the cooks had not got the swing of them, and a hungry crowd waited clamouring for their evening meal. When Last Post was sounded it was discovered, too, that some fifty men would have to spend the night without bunks or hammocks.

This latter misfortune was not altogether the fault of the authorities. The strength of the contingent was supposed to be one thousand and nineteen. When the final medical inspection took place at Quebec Surgeon-General Neilson made twenty-nine, who were not the regulation height, fall out of the ranks as unfit for service ; but the lads took it so much to heart—some of them actually shedding tears—that a sympathetic officer appealed on their behalf and all of the twenty-nine save three were allowed to pass. The regiment then numbered ten hundred and nineteen strong, but when the roll of the company was completed it was found that there were ten hundred and thirty-nine on board.

The officers could but wonder where the other twenty came from. So eager were Canadians to join in England's war that some of these men had either stolen on board with the troops or stowed themselves away among the cargo. No one seems to have repented having enrolled his name in the contingent as there has been no report of desertion among the recruits.

At 6.50 a. m. the Sardinian reached Rimouski and at 9.20 took her last farewell of Canada.

Military discipline and military duties at once began on board. Colonel Otter issued regulations ordering daily drills and lectures for both officers and men; but unfortunately for his regulations he could not command the elements. Scarcely had the Sardinian passed into the Gulf than she began to stagger, and pitch, and roll. Very few of the men had ever taken a sea-voyage before and soon a thousand sea-sick soldiers set all regulations aside. To make matters worse a gloomy, thick fog, chill and saturating, settled down on the rolling ocean. So dense did it become that at night steam was shut off for a time and the sleeping soldiers were roused by the stopping of the screw and the ceasing of the throbbing heart of the steamer. All next day the storm continued and the weather remained dull and wet. Seas occasionally came crashing on the deck. Two of the boats that had been insecurely lashed tumbled from their davits; but the stubborn old steamer went sliding up great green waves and plunging into valley depths fearlessly shaking the waters from her. The soldiers were getting properly initiated into sea life and were being somewhat rudely taught what was meant by the saying

"Getting ones sea legs;" but they saw little hope of getting any drill.

On the fourth day out "Teddy" Deslauriers died just after reveille. The waking bugle had but sounded when he heard Last Post. He was loved by all who knew him. He was a promising soldier with eight years experience in the Princess Louise Dragoon Guards; a strong cross-country rider, and it was generally conceded that the horse that "Teddy" Deslauriers could not break would never carry a saddle. His death cast a gloom over the whole ship. This contingent was to see much of death and suffering, but no loss was to impress the soldiers as deeply as the sudden death of their comrade in arms that gloomy, stormy, squally, November day on the angry Atlantic.

In the afternoon he was buried; the Rev. Father O'Leary, who by his nobleness of heart and his dauntless courage on the battlefield has since made himself dear to every man in the contingent, conducted the funeral service. There was scarcely a throat that was not choking, scarcely an eye that was free from tears as the men stood round the body shrouded in its canvas covering over which lay the British flag. All turned away heavy at heart when the sudden splash in the stormy sea told that the first among them to be taken had been consigned to the deep. They now began to realize how near death was to them, and it dawned upon them that doubtless before another year had sped many of them would be resting in the pathless ocean or on the far veldt.

But they were young and strong and the gloom of November 3 vanished to a considerable extent with the bright sun and the smoother seas of the

THE CANADIAN CONTINGENT LEAVING QUEBEC FOR THE CAPE.

Never was such a scene of excitement known in Quebec as when the Contingent, gathered from all the Provinces of the Dominion, embarked on the "Sardinian" for the Cape. As the vessel left, the National Anthem was sung by a crowd of over 40,000 people.

A CANADIAN CONTINGENT FOR SOUTH AFRICA. THE MANITOBA VOLUNTEERS BEING ADDRESSED BY THE MAYOR.

It was in front of the monument erected to the men of the 90th regiment who fell in the Rebellion of 1885 that the

following days. Drill could now be begun and when the squads were lined up it was seen to be much needed. Many of the men were utterly ignorant of the rudiments of military movements, many had never handled a rifle, and the task before the officers was indeed a difficult one. It was soon seen that their enthusiasm for arms and their fine intelligence would make them easy men to drill, even on the difficult parade ground, the deck of the rolling Sardinian.

The first Sunday out was a day of services. They began at 10.30 and continued until 8.00 at night with only intervals for meals. The proximity of the church to the home made all good church-goers, and their solemn mission made them give an attentive ear to the striking words that fell from the lips of the different chaplains.

For a week they had been forging southward through heavy seas. The screw beating, beating; the engines throbbing, throbbing; the whole ship from stem to stern pulsating and trembling as she sped along at the rate of about two hundred and sixty miles a day. She had now reached a warmer climate. Fogs, chill winds were past and she sped through sunny seas with a light breeze playing about her. But the weather began to tell on the stokers and it was soon discovered that the engines were not doing as good work as at the commencement of the voyage. The average daily run was now reduced to about two hundred and thirty-nine miles.

A new species of drill was invented, suited to the crowd, the weather, and the climate. After reveille the men were assembled for parade in their shirts and trousers, and bare-footed and bare-headed went scampering around the deck. When well warmed with the exertion, they shed their scanty clothing, and stood like Adam in Eden before the fall, while a full hose was turned on them individually and in groups. The exercise and refreshing coolness of the bracing salt water made them "as hungry," as one of them said writing to his mother, "as alligators."

The nights too had become hot and the bunks crowded in the hold below the water line, ventilated only by means of canvas chutes, became almost unbearable. At the outset they had been glad of the warm blankets that had been given them, but now they felt even their pjamas a burden.

But they were kept too busy to worry much about the heat. Squad drill and arm drill, writing letters home and making acquaintances, fully occupied their time and before the second week had ended they were thoroughly accustomed to their new life. They had indeed begun to enjoy it, and as they went about the deck with the hardy roving air of a Micawber they began to feel much like "'Er Majesty's Jolly Soldier an' Sailor too!"

Their friends had not been forgetful of them and the barrels and boxes of fruit, of biscuits and other luxuries that had been sent in great quantities helped at times to make them forget that the regular fare was boiled beef, potatoes, and "punk," as they scornfully termed the bread. At first they had an abundance of cigars and cigarettes, but before the end of the voyage the gifts of tobacco that had been bestowed on the contingent by the wealthy tobacco manufacturers of Canada, had almost entirely disappeared; and a soldier with a package of cigarettes was never without friends. The thousand youthful smokers did not take long to consume the ten thousand cigars, the twenty thousand cigarettes, and the thousand pounds of tobacco that had been sent on board the Sardinian. Another day at sea and there would have been a literal tobacco famine on board—a horrible thing to contemplate.

If the pipe helped to wile away the time, the store of books that had been contributed did much to make life less tedious. Many, however, never opened a book; the fascination of the ocean was upon them, and they would sit for hours looking over the great blue sea, dreaming of—they knew not what. The infinite vastness of the multitudinous sea held them under its mysterious charm. There were others, however, who were never without their book in hand, and, it must be added, their pipe in mouth. Kipling was their favorite. His sturdy vigour, his rugged force appealed to these strong young men, while his enthusiasm for the Empire touched at this time a responsive chord in their hearts. They understood now for the first time his "Song of the Sons:"

> "One from the ends of the earth—gifts at the open door—
> Treason has much but we, Mother, thy sons have more!
> From the whine of a dying man, from the snarl of a wolf-pack freed,
> Turn, and the world is thine, Mother, be proud of thy seed!
> Count, are we feeble or few? Hear, is our speech so rude?
> Look, are we poor in the land? Judge, are we men of The Blood?
> Those that have stayed at thy knees, Mother, go call them in—
> We that were bred over seas wait and would speak with our kin.
> Not in the dark do we fight—haggle and flout and gibe;
> Selling our love for a price, loaning our hearts for a bribe.
> Gifts have we only to-day—Love without promise or fee—
> Hear, for thy children speak, from the uttermost parts of the sea!"

They have done more than speak, they were acting. They were ploughing their way across the limitless ocean to prove England's words, "Truly ye come of The Blood," and that they were, "Flesh of the flesh that I bred, bone of the bone that I bare."

Kipling did much on this trying journey to nerve the arm and strengthen the sinews of these Canadian Soldiers of the Queen.

They had other recreations besides reading and smoking and brooding. The first few days out watching the horizon for sails kept many amused, then several whales hove in sight and sent great streams of vapor high in the air; sea-birds, too, screamed about them, and occasionally the dorsil fin of a shark, the grim wolf of the ocean, was seen cleaving the sea like a knife. But these companions of their way grew rarer and rarer, and at last their only comrades were the flocks of "Mother Carey's Chickens" that flew after them waiting for the refuse of the galley and the crumbs from the table. These, too, left them in time and for several days they sped along with naught to relieve the monotony of the blue sky and bluer ocean. They were travelling an unfrequented course, taking a short cut across the Atlantic and no sail was sighted after the first day or two.

On their sixth day out they were to have a strange visitor. "A fluffy little bunch of feathers" was seen perched in the rigging. A friendly fearless bird! He had no doubt frequently experienced the hospitality of lonely ships in mid-ocean, and knew that he was in no danger. He stayed with them for some time, the cynosure of all eyes, going over every part of the boat. When he had thoroughly investigated this strange craft, from truck to parade deck, he pruned his feathers and flew out into space. There was not a man on board but would have given his month's pay to have had the little fellow back again. How strange is the human heart! Here they were going, armed to the teeth, for war, longing for the chance to hunt Boers, and yet they almost wept at the thought that some harm might befall their little visitor on the broad, lonely deep.

Early in the morning of the twelfth land was sighted. It was the Cape Verd Islands, a barren desolate spot, but a relief from the world of waters. As they sped past St. Vincent a British war-ship and several transports were observed and signals interchanged. Some of the soldiers already had lengthy letters written for their friends at home and hoped that a moment's stop might be made, but they were disappointed. Soon the misty islands about which the north-east winds play everlastingly were but a speck on the horizon and then vanished from view.

Not half way! O the weary waste of waters that had yet to be crossed before Table Mountain would tell them that the end of the journey had come. They could expect but one more glimpse of land before their journey's end. St. Helena, that historic island which the French soldiers on board longed so earnestly to see, towered high out of the ocean two thousand two hundred and eighty six miles farther on.

In the meantime all had been kept busy. An iron shield had been erected in the bow of the ship, Morris tubes fitted to the rifles and daily practice begun. It was sadly needed. The war this contingent was hurrying to, was, in the initial stage at least, to be a war where the steady arm and sure eye would be most needed. The intricate evolutions of the parade ground would be of little avail; good marksmanship was worth far more than much wheeling and turning. No doubt the daily practice on the Sardinian went far to make these soldiers capable of keeping Cronje's men in close cover in the bed of the Modder during that trying week of fierce fighting in February.

The soldiers, too, had to be vaccinated, and the four nurses were kept busy making bandages for the arms of the victims. To the disgust of the surgeon, and, it is to be feared, to the delight of many of the men, the supply of vaccine ran out when only one hundred and eighty-three men had been vaccinated, and when there was still three hundred to undergo the ordeal.

Stores, too, had to be overhauled. The Sardinian had been fitted up at a moment's notice; the loading had been done with even greater rapidity and many important articles were missing, or known to be buried under piles of baggage that would not be needed till Cape Town was reached. But the energy of the officers and the experience of Captain Todd, who was on his way to join his regiment at the front, and who had been appointed acting quartermaster for ship duties, soon had these difficulties straightened out. One thing they could not straighten out however. There was not sufficient khaki on board for the regiment. If they had only been able to change trousers into tunics all would have been well, for in some mysterious way six hundred pairs of trousers that were not needed were sent and two hundred and sixty tunics were found wanting.

The vessel had now got into the tropics. What a

change it was from the bleak autumn winds of the Gulf and the St. Lawrence. No rain, no sleet; warm winds and a burning sun. Coats and boots were a burden and the men were permitted to go coatless and bootless between nine in the morning and retreat. In a few days the privilege with regard to the boots had to be withdrawn. Blistered feet, sunburnt arms and legs were the order of the day. They were now as brown as Indians and were rapidly becoming fit for the hot sun of South Africa.

Sore feet was not the only trial brought by the fierce tropical sun. Thirst, thirst, unquenchable thirst stayed with them from sunrise till sunset. The unfortunate part of the tropical thirst is that it delights in being fed. The more water they drank the more they seemed to require. A thousand thirsty men managed to consume enormous quantities of fresh water and by the end of the second week at sea the captain reported that there was danger of the ship's water supply running short. The men were warned of the evil of giving way to thirst, but they heeded it not, and it was found necessary, first to threaten that unless more care were taken with the water they would have to be put on allowance; and finally a guard was posted over the tanks.

Four long, weary, hot, thirsty days had passed since St. Vincent was sighted; four tiring, monotonous days. On the fourth, however, a little after five in the morning, and when the men were busy at their running drill, all were startled by the cry, "A ship in sight!" From lip to lip the word passed, from deck to keel, from stem to stern; through the men's quarters it was carried, into the officers' rooms it found its way, and soon every soul on board was on deck straining hungry eyes to catch a glimpse of the vessel bearing, like their own, human souls for peace or war.

It proved to be the Rangatira bound for Southampton. At first she steamed away from the Sardinian, and no wonder. The Sardinian cut a figure that was calculated to alarm any ordinary craft. She was strangely fitted out with her high-built decks, her rigging was lined with drying clothes and haversacks, and from forecastle-head to quarter-deck she was a sea of faces. The Rangatira had been on the Atlantic for several weeks and she could not but fear that European complications might have arisen in the war in the meantime. The Sardinian might be some foreign foe, or one of the privateers to which Kruger was said to have given letters of marque at the beginning of the war. Whatever she thought, she at first seemed inclined to give the Allan Liner a wide berth. But she, too, was no doubt lonely with weary plunging across the thousands of miles separating her from England, and so she drew nearer and nearer until less than a quarter of a mile was between the two vessels.

She was a welcome sight with her heavy, broad, black hull and her dirty yellow smoke-stack. An ocean tramp, but no Atlantic ocean-grey-hound ever seemed so fair! She could be their messenger home. All had some word to send to relatives, friends, to lovers, and not a few to the papers. Indeed almost every local paper had its own "special correspondent" on board. Two big, fat bags of mail matter were gathered together, one of the life boats lowered, and the precious load of glad messages borne over the smooth tropical sea to the broad-hulled freighter.

ON THE "SARDINIAN"—A GROUP OF CANADIAN OFFICERS.

ON THE STEAMSHIP "SARDINIAN," A GROUP OF CANADIAN OFFICERS.

No time was lost. Soon the boat returned with gloomy news from the seat of war. A copy of the Cape Town *Times* had fortunately been preserved on board of the Rangtira, and the news it contained went like an electric thrill through the ship.

The British had met with severe reverses; Ladysmith was in danger; a fierce conflict had been waged outside that military centre, and although the Boers had been repulsed, the British, under Sir George White, had been forced to order a general retirement, and the whole army on the Natal border had fallen back on this fortified encampment. Glencoe, Elands Laagte and Rietfontein had been barren victories. This was not the worst news. A column had been sent out to seize Nicholson's Nek. Lieutenant-Colonel Carleton was in command of a force of one thousand two hundred men, consisting of four and a half companies of the Gloucesters, six companies of the Royal Irish Fusiliers, and the Tenth Mountain Battery. A few rifle shots from ambushed Boers frightened the hardy little mules bearing the mountain guns, and a general stampede had followed. Battery mules and infantry ammunition mules broke away from their drivers, and the soldiers were left to face a host of enemies with only the cartridges they carried in their pouches. For over eight hours they had held out against the enemy, but when dawn came and the last cartridge was fired they were forced to surrender. Over a thousand British troops seized by the Boers in one haul—it was hard to realize.

The news of this reverse was read by everyone who could get hold of the precious copy of the Cape Town *Times* with mingled feelings. All were sorry for the Gloucesters and the Fusiliers and the Mountain Battery, but they were strangely pleased at the thought that there was now no doubt about their future. They would see war, and plenty of it. These weary leagues of barren sea would not have been traversed in vain.

Sir Redvers Buller was at the Cape, and was about to hurry to Durban to take charge of the operations on the Natal border, and if possible to save the fine troops and valuable stores now shut up in Ladysmith. War was near at hand! With this thought the soldiers went to their drills with new ardour, and the music of the grindstones as they sharpened the bayonets had a new meaning.

War was now a sure thing, and they must be ready for it. The white helmets had to be dyed as nearly khaki color as possible, so had the haversacks; and at last a mixture of coffee and diamond dyes was found that would answer the purpose. When the work was completed, however, there was a variety of shades, and not a few were marvellously streaked.

In the midst of their bayonet sharpening and helmet dyeing the Equator was reached. It is Neptune's custom to come on board as a vessel crosses the Line and shave all who have never before been in his domain. But Neptune evidently had never seen so many Canadian men on one ship, or perhaps he saw no room on the crowded boat for setting up his barber shop, and so did not make the customary visit. It would never do, however, to pass this celebrated spot on the globe's surface without some manifestation of interest, and the whistle was blown and several rockets were sent up, and the good boat found herself no longer in Northern waters. Passing this point seemed to indicate that the journey was drawing to a close. This lonely, long journey with no companions save the silver-colored, broad-finned flying-fish that swam and leaped and sailed high in air about them.

Hot, blistering weather was anticipated; but after passing the Line the sky became clouded and the air pleasantly cool.

The ship continued to be a veritable bee-hive. The nurses were occupied covering the water bottles with khaki; the men with two parades each day instead of one, the usual thing on ship board, with dyeing helmets and haversacks, making puggarees, sharpening bayonets, and practising at the rifle range with the Morris tubes; the officers at drill and at lectures, and at revolver practice. Through it all Bandmaster Tresham's band, which had now by dint of constant practice become to the minds of the soldiers a not unworthy rival of Sousa's, kept the spirits of all buoyant with airs from the land of the pine and the Maple Leaf.

Captain Bell, too, had got his Maxim gun out of the hold and his special squad well in hand. From the gun's position on the stern of the boat a shower of bullets would occasionally go crashing into the barrel that bobbed about on the tossing waters far astern.

Everything spoke of war, and the eagerness of the men to be ready for the inevitable fight. The stir and bustle of the boat stood out in striking contrast with the ocean, which was at times smooth and calm and blue and silken by day, sparkling and phosphorescent by night.

All now seemed to enjoy the voyage and the work excepting the officers' unhappy horses in their cramped quarters. It was pathetic to watch them standing day and night through those long hot weeks, never allowed to lie down, only getting occasional relief from the slings in which they slept.

But there is an end to all things, and when on the 27th the target for rifle practice was taken down and preparations for disembarking began everyone knew that Cape Town would soon be sighted.

The water had now became a little rougher, and the boat rolled villainously. She was getting top-heavy. Her coal bunkers were nearly empty, and the thousand hungry mouths on board had devoured the greater part of her cargo. So she wallowed and rolled onward seemingly tired and staggering after her unwonted voyage until the morning of the 29th, when like a clear clarion of victory the cry rang out, "Land, land!" and through the morning mists far, far ahead loomed up the bold top of Table Mountain.

CHAPTER V.

AT CAPETOWN.

At the sound of the word "land," the ship became alive with murmuring voices and hurrying feet. Soon all excepting those on duty crowded the deck of the rolling Sardinian to watch the distant shore. The clear South African air was very deceptive. For hours the vessel plowed on and on, and never a foot nearer did the ship seem to be to land; but at last the surrounding country stood out and even the houses could be discerned. In a few hours they would be on firm earth once more. To their impatient spirits the old boat seemed very slow indeed, and it was not until they passed Robben Island that they realized they were in the land of their dreams.

The first glimpse of it was foreboding. Robben Island, barren and flat and parched, was a type of much of the country they were to spend the greater part of the next year in. When they learned that it had been the home of convicts in by-gone years, and was now the abode of lepers, they shuddered at the first glimpse of Darkest Africa that greeted them.

There, too, before them stood out, bold and grey against the sky, Table Mountain. As they gazed upon its wooded sides and its bald sandstone top, it seemed, as they thought of war and death, as it had seemed a few weeks before to G. W. Steevens, more like a gigantic coffin than a table. On either side of it stood its buttressing hills; Devil's Mountain rising in irregular peaks on the left to a height of 3,315 ft., and on the right the solid, gloomy, scarred mass of Lion's Head.

Many on board had got their ideas of Table Bay and its surroundings from the quaint old woodcuts so common in books dealing with South Africa. For once the woodcuts had not lied. Stiff, wooden, unpicturesque stood out these barren hills with severe harshness of outline against the clear dome of the South African sky.

But for them the landscape had one pleasing quality. That broad town nestling apparently in the distance right up to the foot of these towering hills sent their minds back to Old Quebec. As they thought of that dear old fortress and the shouting thousands not a few felt a sudden pang of homesickness It was only for a moment they were following the paths of glory; somewhere through those barren hills they would march to glory or the grave—and for them the march could not begin too soon.

At noon the sudden clattering of the steam winch and the din of the rattling cable as the anchor sank into the deep waters of Table Bay told them that the end of their journey was reached. The Sardinian grim and tired had staggered and rolled her way for about seven thousand and three hundred miles. She seemed to have got the habit of rolling, and now as she lay tugging at her anchor chains she threw herself from side to side on the smooth swells, till many of the young soldiers thought she was about to roll over.

What a picture of war was presented. The bay was crowded with ships, transports heavily laden with munitions of war lay on all sides; transports crowded with men rolled proudly under the shadow of the hills, weary with their long journey from Southampton and Australia and New Zealand—from the ends of the earth; men-of-war with their well-protected hulls and their frowning black-lipped cannon could be seen here and there among the fleet of "liners" turned into "cargo-boats." English all, or nearly all; and each one had come in England's hour of need, for from every peak the Union Jack rose and fell on the light sou-easter.

The welcoming cheers of the fleet told that the Sardinian was recognized, and as she swung on her anchor trying to steady herself the same music that had sounded farewell to her under the dark gray heights of Quebec echoed over the waters of Table Bay. Rule Britannia, God Save the Queen, and Soldiers of the Queen, told Canada's Sons that the spirit of Quebec was the spirit of Table Bay. The cheers of the Australians and New Zealanders, who had just arrived, the cheers and shouting and piping of the Dargai Highlanders, who had come to prove that what they had done on ridge in Northern India they could do on kopje in South Africa; the rollicking shouts of " 'er Majesty's Jollies," whose comrades were playing such an important part with the naval guns about Ladysmith and on the Kimberley route, all told them, they were expected and needed. It was a royal greeting and well repaid them for the privations and hardships of the four hot, cramped, lonely ocean weeks.

The day was somewhat hazy, but still a good view of Cape Town could be had. There it lay, the big, straggling town, looking out towards the ocean, the meeting place of two worlds; the lazy, mysterious

East, and the bustling, energetic West. It seemed, however, a small city, dwarfed as it was by the great flat hills towards which it sloped. The houses were not tall and towering, but low, and broad, and flat like the mountain in the rear. Avenues of trees could be seen, oak and pine and poplar planted by the early Dutch settlers of the last century. These trees presented a strange appearance. They did not grow tall and stately as in other lands, but were bent and flattened at the top by the steady winds that blew up the misty haze from where the Mozambique current meets the cold Antarctic stream.

The attention of the men was soon drawn from the transports, the men-of-war, the hills, houses, and trees, and broad red roads intersecting the low lying town, to a heavy-built side-wheeled tug that came speeding towards them. It was the official boat with Sir Alfred Milner's A. D. C. on board, and with him came Lieutenant Duffus, a Canadian in the Imperial Service in South Africa.

It soon became known that the Regiment was to be sent to the front at once. The war was being waged with vigor on the Natal Frontier, throughout Cape Colony, and on the road to Kimberley. News of the battles had been shouted from passing boats and the Canadians knew vaguely the situation, but with the coming of the tug, newspapers drifted on board and were eagerly devoured.

What a bloody week the last one had been! From the 23rd to the 28th there had been one round of battles. Methuen had driven back the Boers at Belmont; had met them again at Graspan and seized, with incredible bravery, the kopjes on which they were entrenched, and forced them back on the

TORONTO MEN SHARPENING BAYONETS ON THE "SARDINIAN."

GROUP OF OFFICERS OF CANADIAN MOUNTED RIFLES (NORTHWEST SQUADRON).

For Active Service in South Africa.

AT CAPETOWN.

Modder River. Here a last bloody, hot, thirsty fight had taken place with a final victory to the British. Three fierce, well-contested battles in five days—this did indeed look like war, and all of these fights had been bloody and trying. On the East at Willow Grange the Boers had been beaten after a hard struggle. General Gatacre had successfully occupied Bushman's Hoek; brilliant sorties were being made from Kimberley; Mafeking and Ladysmith, though sorely pressed, were holding their own against a numerous foe. Through the length and breadth of the affected districts the war was being actively carried on, and though the British soldiers were proving themselves successful, they were suffering great loss and were forced to fight for every foot of ground they won. For seven weeks the struggle had gone on and yet not a single shot had been fired on the territory of the Republics.

These tidings effected the Canadians strangely. They were now brought face to face with war and death. On the morrow they would be landed and in a few days they would be at the front. They had deemed the work and privations and heat on the Sardinian hardships, but these things were luxuries compared with what the men under Gatacre and Methuen and Buller were enduring. But they felt no regret. They rejoiced that they had come, and impatiently awaited the morrow when they were to be marched to camp.

At six o'clock their boat moved into the dock. As they neared the landing place the steamships whistled and the crowds on their decks shouted themselves hoarse. The Canadians filled with the spirit of their country and the Empire, burst into a rousing chorus and "The Maple Leaf" and "Canada Forever" rang out over Table Bay. When the long dock was reached the dense crowd that cheered wildly showed how Canada's action in sending this contingent was appreciated. Amidst shouting, whistling, singing, and the playing of martial airs the lines were thrown ashore and the Canadians felt themselves a part of the African Continent.

Many in the crowd were disappointed at their appearance. They had expected a different race of men. Canada, through the pictures in English papers that had reached them, was a region of snow, half-breeds and wild Indians, and they were somewhat surprised to see this body of men like unto themselves, a little taller as a whole, a little more wiry and athletic, but English all, in appearance, refined and intelligent. No tomahawks here, no scalping knives, no war paint, no blanket-encased figures.

The lads, however, soon won the hearts of the crowd—this strangely mixed crowd, black and white and yellow and brown; Malays, Hindoos, Kaffirs, and Europeans all mingled together. Truly Cape Town was the meeting place of two worlds and of all races and colors. The pickaninnies seemed to predominate and the Canadians threw them handfuls of coppers; a scramble began and a shower of coppers rained all along the dock. The crowd stared open-mouthed. Here was a new breed of "Tommy Atkins," a Tommy with money to throw away. Extravagance, recklessness, is ever appreciated, and this simple act, done in a spirit of fun, won even the hearts of the Boer-sympathizers in the crowd; and many began to throw on board the Sardinian papers, cigarettes and cigars.

AT CAPETOWN.

The men were not allowed ashore that day, or rather were permitted merely to stretch their limbs for a couple of hours within the limits of the dock. A few, however, obtained special permission to visit the town, and at last-post brought back wild tales of the sensation they had created in the city.

There was but little sleep that night. A continuous bustling and rushing and shouting as the accoutrements and horses and guns and baggage were disembarked, kept nearly every one awake; and it was a tired and sleepy, but excited lot of men, that rolled out of bunk and hammock at the sound of reveille at 4.30 in the morning.

All were kept busy for several hours packing up and sorting their valuables, wondering what to take with them and what they would be forced to leave behind. Friends had been generous; precious little keepsakes had found their way into every haversack, but every article, be it ever so small, added to the weight the soldier would have to carry; and besides paper, books, and keepsakes took up room that on the march would have to be given to food.

By breakfast time they were ready to answer the call to fall in. There was a certain sense of regret as they left the old Sardinian at 8.30 and fell in by companies on the crowded dock. The close quarters on the ship had brought the men of the contingent very much together, and friendships such as are formed only at school or college were made. Besides she was a link between them and Canada—a Canadian ship. But they had no time for sentimental broodings. To Green Point about four miles from the city they were to be marched, there to await further orders, for on the morrow they were to be sent to the front.

As they fell in there were three thoroughly disgusted companies. While the remaining five were fresh, modern, and gorgeous in their new khaki uniforms; these three through the blundering of someone had to fall in in their dull, dirty-looking rifle uniforms, which through the new developments in war had been consigned to the dark ages along with the Snider rifle and the smooth-bore cannon. The three, F. H. and G., were not a little pleased when they were told that they would not have to march through the streets with the others but were detailed for regimental duties with the baggage and otherwise.

After inspection the men weighted down with their heavy kits were marched through the crowded streets to Green Point. On the line of march a vast multitude had assembled to greet them—and curse them too; for in the crowd were many frowning faces, gloomy at seeing the children of the Empire thus standing by the Motherland. They were in sympathy with their fellow-countrymen, one in blood and tongue, in the Transvaal and the Orange Free State. So far they had hoped for victory for their race, but Canada, Australia, and New Zealand were doing more to kill that hope than all the regiments of England.

Through the crowd the lads from the Land of the Maple Leaf marched, looking neither to the right nor the left. Steady as veterans they went, and the crowd cheered and cheered and shouted words of praise and greeting. The Maxim gun squad attracted a great deal of attention, for in the place of horses Privates Hendrie and Machim dragged the

AT CAPETOWN. 101

gun through the streets. From every window, flying across the street, floating high overhead, were words of greeting, decorations, and flags. Even the post-office flew the British flag. So bitter had the war feeling been in Cape Town, and so strong was the influence of the Afrikander Bond up till this time that the Government had not ventured to raise the British flag to welcome the troops coming to battle against the Republics.

There is an end to all things, and there was at last an end to the weary, trying march to Green Point. The men had not yet lost their sea-legs, and the hot tramp and the heavy burden each had to carry—almost a hundred pounds per man—made them glad indeed when the charming camping spot, fronting the cool sea and shaded by the hills, was reached.

There was no time to rest however. Tents had to be pitched, camp duties performed, and when this was done khaki frocks were got out of stores and distributed to F, H and G companies. Boots, too, English army boots, had to be handed out to the men, and a thousand serviceable clasp knives. All this took time, and it was evening before the regiment could think of stretching itself at ease on the green plain swept by the cooling breezes of the ocean.

It had been a hot day, and the men were wearied with the long, cramped journey on the Sardinian, the scorching march through the city and their camp duties; but Cape Town had been their Mecca. On the morrow they were to depart from it, perhaps never to see it again, and so many got permission to leave camp. Some had during the afternoon visited the surrounding country, and even investigated the moist valleys at the spongy top of Table Mountain. The shade of the trees familiar in their native land —the oak and poplar and pine—was like a summer breath from Canada. But what interested them most was the silver tree which stood out on the landscape in such striking contrast with its European comrades which had been transplanted in the early days of Cape Colony. The leaves covered with their silvery hair-like down were collected by many to be sent over-seas as curiosities.

In the city the Canadians were the observed of all observers. Australians and New Zealanders were more or less familiar to the Cape people, but these men from Canada were unfamiliar beings. The wonder of the inhabitants did not cease at the way the boys spent their money. Some were rich, and all were young, thinking only of the present, and the money slipped through their fingers like water. The more observant among them gathered much information about the conditions of affairs in South Africa.

The war was not likely to be finished for some months, and there was grave danger that England would have to contend with a second American Revolution. Public opinion in Cape Town was sharply divided. While on the one hand the action of England in attempting to bring Kruger and the Volksraad to their knees was applauded; on the other England and her soldiers were execrated with curses both loud and deep. The pro-Boer party was decidedly outspoken, and the hope was openly expressed that a general rising throughout the whole of Cape Colony and Natal would take place in the interests of the Republics.

These were too serious thoughts, however, to

occupy much place in the young soldiers' minds, and their attention was more taken up with the cold sparkling champagne that flowed like water, the cooling beer, and the refreshing strawberries and cream—strawberries and cream in December!

The streets, too, so different from the thoroughfares of Montreal and Quebec, interested them greatly. The white cabs, each named after some hero, statesman or steamship; the blood-red trolley cars; the pictured omnibusses; the Malays, the Hindoos, the blacks, the whites from every land—all these things were of an absorbing interest. The cabdrivers and porters, some in turbans, others with high-pointed straw hats rising like "Pagodas," made them realize that the West was behind them, that they were at the gateway to the burning East.

Tired, sleepy, utterly exhausted, all returned to camp in good time and threw themselves down to sleep as they had not slept for a month.

On the morrow preparations began at reveille for their journey to the front. At noon everything was ready for their march through the town to the station. Past the summer residences at Green Point and Somerset Road the regiment marched, and cheers and greetings and applause accompanied the men at every step. Along they marched with steady, confident step, these representatives of a young nation. In two divisions they marched with the Maxim guns separating them. The first division was headed by a bugle band and pipers, and above the shouting, and the tramp of the marching thousand, shrilled out the bagpipes at the head of the column. The second division was headed by the Cape Garrison Artillery Band, the khaki-clad men, marching steadily, steadily; the surging crowd shouting and waving; the set, determined, yet happy expression of the soldiers in the ranks—all presented a sight never to be forgotten. That day the Cape *Argus* and *Times* went into raptures over Canada and her men. The *Times* well voiced the feelings of the onlookers.

"Surely never before did such a gigantic throng of people gather in the streets; they began in thin fringes at Bree Street and ended in immovable masses of men and women in Adderley Street. From Parliament House to the station—immovable only as far as change of place goes. Packed in rows on footpath and roadway they greeted the men off to the front with volley after volley of cheers, waved hats, handkerchiefs, sunshades, hands. Not a soul was silent, but each vied with the other in giving voice to the admiration and half-sorrowful regret they felt for the gallant sons of the "Lady of the Snows," going light-heartedly to grapple with those who would dare assail the Old Lion. It is no stretch of language to say that the city was moved as it never before was stirred, and the troops caught the contagion."

At 2 o'clock the station was reached. Almost simultaneously Sir Alfred Milner, the man next to Joseph Chamberlain most prominent in the Empire's eye, arrived to bid the contingent God-speed on the way to the front.

All strove to get a glimpse of the man whose action had brought them from Canada. On his shoulders rested the weight of the war; his diplomacy made it. It was an appalling responsibility, and and whether he had acted wisely or foolishly no man could know till the struggle the contingent was now about to enter upon was finished. Evi-

DEPARTURE OF THE CANADIANS FROM CAPE TOWN TO THE FRONT, DECEMBER 1st.
Sir Alfred Milner shaking hands with the Officers, Col. Otter, O.C. is on Sir Alfred's right.

THE CANADIAN CONTINGENT PASSING UP ADDERLEY STREET, CAPE TOWN

dently the responsibility did not sit lightly upon him, and the lines of care in his face, the stern, determined lips, told that he felt keenly the bloody engagements that were taking place in Natal and to the North.

The ringing cheers of the crowd, the whole-hearted singing of the National Anthem, the manly rendering by the Canadians of the Maple Leaf, drove serious thoughts of war and death from the minds of all, and when at last the whistle shrieked out above the shouting of the pressing multitude, and the train began to move slowly, slowly on its Northward way, the bands and the crowd reached a climax of enthusiasm in the strains of Auld Lang Syne. Hand grasped hand; Australian, New Zealander, Canadian, South African, Englishman, had united their hearts and their hands under the shadow of Table Mountain.

How strange a thing is history! The politicians had been vainly striving for a solution of the Imperial problem. In London, in Sydney, in Ottawa, they had disputed, almost fought over it. Suddenly the spirit that broods over history solved it in far Africa. Shoulder to shoulder the hour of need had brought them, and without the aid of Parliaments, or laws they found themselves one. The children of England from the ends of the earth had flocked to prove that Imperial Union was already a fact.

CHAPTER VI.

ON THE ROAD TO THE FRONT.

THE Canadians had had a little more than twenty-four hours of Cape Town and its surroundings and they were glad to get away from its busy, crowded streets. Their desire, their one desire, was to get to the front. They had feared when on the Sardinian that they would be too late for the fight, and now every man of the contingent was anxious to get into the battle that General Methuen was supposed to be planning, a battle that was at once to scatter the Boers on the Kimberley line and relieve that sorely pressed city.

A score or two of very unhappy lads were left behind at Cape Town—one with a sprained ankle, another with a dislocated shoulder, some by the necessities of the regiment, and some as physically unfit to undergo the severe hardships of an African camp. These no doubt were the very ones whom Surgeon-General Neilson had at first refused to pass at the final inspection at Quebec.

Slowly the train—or rather trains, for half of the regiment left about two hours before the rest—puffed and groaned up and up the "dusty stairway" leading to the battlefields of the North. The progress was slow and there were many stops on account of the crowded state of the roads. Ample time was given them to view the country; and the dried up spruits they crossed; the bald, stone-strewn hills they threaded their way among; the great stretches of yellow, brown, and red desert; the wildernesses sprinkled with tufts of wild sage—brought home to them the truth of the lines of a South African bit of doggerel:—

"The rivers of South Africa have no waters,
The birds no song, the flowers no scent."

Nothing so well describes the South African landscape as a paragraph from the late George W. Steevens' book, "From Cape Town to Ladysmith." To him as to hundreds of others these deserts had a mysterious charm, and in a few illuminating sentences, such as only a man of transcendent genius could have written, he gives this charm :—

"Believe it or not, this is the very charm of a desert—the unfenced emptiness, the space, the freedom, the unbroken arch of the sky. It is ever fooling you, and yet you forever pursue it. And then it is only to the eye that cannot do without green that the karroo is unbeautiful. Every other color meets others in harmony, tawny sand, silver-grey scrub, crimson-tufted flowers like heather, black ribs of earth, puce shoots of screes, violet mountains in the middle distance, blue fairy battlements guarding the horizon. And above all broods the intense purity of the South African Azure—not a colored thing, like the plants and the hills, but sheer color existing by and for itself."

Under such a sky, through such a country, the Canadians were travelling—every hour bringing them nearer battle, so they thought. The mystery of this strange new country, resembling either a half made world or one that had worn itself out in ages gone by, seized them. The spell that possessed them was not unlike the feelings that swept over their minds as they had viewed the weary miles of barren sea stretching from horizon to horizon for those four tiring weeks on the Sardinian.

The excitement of the day had, however, thoroughly played them out, and when cooling night fell they were glad to shut out veldt and kopje and snatch a much needed sleep. How strange Africa seemed to them! The land, the vegetation and the streams were unlike any they had ever experienced before, and now this sudden refreshing coolness after the intense, parching, thirsty heat of the day was yet another marvel.

Next morning they were awake with the sun and their grimy, hot train still bore them upward through the never-ending stretch of hill-strewn veldt. Here and there a railway station, or a corrugated-iron store attracted their attention. They counted the miles by the telegraph poles and the camps of the men guarding the track. What a job England has on hand, they thought, as they saw, every mile or so, the tents of the Cape Volunteers who watched night and day to see that no rail was loosened, no obstruction placed in the way o f the ever-passing trains which carried to the front supplies and a seemingly endless host of men. As they thought of the vast extent of South Africa and the long stretches of railway from Durban to Ladysmith, from Port Elizabeth to Colesburg, from Cape Town to Kimberley that had to be guarded with such vigilance, against, not the Republics, but the Boer sympathizers on British territory, they knew England would have no holiday march to Pretoria, and they saw before themselves months of camp and field.

All day Saturday they climbed the Great Karroo weary of the heat and the grime and longing for the refreshing night. Through the darkness they sped, and at 3 o'clock on Sunday morning after a ride of almost forty hours they reached De Aar station where they were to detrain and await further orders. The right-half of the Regiment was the first to arrive and an hour and a half later the left-half joined their comrades.

They were at once led to the portion of the camp alloted to them. Tired with their long railway journey, tired with the excitement of their brief stay in Cape Town, tired with the hurry of disembarking, thoroughly exhausted—when the command "Stand at ease" was given they threw themselves down on the soft yellow sand to snatch a brief moment's rest before the heat of the day would make sleep impossible.

The regiment was now in the field, and in good company. The Duke of Cornwall's Light Infantry, with whom they were afterwards to be associated on that hot trying day in February before Cronje's trenches, was on the right, and on the surrounding hills were the Royal Engineers. With such regiments the Canadians began to feel like veterans, and when the tents were detrained they went about the work of pitching them with an air of having done it all their lives. They were, however, thankful when the tents were up and never heard a more welcome sound than the call to rations. Luxurious fare they were to have for men who had travelled for five hundred miles up the sweltering karroo. Coffee or water and biscuits—hard fare; but there was no complaint. This was war and the sooner they learned to do with the hardest and most meagre fare the better.

The fast broken they began to settle themselves

for the enjoyment as best they could of a quiet Sabbath. A light breeze began to play among their tents, and little eddies of dust, dust imps, whirled into their tents and beat against them. The wind increased, and the eddies grew till they were regular "Dust Devils" and soon the whole air was one thick mass of driving sand. It choked them, it blinded them; it penetrated their clothing till they felt as though they were wearing sand paper; it worked itself into every part of the tents. There was no escape from it. So thick was it that the houses half a mile away were hidden from view, and at times it was impossible to distinguish objects fifty yards distant. The men lay in their tents almost suffocated and only those who had goggles were able to face this blinding blizzard. Sand, sand, sand! in ear, in mouth, in eye; in food, in clothing; in tents and bedding—no Turkish bath they felt would ever be able to rid them of the yellow and red and brown earth that had worked into their bodies. There was neither work nor worship that December Sabbath, and as the blinding pestilence hurled itself across their camp from morning till night they were unable even to parade.

Next morning a cool breeze was blowing through the tent streets and they rose refreshed for parade at six o'clock. They were to be prepared for Paardeberg and extended order began at once. With their regular drill they again began to clamour to get nearer the front; this burning sand, this everlasting thirst, this scorching, blistering sun could be borne patiently if only at the end of it all there would be a chance to distinguish themselves in battle. For three days they drilled and sweltered at De Aar hearing vague rumors of heavy fighting. So strict was the censorship that even the soldiers on the way to the front had to depend on passing trains and stray visitors for the state of the war. If their officers knew the truth they kept it to themselves.

On the third day of this monotonous existence word came that the regiment was to proceed to Orange River at once. That night all the transports were loaded and at three in the morning while the night chill still lay on the sleeping plain reveille sounded and in an hour and a half's time the regiment was at the busy station. Coffee and biscuits were served to the soldiers after they had entrained, and by half-past six the entire regiment in two trains was climbing northward.

It was not until near noon that the men from their "observation cars," as they laughingly called the flat cars that bore them up the wilderness, saw the cluster of houses about Orange River station. In the distance they could see the white tents of the British soldiers. They dreaded another De Aar and were in hopes that the rumour that passed from lip to lip would prove true—that they were about to be sent on to Belmont at once; but the Dargai Highlanders vigorously objected, and as their experience gave them precedence over the Canadians, they were sent forward and the contingent was marched across the veldt towards the wide cluster of tents dotting the plain under the shadow of the surrounding kopjes.

They were to occupy a spot the Australians had just left and found themselves next to the Shropshire Light Infantry in a camp made up of Cape Artillery, Gordon Highlanders, Royal Horse Artillery, and Shropshires. These regulars were excellent company and gave the men every opportunity of learning the

WITH THE ROYAL CANADIANS IN SOUTH AFRICA. LIEUTS. MASON AND TEMPLE GOING OUT ON PICKET DUTY FROM THE CAMP AT BELMONT.

THE NEW BRUNSWICK QUOTA OF THE SECOND CANADIAN CONTINGENT
SECTION OF "B" SQUADRON, C.M.R.

ways of the genuine "Tommy Atkins." "Tommies" they had to become if they were going to be that splendid fighting-machine a British soldier.

Orange River was another De Aar; sand grinding under foot, sand whirling through the air; if a squad marched across the plain its course could be followed by the sand that rose at every step. From kicking mules, from moving men, little bursts of sand made this camp deserve the name Julian Ralph had given it, "The Dust Bin of Creation."

And what a country they had come through—sand, wilderness, rockstrewn hill, dried river-bed, greeted them at every mile. Cavalry patrols here and there; hot, dusty camps guarding the track relieved the monotony of this journey. Flocks of sheep nibbled the dry grass that grew between the stretches of sand; flocks of goats cropped the brown plains or browsed among the rocks on the unpicturesque kopjes. O for one acre of the restful green of a Canadian field! Farm houses—so they were called—were dotted on this everlasting wilderness at intervals of about six miles and each farmer gloried in the broad domain of from twenty to forty thousand acres. Occasionally a few green trees, a green patch by some water-mill, would remind them that even this desolate wilderness might become green and beautiful if only it could be properly irrigated. Their own torturing thirst made them sympathize with this baked, dried, parched, barren veldt.

The tents did not reach the camp until six o'clock, and the work of pitching them began with vigor. The sound of the clinking hammers rose above the murmurs of a resting army. Only a few tents had been pitched, however, when black clouds began to beat up over the surrounding kopjes—black clouds heavy with rain. Dust, suffocating dust, began to choke the toiling soldiers, and then great cooling blobs of rain smote upon them.

Soon the windows of the heavens opened (only a writer familiar with an African rain-storm could have used that metaphor) and a solid-wall of rain beat down upon the camp. While the rain descended and the winds blew and beat upon that camp no work could be done. It took just about a minute to soak the men to the skin. This was their second experience of South African weather, evidently Nature was going to help the British officers to harden the boys from Canada, as both the sand-storm at De Aar and this rain-storm at Orange River were of unusual severity. But it was too violent to last long, and the chilled and shivering men were soon hard at work again getting up their tents.

Their first night at Orange River was not to be one of luxurious ease; it was to be a soldier's night. The enemy were in force not many miles away. Methuen's line of communication had been cut only a short distance farther up the track. A night attack might be made at any moment, and so they were ordered to sleep in their clothes and to be ready for a call to arms. Wet, tired and hungry as the soldiers were they lay down happy with the thought that they were perhaps on the eve of battle; that on the morrow their friends over seas might be scanning the bulletins to see how they had acquitted themselves.

That they were not playing at war was brought home to them that night. The pickets had been ordered to allow no one to pass, and, if the promptest answer was not given to their challenge, to shoot, and to shoot to kill. One of the Shropshires passing into the lines made a careless reply to a picket, and for his thoughtlessness was instantly shot down. The sound of the firing woke the camp, and many of the Canadians sat up and clutched their rifles, but no call to arms followed.

The chill of the African night was upon them, and their teeth chattered as they tried once more to get to sleep. What a land of contrasts! These extreme changes were sufficient to break the strongest constitution. Blistering sun and a freezing moon; as Julian Ralph has said, "To be happy in Africa one would have to have a fig leaf for a daytime costume and a Laplander's suit of furs for the night time."

Next day was a busy one, but the curious Canadians had time to view their surroundings. Every kopje was fortified, and at some distance was a well-defended fort. From this fort the distant hills around Belmont could be seen, and when on November 23 General Methuen with the Guard's Brigade and the 9th Brigade had driven back the Boers at Belmont the bursting shells were seen by the soldiers from Fort Munster.

The Canadians were in a safe, well-guarded camp doing fine work, most useful work, guarding the line of communication; but they were as impatient as young colts to be off to the front. They wanted to win glory, none of them thought of death. No doubt some of their comrades would fall, but each one felt that he would return with honor to the land that had sent him forth with such pride. The soldiers, however, had to learn that war meant a good deal more than dodging bullets and sniping foes.

The day at Orange River was a busy one. The men were detailed for fatigue duties, and two hundred of the regiment under Captain Barker constituted a working party to put in sidings and build platforms near the station. The lads were neither "duke's sons" nor "sons of belted earls," but they were in many cases from the best and wealthiest families in Canada. However that seemed to detract nothing from their energies. They would show the regulars how they could work; off went coats of officers and men, and in the blazing heat—over a hundred in the shade—they toiled, swinging pick and wielding shovel till they had constructed three-quarters of a mile of track with ties, laid one-quarter of a mile of rails, and built a safe, substantial platform of one hundred and fifty feet by fifteen; not a bad day's work.

As they completed their task a train drew into the station and a light, active figure alighted. Some of the Royal Military College men recognized the officer. It was Lieut.-Colonel Girouard. Girouard of Soudan fame, Girouard of Canada, who had by indomitable energy made Kitchener's victory over the Khalifa an easy thing, and who, in the time of the Empire's need, had been chosen out of the Empire to make the way from Cape Town, Elizabethport and Durban easy to Pretoria. He was leaping hither and thither over the African continent; to-day in the East, to-morrow in the South, and then away to the North. The breaking of the track by the commando of a thousand Boers between Orange River and Belmont had brought him for a brief moment in contact with his fellow-Canadians.

All the men rejoiced to see him, and particularly his old military friends. As he viewed with his critical eye the work the contingent had just completed he praised it with no stinted praise. Regulars could not have done better, and none but Canadians could have done it in so short a time. Then on his train he leaped, and away he sped northward to clear the road to Kimberley. This passing glimpse of so stirring and energetic a Canadian officer put new life into all who saw him, and they longed to follow him up that thin thread of track that wound among the hills and over the veldt.

That night two hundred of the men with six officers did outpost duty, and the fact the Boers were said to be in the vicinity kept them very wakeful; but morning dawned without any alarm having been given, and the soldiers began to fear that the monotony of drill, fatigue, and outpost duty, without any real fighting, was to continue. While on this outpost duty some of them got their first contact with the fighting line. It was distant contact, it is true, but nevertheless very real.

About half a mile from camp was the tall, bald top of Mount Cheviot kopje. On this hill Lieutenant Armstrong with twelve men on outpost duty kept careful guard over the country that lay about them, and watched with the keenest interest the flash light of Kimberley, seventy-seven miles away, playing across the heavens. Message after message came to the signalers beside them on the hill, and Kimberley was brought very near as they read these messages. Yet how far it was away; more than two months of suffering, privations, bloodshed were to pass before that beleagured city now asking for bovril and cocoa would shout its welcome to the relieving forces.

The men had read and heard of the splendid work done by the Highlanders and the Naval Brigade, they had seen something of the trials of a camp which helped to harden men for the severer trials of the battlefield, and while at Orange River they were to be brought face to face with the sterner side of war. There was a hospital here with one hundred and fifty British soldiers and seventy-five Boers under treatment. Fever, exhaustion, wounds, death were what many of them must expect, and as some of them visited the hospital and saw the ghastly sights made by war they wished that it might end at once. They felt no resentment towards their suffering enemies; only pity for the poor fellows who for the most part were fighting honestly for what they believed to be a righteous cause. Victims of ignorance they were; the ignorance of their leaders and their own; and for nothing is man punished more severely. Brave fellows too; for though they could not face a bayonet charge they had withstood for hours in their trenches and on the open veldt the heavy shell-fire of the British and had laughed at the terrifying Lyddite. Stubborn, savage (and the country was enough to make any one a savage) these men might be, but they were worthy foemen. A sentence from a letter by Lieutenant Armstrong indicates how the Canadians felt towards them.

"I talked with several of the Boers and fanned one poor chap who I am afraid looks as if he were done for!"

There, too, behind the tents on the hillside was the little cemetery, fast filling up. Captain Wood, who had gone out from Orange River on November 10 on a reconnoitring expedition, and had met his death, rested there. He was a recent graduate of the Royal Military College and many in the contingent knew him well.

A party of mourners went out to his grave to pay a tribute to his memory. They could raise no marble slab over him, but they bound two railway ties together in the form of a cross and prayed a silent prayer for the repose of his spirit.

There on the Karroo with the gloomy kopjes about him, the burning sun beating down on his rough cross, the dust eddying over his grave, this Canadian hero who had fallen fighting for the Empire would sleep the easier for the kindly tear dropped by his fellow-countrymen.

There was rejoicing in camp that same day when it was learned that communication with Methuen's army had been restored, and that the regiment was to be pushed forward without delay. Fight was in the air; a battle of greater magnitude than either Enslin or Modder River was foretold, and they hoped to share its dangers and its glory with the Scotch and English regiments that had been the companions of their journey up the Karroo.

RIGHT HON. CECIL J. RHODES, P.C., M.L.A.,
Formerly Prime Minister of Cape Colony and Pres. of the British South Africa Company

FRANCIS WILLIAM REITZ,
Late Secretary of State in the Transvaal.

CHAPTER VII.

LEARNING THE GAME OF WAR.

FORWARD was the word; and the men of the right-half regiment piled into the open cars in the early morning of December 9, glad to get away from the heat and dust, and inactivity, from a soldier's point of view, of Orange River. The left-half however was very indignant at being left behind, especially as there was nothing said about when they would be pushed forward. The big battle might take place and they would not be in it; that would indeed be a calamity.

After twenty miles of puffing up the brown treeless veldt and through the kopjes that were now growing larger and larger, and as the front was being reached more threatening with each mile, the contingent detrained at Belmont.

On November 23 a fierce fight had taken place here but General Methuen after a savage struggle had driven off the Boers. On this account it was one of the great landmarks on the way to Pretoria and already had a place in history. It was therefore with a sudden feeling of being in the immediate vicinity of battle that the four companies of the Royal Canadians formed up at the little station to be marched to Van Wycks' farm three miles away.

Belmont was a most important centre, the rear guard of Methuen's forces; and was in danger of an attack at any moment. Indeed it was only two days before that the Boers had swooped down in force and made havoc with the track a few miles north at Graspan, effectually cutting Methuen's communication with the rest of the world. As a result of its important position a goodly force of Highlanders, Munster Fusiliers, Australians, and Royal Horse Artillery, had their tents dotted about the station. The Canadians expected to be located with these older regiments, but water was scarce and on this account they were at once marched to the Farm.

They were indeed lucky. The place where they were to spend the night was a genuine oasis in the African desert. Since leaving the cool breezes of Green Point Camp at Cape Town, they felt as though they had had nothing to eat or drink or breathe save dust. The food they ate was grity with it, the water they drank was almost the color of the soil, and the air was filled with innumerable particles of this ever present pest. But here was a place of green grass, soft green grass not unlike their own Canadian fields, and a fine windmill which told of cooling water. They drank and were refreshed; but this was not enough: they scooped out holes in the sand and borrowing the waterproof sheets from the transport wagons improvised baths, filled them and splashed and splashed and rose up new men; clean in body and clean and wholesome in spirit. After their bath they were able to sing the songs that had grown into their hearts in Canada with new vigor under the clear stars of the first African night they had been able to enjoy since leaving Cape Town.

But the regiment was not to have a loafing time

LEARNING THE GAME OF WAR. 129

in this agreeable spot. They had to sleep in their uniforms to be ready at a moment's notice to spring to arms. They were a step nearer war and the duties of the soldiers became more rigorous and trying.

The men had had some experience of outpost duty at Orange River but they were now to begin this important duty in earnest. Their camp had to be protected from surprise, and through the night watchful pickets guarded the surrounding country. No enemies were sighted but the parties under Lieutenants Ross and Mason succeeded in bringing in a suspect—a poor stunted little negro, black as the night, but not black enough to escape the vigilant eyes of the Canadians. It seemed a ludicrous capture, but too great care could not be taken as the Boers were making the natives do excellent work for them as spies.

In the morning they learned that this oasis in the wilderness had been but a temporary resting place. They were to leave it at once and so struck tents after breakfast and marched back to Belmont station. They found the encampment of the night before greatly changed. The Highlanders had gone, and so had the Australians; and the Munsters were but waiting the arrival of the train bringing the remaining four companies of the Royal Canadian Regiment from Orange River to depart for Honeynest Kloof, an important position about nineteen miles further up the line. As the Canadians were to go into camp a united body once more on the ground occupied by the Munsters, the right-half was led out on the battlefield where they piled arms and lay about to await the train.

Nature had tried the regiment with "dust devils"

as they went into camp at De Aar; with a rain devil as they pitched tents at Orange River and now they were to have a somewhat similar experience. Half an hour before the train with the second half arrived, the rain came down in torrents and drenched the men on the open veldt. At noon while the rain was still pelting down the remaining companies arrived in open cars looking like drowned rats but glad to be once more with their comrades.

No time was lost. The Munsters struck camp, hurried on their northward way, and the Canadians took up the ground they vacated in front of the station and became the important factor in this important position on Methuen's line of communication.

They were now to become thoroughly familiar with every part of a soldier's life, except actual warfare. With the Mounted Infantry they patroled the track from Wittiputs to Graspan, a distance of twenty miles. But perhaps their most trying duty was the outpost work on the wide range of Belmont battlefield. It was far from a pleasant duty to have to stumble over the rugged plain and up the steep, boulder-strewn kopjes, where but thirteen days before a bloody battle had been fought from ridge to ridge.

Occasionally they would come upon a heap of stones and as the night wind blew across it they knew that beneath lay the dead bodies of some of their enemies. The days, too, were exhausting with the heat and work of entrenching; and at times it was hard to keep their eyes open. In the cold grey light of dawn, too, they would sometimes catch sight of an arm or a leg protruding from the rough burial mounds---gruesome sights that made a shudder pass

LEARNING THE GAME OF WAR. 131

through them as they thought that it might be their turn next. Carcasses of mules and horses lay here and there, and it was not uncommon to frighten away a flock of vultures as they gorged themselves on the carrion. There was a taint of death in the air and these birds of battle, swooping down on the plain, circling in the heavens, made the one thing needful to complete the ghastly picture. But after all they were friends, devouring the foul contagion that otherwise might have bred a pestilence.

In places the fight had been particularly stubborn, and up the steep kopjes where the Scots Guards, the Grenadiers, the Northamptonshires, the Northumberland Fusiliers, the King's Own Yorkshire Light Infantry, and the Coldstreams had so gallantly charged, they came upon abundant reminders of the fight. Shells unexploded, scattered fragments of shells that had done such fatal work, broken belts, snapped bayonets, smashed rifles, empty cartridge-shells—all told what war really was. From the gloomy horrors of these nights of outpost duty they were glad indeed to be led back to camp as the little dikkops, or thickheads, rose in innumerable flocks from the dusty plain with their cries of "Hui" or more probably, let us fancy, "Pluie,"—crying plaintively to the heavens for rain for the thirsty earth.

For three days this round of patrol and outpost duty went on, relieved by work with the pick and shovel in the trenches on the north side of the camp. Drill was practised too—drill of a kind made by the necessities of this war. It was a weary round of monotonous work relieved by occasional whirls of dust and fierce thunder, accompanied with rain such as falls only in South Africa.

Meanwhile they had an excellent chance to view the little settlement about the station. It was only a cluster of six cottages and an hotel. What a fierce fight had been waged here! The battlefield gave them abundant evidence in the fragments left by the whirlwind of war of the fierceness of the struggle, and there were more traces of it in the village. Every building showed that the shrapnel had splashed against the walls and roofs and a huge opening or two stood as evidence that heavy shells had there fallen with destructive crash. Innumerable small holes told what a hail of rifle fire had played about this little cluster of buildings. These evidences of war were giving them a realization of what they might expect when the time came to move into the advance guard. Indeed at any moment a similar bloody hail might play across their camp. The Boers were reported in force near at hand and they had not only to keep a most careful guard but go on constructing an impregnable line of trenches.

In the early morning of the twelfth a report ran through the camp that an army of the enemy had been located. The outposts were strengthened, the guns paraded, and the regiments drawn up in line of battle. But it proved to be a false alarm, and a little after five in the morning the troops were dismissed, but the entrenching went on with greater vigor than ever.

This same day brought gloomy news to the camp. General Methuen's advance had been checked—checked with terrible loss. He had climbed up the succession of kopjes leading towards Kimberley in a series of bloody contests at Belmont, at Enslin, at Modder River, losing heavily it is true, but in the end winning with irrestible dash. He was almost within speaking distance of Kimberley when he met the enemy strongly entrenched at the Magersfontein hills. The Highland Brigade under General Wauchope was given the task of storming the trenches; but the Boers had anticipated the attack—with searchlights they exposed the advancing Highlanders on that dark December morning ; with wire entanglements they entrapped them, and one of the bloodiest fusilades in the history of war played down that slope. For a moment the British were stunned by the suddenness of the attack, then Gordons, Seaforths, Black Watch—the flower, not of Scotland only, but of the English army—dashed forward to victory or death. Hundreds fell, and among them, with a dozen bullet wounds, the gallant Wauchope stumbled on the veldt still cheering his men forward, but they were beaten back.

This was dreadful news for the Canadians. Only thirty miles away hundreds of fellow-soldiers lay dead, and hundreds of others were wounded, many fatally. But they shuddered not at the news, they only hoped that now they might be given a chance to help relieve Kimberley. They had almost been in this fight, and had such been their ill-fortune the loss to the regiment would have been very great. Young, inexperienced as they were, wishing to emulate the tried soldiers they would have exposed themselves needlessly to the fire that mowed down the Highlanders as though they were grain before the reaper. This enforced waiting time was excellent experience. The mistakes of the well-known regiments were splendid object lessons of how not to attempt to storm the Boers' positions.

While they were ruminating on the news of the great loss England had sustained in the battle o

Magersfontein, three cars loaded with wounded passed down on the way to De Aar and the Cape. The grim awfulness of war was brought home to them as they saw the pale, agonized faces of the strong men, many of whom had been with them in their first camping grounds at De Aar and Orange River. And yet there was no desire to turn back, even had it been possible, no regret that they had came; their only word as they heard of the heavy list of dead and saw the wounded was, when shall we have our chance?

On the following day, while the memory of Magersfontein still hung like a black pall over the camp, Private M. C. Chappell died. His death was the first break in the contingent since it landed on African soil, and all, especially his comrades of G Company, felt it keenly. It was hard to have come all these miles to die without ever having a chance to strike a blow. Out on the veldt he was buried, on the battlefield of Belmont, and the spot selected was the ground over which the Guards had so gallantly and successfully charged with such terrific loss—a fitting place for one who had come to Africa to fight the battle of the Empire to rest, a place hallowed by the best blood of the English army. A heap of stones was piled over his tomb, and at his head two larger ones, on which are enscribed the words: "In memory of Private M. C. Chappell, Canada, Died December 12, 1899. Erected by G Company. Our Comrade." So rests this Canadian in the bosom of the bare, brown, dry veldt, far from the green fields of his Nova Scotian home.

After this day of mourning the dull routine of the camp continued. Now and then a Boer suspect would be brought in, and on one occasion five natives

MARTHINUS THEUNIS STEYN,
Late President of the Orange Free State.

THE HON. JAN. HENDRICK HOFMEYR.
One time Member of the Government of Cape Colony.

were tried for stealing and sentenced to nine months in the Hopetown jail. Several times the mail arrived, and these were days of rejoicing. But most welcome were the frequent visits of that splendid body of men, Rimington's Scouts, driving in cattle and sheep and goats. But the utter absence of news from the front, the sudden suspense of operations, the seeming paralysis of Lord Methuen's entire force were wearing on the spirits of all.

Sometimes the call to arms would be sounded, but it always turned out to be a false alarm; a body of Colonials with hats like those worn by the Boers, the shooting of buck by the Rimingtons, the accidental discharge of the rifle of one of the outposts, such things as these were invariably the cause. The call to arms was usually given at three in the morning, for with daylight an attack was to be expected, as it was part of the Boers' tactics to steal up in the night, and with the first light of day to get in their destructive work.

While the regiment was impatiently groaning under this enforced absence from the front, they were becoming brown and hard and capable of enduring much. This hot sun, these frequent rainbursts, the sudden leap from the tropical weather of the daytime to the cold nights, not unlike a crisp Canadian November morning, were making them fit for the terrible hardships they were to endure after leaving Belmont. They slept in the open as often as under canvas, and heeded not the occasional lizard that crawled clammily across them.

The worst thing they had to endure, however, was the dirt. Water was a scarce article and sometimes they had to take their evening meal of hardtack or sour bread without even the muddy water of South

Africa to wash it down. The springs and streams in the region of the camp had been poisoned and it was necessary to bring the water from Orange River in tanks by rail. Every drop was precious, a bath was out of the question, and even a wash was a luxury. They crowded around the engine as she snorted and panted at the station, caught the steam from the cylinders and rubbed off some of the dirt.

But these privations and hardships, loss of sleep and poor food, seemed to have effected them but little, for at the end of December, after the Christmas festivities too, Colonel Otter's parade report shows that there were only nine sick men at the camp at Belmont, a good showing for any body of men a thousand strong.

While they were learning lessons of war that made them fit to endure much, they were likewise unremittingly learning how to fight under the conditions of the modern battlefield. Drill, incessant drill, heat nor storm stopped it, went on during the entire month.

The first thing noteworthy about this new drill was the apparent absence of officers, and were it not that some men on the field could at times be seen evidently coaching the lines it would have been thought that the soldiers were acting like so many automatons, knowing their parts and doing them without sign or word of command. The officers were there, however, but in no way were they distinguishable from the men. The Boers had learned that an army, or a regiment, or a company without a head was but a blind force easily resisted, and so they made the officers their especial mark, pouring volleys upon them wherever they appeared on the field. After the battles of Eland's Laagte and

Dundee, after Enslin and Magersfontein, and the lessons they taught, it was deemed prudent to make it impossible for the foe to recognize any officer in the field.

As early as November 10 Julian Ralph wrote thus from Orange River as he saw the dead body of that fine soldier, Lieutenant-Colonel Keith-Falconer, and the dying form of Captain Wood, a late graduate of our own Royal Military College, carried from the the train:

"'They will not play the game fairly,' said a soldier, when we got the news that three officers and two privates were shot.

"In the camp during the next day much that was interesting was said about the means which must be taken to give the officers an ordinary measure of protection. Look at any reproduction of a photograph of British officers in khaki uniform, which has been published in the London weeklies, and you will see that their buttons and golden insignia of rank gleam like diamonds against their uniforms. As you see them in the pictures the Boers see them in the blazing sunshine on the veldt. "Tommy" has few such points of metal, and these he is forbidden to polish. He must keep them dim. He must paint the sheath of his bayonet brown, and he may not even polish his boots. His rifle is his protection just as the absence of a rifle marks an officer before the enemy. It is now under discussion to have all officers who march with their men provided with light carbines. In that case the swords, whose silver handles now gleam like electric lights on the field of battle, would be discarded, and so would the colored collar-bands and shoulder ornaments, which make such shining marks. Such matters as these the Boer does not have to consider. He fights behind rocks, and except in the case of his blue-clad artillery he fights in his civilian dress."

Swords, as useless for any but cavalry officers in this war as the ancient javelin would have been—more useless in fact—were left behind; and each officer bore his rifle like the men. Helmets were covered, every mark that distinguished them was torn off, or concealed with the all-pervading khaki. In many cases the men were scarcely distinguishable, even when near at hand, from the sandy desert over which they trod.

The drill was the most interesting part of this wearing month. Mr. C. Frederick Hamilton in one of his interesting letters gives an excellent idea of the method of drill evolved by Major Buchan to meet the tactics of the wily enemy in the new environment.

"More than that, the officers and non-coms. now get into the ranks, and the word is passed along in lieu of the signals which make the leader so conspicuous in the deadly clearness of vision given to the battlefield by the devilish smokeless powder. And so our men daily skirmish up the kopjes in long extended lines, officers and sergeants in the lines, to be distinguished only by the neater fit of their uniforms and the coaching which they give their men. The formation adopted so far is much like what I think I have seen in some disquisitions described as the "wave" method. A succession of thinly extended lines advance upon the enemy, one line behind another, each so extended as to present the minimum target. As the objective point is reached the rear "waves" come up and join the "wave" in front, thus feeding the firing line and developing its fire with gradually increasing intensity. Roughly speaking, this describes the general idea. In carrying it out various methods may be adopted. On one occasion the front and rear ranks of one of the companies worked separately, each furnishing a wave. On others the advance was made by alternate half companies or sections. The formation which is most favored, and which we may count upon as being adopted, is as follows: The rear rank supports the front rank at a distance of thirty paces. The men in each rank are at intervals of not less than five paces. The companies in rear follow in the same formation at a distance from each other of from eighty to one hundred paces. Thus a half battalion of four companies advancing on the enemy would present eight waves of thinly scattered men."

Along with this study of formation rifle practice went on diligently. An ant hill, a bush, a white stone would be selected by a section, the distance judged and volleys poured upon it. They needed no marker to tell them how close they came to the target. The dry soil of this "dust bin of creation" told where a shot hit. Under this exercise the men rapidly became excellent marksmen, and acquired that steadiness of eye and hand that enabled them to kill the Boer fire first at Sunnyside kopje, and again in that black week in February when Cronje was run to earth.

So passed the days in a round of drill, digging entrenchments, building walls, watching passing trains; their nights in listening to the sentry's call "All well!" passed along their line, or in doing outpost duty over the grim battlefield. An outing or two into the surrounding country to look after rebels; an occasional shot at skulking Boers and patrols were all that relieved the monotony of this camp in hot, thirsty, hungry Belmont. But they had grown black as Kaffirs, with a fringe of beard around the most boyish chin, and they could stride across the veldt for miles without feeling exhausted. It was a trying time, but the regiment needed the discipline. It was weary waiting, nevertheless. It had been prophesied when they left Canada that they would eat their Christmas dinner in Pretoria.

Christmas was with them, and they were practically no nearer Pretoria than when they reached Capetown, and there was no word of an advance; no hopeful news came from any quarter of South Africa. In Natal, in Cape Colony, by the Modder, operations were at a standstill, and the three beleaguered positions, Ladysmith, Kimberley and brave little Mafeking, saw no early hope of relief.

CHAPTER VIII.

CHRISTMAS WEEK.

SUNDAY, even in a South African base camp where there is the same routine work to be gone through as on a week day, has a feeling about it that stamps it different from the rest of the week. A calm is in the air, and a holy quietness seems to hang even over the toilers; voices are less loud, the curse has a less harsh sound, and is not heard so frequently. Consciouslessly or unconsciously all are worshippers. Sunday December 24 of last year will ever be a memorable day with the Canadian soldiers who return from South Africa. Their minds were full of thoughts of Christmas cheer, of the friends in the homeland, and they were busy making preparations for the morrow. In the early morning at six o'clock mass was held, and as fully half the Munsters were Catholics as well as a large proportion of the Royal Canadians, the parade was a big one and the service most impressive. There stood the soldiers before the rude altar—a dressing table answered the purpose—listening to words about the Prince of Peace; there they stood or knelt, armed, ready for battle. A morning attack was feared and each man went to the altar rifle in hand.

Nineteen hundred years had passed since Peace and Good-Will to all men had been brought to earth, nineteen hundred years crowded with strife and wars; and this Christmas on the morrow would hear the bells ringing out Peace and Good-Will, Good-Will and Peace, while the two most civilized Powers in the world, England and the United States, were waging bloody wars; the one in the far East in the Philippines the other throughout the length and breadth of South Africa. Instead of the sword being beaten into the ploughshare, and the spear into the pruning-hook, the manufacturers of military engines were never so busy. Great warships were in the ship-yards of every nation in process of construction, the factories of Europe were busy night and day turning out monster guns of diabolical destructive power; the best mechanical genius of the human race was being directed to the invention of engines of destruction. The wars of Darius and Xerxes, of Pyrrhus and Alexander, of Hannibal and Cæsar, seemed mild and gentle when compared with these modern struggles with their quick-fire guns and deadly explosives.

Such thoughts as these could not but flash through the minds of the more thoughtful among the soldiers as they stood round the altar on that hot Sabbath morning with their bandoliers filled and their rifles ready for the fight. Throughout the day their minds were on Canada and the morrow; and as they patrolled on outpost duty over the veldt and up the kopjes they occasionally stopped to sit and talk together of home. In the evening as if to tell them in no unmistakable voice how far they were from the home that held their thoughts, crashing thunder rolled across the sky.

Throughout the day the preparations for the morrow went on despite the heat—something over a hundred in the shade. It was hard under this hot

LIEUT.-COL. SIR FRED. MIDDLETON, K.C.M.G., C.B.

MAJOR-GENERAL RICHARD G. A. LUARD.

sun, with no green thing about them, with lizards and centipedes, scorpions and tarantulas crawling around their camp, to realize that Christmas was coming. How they longed for a Christmas tree; children could not have been more eager for one. In nearly every tent some attempt was made at a substitute—a poor, white, dry desert bush—but it was a bush and imagination could do the rest.

Christmas broke clear and fine with every promise of a scorching day. That Peace had not yet come to earth they were made to realize by the usual call to arms at 3.30 in the morning. It was to be a holiday, but the Royal Canadians were taking no chances. On just such a day when a less careful guard might be expected, the enemy might attack. But no enemy appeared, and a holiday was proclaimed.

It was a treat to have one day off from the wearying fatigue duty of this broiling camp. At five in the morning the Toronto company paraded and marched to Van Wyck's farm for a bath and swim in the sheep-wash, and no doubt to catch some of the abundant frogs to add to their Christmas cheer. They had the usual breakfast of coffee and bread, and then lay about to loaf and anticipate the luxurious feast of chicken and duck and turkey they were to have in the late afternoon.

A thousand pounds of fowl had been ordered, but when the train with the Christmas cheer drew up at the bullet-scarred station, it was found that only four hundred pounds had been sent. The fowl too were not dressed for the cook, but came into camp clucking and quacking and gobbling. Off came their heads in quick order and the inhabitants of

"Hungryfontein," as some of them had christened their camp, soon got rid of the feathers.

What a strange Christmas this! But the strangest part was to come. As the dinner to which all had been looking forward was being prepared the sky grew dark on the horizon, a wind played over the camp, then a howling, blinding dust-devil tore through their midst, swirling about in its mad career, its funnel like shape threatening to sweep the tents from the path. At its approach all fled before it—there is no Christmas comfort in the track of the South African dust-devil! When it had passed and they could breathe the sultry air once more without choking, black clouds spread over the sky and out of these clouds great rain-drops beat down, cool and refreshing.

While they lay about in the heat of this strange Christmas a magazine with pictures of hockey and other winter sports was eagerly scanned. Not a few felt the tear come to the eye as they thought of the home where these sports were and would have given a year of their lives for one clear, cold touch of bracing Canadian air. Nothing here but dust, dust; and not even a cold drink to wash out their throats. Stay in Africa! They would as soon think of becoming settlers in Greenland.

At four o'clock the men were assembled and Major Buchan who had had command of the regiment since it came to Belmont—Colonel Otter having the more important duty of Station Commandant to perform—addressed the men congratulating them on the excellent work they had done and reminding them of the eyes that were upon them in the homeland and wishing all a Merry Christmas. He was enthusiastically cheered and then these men enjoying their Christmas with shirt sleeves rolled up to the elbows, in canvas shoes and slippers for the most part, tramped to the hogsheads of beer. Six hundred quarts had arrived for the regiment; six hundred quarts, seemingly an enormous supply, but when it came to be divided among a thousand men, each one had a small quantity indeed.

The dinner was a change, but it was hard to cater for such a hungry host; and as there were over a hundred thousand men in South Africa, all equally anxious to have a fine spread, each man had turkey, duck, chicken and fruit mainly in name. But the plum pudding that after all gave the feast a Christmas character was in abundance, even if it had to reach camp in hermetically sealed tins. But what made the dinner one to be remembered lovingly by all was the spirit in which it was eaten. There on the veldt under the broiling sun they joked, they sang, they laughed; but under the laugh lurked the tear as they thought of Canada, its frozen rivers and lakes, its evergreen forests, its jingling sleigh-bells, the ruddy faces of the happy children.

How thoroughly they saw the humor of their feast is well shown by a little poem, written by one of the contingent, which drifted across the ocean shortly after this Christmas dinner. It is dedicated to the regimental Quarter-Master by "Magloire Laframboise—the *nom de plume* no doubt suggested by the extra issue of jam given the regiment on this occasion. How much the writer's heart was in Canada! and how well he has caught the spirit of the laureate of the Habitant, Drummond :—

"On dit, dat dis is Creesmas Day!
Ma foi! it seem to me
To be more lak Saint Jean Bapteese
She was so hot, you see.

"De Gouvrement she's feed us fine,
   Oh ! yes, I dont tink so :
One small cheeken mong thirteen men,
   How you lak dot, mon Joe ?

"De fruit she's libral, too, also ;
   If every compagnie
Would give hees fruit to one small boy
   She's maybee get plentee.

"Dere's one good ting, dat we was get,
   And dat's the plum puddeen ;
Tanks for dat precious leetle bite,
   We geeve our gracious Queen.

" At four o'clock dey cry 'fall in,'
   To get your Creesmees beer,
And so we bring our pannikin,
   Dere's no one missing here.

"Jus one small pint, das all you get,
   For fear you get en fete ;
To-night you'll get a glass o'rum,
   Eef you can all walk straight.

"So pretty soon we go to bed,
   And dream of 'soup au pois,'
And hope next Creesmas day we spend
   Will be in Canadaw."

The officer's dinner at the Headquarters of the Staff Officers in the cottage hotel was a somewhat more extensive affair; but no happier than the frugal meal of the privates and the non-coms. Wherever a Canadian officer could be found—at De Aar, at Orange River, at Modder River, at the Cape—he had been invited, and sixty in all sat down to a table laden with turkey, duck, chicken, beef, springbok, vegetables, plum pudding, and wine. A jolly and yet serious time was spent. Into their speeches crept the cause of their spending this

Christmas far from loved Canada and merry England. Voices from the Homeland came to them; messages from every part of the Dominion, and to crown all a Christmas greeting from Her Majesty Queen Victoria.

Her Majesty's health was drunk with enthusiasm. Not until South Africa is subdued permanently, and a prosperous Federal Government is established there, in touch with the rest of a united Empire will it be known what an important part the name Queen Victoria has played in this struggle. The British people are no longer a monarchical people in the sense they were in the time of Queen Elizabeth and the Stuarts, but the chivalry of the Elizabethan age is not yet dead. It was as much the feeling that they were going to fight for the Queen as for the Empire that made so many respond to the call to arms. The very name "Soldier of the Queen" shows how deeply this feeling is rooted. It is the thought that she, the noblest Monarch that has occupied the throne since the days of Good Queen Bess, and the best that ever held the sceptre of England, will applaud their deeds that nerves the arm of many an officer and soldier in the deadly battle-hour. Her name has made heroes, has ennobled the home-life of the Anglo-Saxon world, has kept anarchy, communism, nihilism, and all the other isms that have cursed Europe out of England, and it only needed this war to show what a unit that revered name had made the Empire.

When the feast and the speeches were over, the party enjoyed a smoking concert on the broad piazza of the hotel; a jolly entertainment that warmed the spirits of all.

In the meantime the men had been enjoying

themselves. Dinner over they tried every conceivable sport. The West of Canada pulled against the East in a tug-of-war, a quoit match was played; a game of ball with a bit of limestone for a ball; the fun grew fast and furious; but when the Toronto lads marched out of their quarters with a hobo band—tin whistles, tin kettles, iron pans—everything else gave way. To the officers' quarters they marched, serenaded them with hilarious mirth and then betook themselves to the little square in front of the station, where they kept up their character songs, dances, and cake-walks, till "lights out." The Boers had heard of the Canadians, and a rumour had gone abroad through South Africa that they were half savage and scalped their enemies. If they could have seen them on this Christmas night they would have firmly believed the rumour. They were a motley crowd—in rags, in blankets, dressed as uncouth Highlanders, as tramps, as wild indians; in war paint and adorned with waving ostrich plumes, they sang and shouted and leaped like a lot of unfettered school boys. It was good to be young on this Christmas. They forgot their hardships and privations, they forgot for a moment that front only a few miles away where battle and death awaited them, and they spent the oddest and merriest Christmas of their lives; and wandered back to the lines when the day's fun was over, happy but as tired as if they had been digging trenches for twenty-four hours.

On the following day the men awoke to find a new state of affairs in camp. Colonel Pilcher of the Bedfordshires had arrived to act as station-commandant and Colonel Otter once more took command of the regiment. The three weeks had been busy ones, and Colonel Pilcher found that the camp was thoroughly entrenched and so could devote more time to field work. All those weary, hot days the men had been erecting stone sconces on the kopjes till each was an almost impregnable fort, or digging wide, deep trenches where they might lie and "snipe" any approaching foe. So well was the work done that as Colonel Pilcher viewed it he felt that behind these works the little garrison could repel an attack by an army ten times it strength. Nevertheless he added to the camp two companies of the 2nd Duke of Cornwall's Light Infantry under Major Ashby with a machine gun, and conceived a plan by which he could thoroughly test the force at his disposal.

After Christmas the camp had settled down once more to the ordinary humdrum of fatigue and outpost duty. Tuesday passed; Wednesday was dragging by, and no word came to them of an advance—the new station-commandant had not brought them any nearer to war. On Wednesday afternoon, however, just as they were making preparations for their evening meal the bugles rang out an alarm. No time to wait. Each man seized his rifle and rushed to his assembly ground. They moved with precision, and yet how odd they looked in many cases; some with but one puttee on, some buttoning their tunics or pulling them on as they ran. Each company had its allotted place and over the wide range of Belmont battlefield the columns could be seen doubling to take up their positions in the trenches, on the redoubts, or behind the sconces. Soon every important position had its defending force. Khaki clad men on Kaffir Kopje, Kidney Kopje, Belmont Kopje, Guards' Kopje, Scots Ridge, swept their keen eyes over the surrounding country but no foe appeared. The artillery and mounted infantry were not in this defence parade. All the horse were three miles away for water when the bugles rang out, and just as the infantry had taken up their position the rapidly approaching cloud of dust told that the drivers were losing no time in getting into the field of action; but before they had formed up the bugles once more sounded and the men hot, tired, and happy—they had sniffed battle from afar—were marched back to their tents with their appetites considerably sharpened by this vigorous outing.

Colonel Pilcher was pleased with the speed at which the men responded to the call to arms, but determined to put them to a still severer test on the morrow. He no doubt had already planned the Sunnyside affair, and wanted to fully try the men he would have to rely on, and as near as possible to put them through the manœuvres they would probably have to perform when brought face to face with a strongly entrenched foe.

A route march was planned for Thursday morning, a route march that was to end in an attack drill. After reveille the men were given coffee and cocoa and a bite to eat. Every department of the army was to have a share in this drill. The force was made up of four companies of the Royal Canadians, two companies of Cornwalls, two guns of P Battery, Royal Horse Artillery, under Major De Rougemont, the Mounted Infantry and the Maxims. Along with them went a train of ammunition waggons, buck waggons and stretcher-bearers. They were playing the game of war, and none of the pieces necessary for a good game were wanting. In

QUEEN VICTORIA ON THE MORNING OF HER ACCESSION.
JUNE 20TH, 1837.

COLONEL SIR CASIMIR S. GZOWSKI, K.C.M.G.

a long line they marched over the veldt on that clear January morning until they had gone several miles, and then the "attack" rang out.

Instantly the whole winding line broke up into parts. The mounted infantry galloped furiously across the plain; the artillery thundered off to an elevated position two thousand six hundred yards from where the foe was supposed to be and opened fire; the Cornwalls were detailed to turn the flank of the enemy, and into the springless buck waggons they tumbled, and by a wide detour rapidly took up a position on the right of the foe. In the meantime the Canadians advanced by rushes across the veldt, gradually drew nearer to the objective point, and when within three hundred yards fixed bayonets and stormed the height just as the Cornwalls and Maxims appeared to help in the work.

The whole movement was done with incredible rapidity considering the state of ground to be passed over. The infantry had kept their intervals perfectly, and Captain Bell and his men in charge of the Maxims had carried their guns up what seemed an impossible kopje. He had made the boast that there was no hill too steep for his men to climb; this ascent up the boulder-strewn precipice proved that he had not uttered idle words. There was but one casuality in this mimic fight. By the time it was at its height the sun was high in the heavens, and one of the privates fainted and fell under the fierce glare.

The force was tried and proved, and Colonel Pilcher marched his men back to camp with the feeling that when the battle-hour came, and he intended that it should come very soon, he had under him a body of soldiers second to none in

South Africa. The men, too, knew that they had done well, and scanned the orders to find if any word of praise were given. They were not disappointed. Thus they found it written: "The officer commanding the Royal Canadian Regiment is desired by the officer commanding the troops at this station to express his satisfaction at the intelligent and quiet way in which this morning's work was carried out by the officers, non-commissioned officers and men of the Royal Canadian Regiment." It is good to be praised when work is well done, and the men felt the better for Colonel Pilcher's encouraging words.

Since leaving De Aar they had had occasional dust-devils, but no dust-blizzards. The afternoon of their route march just such another storm as they experienced at their first halting place swept over their camp.

On the following day their force was still further augmented by the arrival of two companies of Queensland Mounted Infantry. Although Kipling has said that the Colonial troops are absurdly jealous of each other, there was no jealousy shown at Belmont. The best of feeling prevailed, and the Canadians helped the advance party under the Quartermaster-Sergeant to pitch the tents of the Australians, so that when the companies arrived hot and tired at ten in the morning they found their camp ready for them. They had not a very comfortable rest however. The storm of Thursday continued. On that day it was thought to be as violent as possible, but with the arrival of the Australians it increased in fury; it rocked the tents; in the blinding dust the men would occasionally have to rush from their shelter to drive the pegs more firmly

CHRISTMAS WEEK.

into the yielding soil. It lashed them, it stung them; it crept into every corner and crevice, and swept like a blinding, driving fog over the desert. It made the Canadians long for a biting, bracing January blizzard.

The end of the old year was rapidly approaching, and no word of action. Yes; a rumour, no doubt occasioned by the call to arms on Wednesday, the route march of Thursday, and the increased force in camp, spread through the garrison that a part of the force at least was to be led out in the direction of Douglas. There were now nearly seventeen hundred soldiers in camp, almost a thousand of whom were Canadians, and every officer and private hoped that the rumour would prove true, and that he would be chosen for the work.

Whatever Colonel Pilcher intended he told no man; but he would give the impatient Canadians who were wishing themselves back by the frozen rivers and lakes in Canada, and away from the eternal dust and heat of the African desert, a chance to prove that they could do something more than play at war; and when the hour of trial would come he would not find them wanting.

CHAPTER IX.

UNDER FIRE

AFTER the Christmas festivities the camp once more settled down to its humdrum life of outpost duty, fatigues, and drills. The soldiers were beginning to lose interest in the war, and not a few of them were wishing themselves back on the gleaming rivers and lakes of Canada and away from the eternal dust and heat of the African wilderness. Towards the end of the week, however, they were aroused from their lethargy and discontent by the good news that a chance for action would be given to at least a portion of the regiment.

For nearly two months the region to the north and east of Belmont about the little town of Douglas had been in a much disturbed state through the presence of a band of bandits—for they could be called by no other name—who had fortified themselves on the kopjes and from their stronghold raided the country round about. They were largely rebels of the worst type, many of them men who were, even since the war broke out, in the pay of the British Government. They had been stealing, looting, commandeering; neither property nor life was safe while they remained banded together.

Nothing could have given the Canadians greater pleasure than to assist in breaking up this obnoxious gang. It was therefore joyful news to them when they learned that Colonel Pilcher intended to make a forced march across the veldt and run them to earth.

On the last Saturday of the year the Queenslanders and some of the guns were sent out in the direction of Sunnyside Kopje, but to the disgust of the men shortly returned to camp. C Company had been ordered to hold itself in readiness and as no countermanding order was given all began to look upon this return to camp as a part of their commanders strategy. The Boers had to be taken unawares, and Colonel Pilcher had learned much during the progress of this war. "Slim" as the Boer it would be necessary to be to do his work and save his men. Magersfontein, the fierce battles in Natal and the heavy losses sustained there made him exceedingly careful. He would give the Boers no chance to form an ambuscade, and he would moreover teach the older generals that successes against such a wily enemy as they had to face must be gained by scouts, by mobility, and by flanking movements.

All day Saturday the hundred men of C Company waited impatiently, eager for the fray. So eager, indeed, were the Canadians to get under fire that many who were not chosen actually tried to bribe others for their places. Sunday came and it was not until the afternoon at two o'clock that the hundred men, four officers, and the Maxim gun section fell in with the other troops for the hard, rapid march across the veldt. They were in good company; with them went two companies of the Queensland Mounted Infantry, two guns of the Royal Horse Artillery under Major Rougement, a part of the Royal Munster Fusiliers Mounted Infantry and other select men,—a splendid body of soldiers the pick of an army hungry for march or battle. C Company had by no means comfortable quarters on the route. Thirteen springless buck-waggons and eight or ten scotch-carts joggled them out of the envious camp.

Thornhill was their objective point, and across the roadless, rough veldt they toiled. At times they were forced by the heavy sandy ground to walk. After over five hours stiff work, and when they had accomplished between nineteen and twenty-two miles, tired and thirsty they reached Thornhill. There was no danger that their expedition would be reported to the Boers at Badenhorst Laager during the night. The camp had been left with absolute secrecy and Colonel Pilcher had prevented the possibility of news being carried along the route by leaving a trooper at every house he passed to prevent white or black from letting the enemy know of his approach.

It was the eve of battle and the men lay on the hard veldt with nothing but their great coats over them. They watched the Old Year out and the New Year in under the clear sky of Africa, with the gleaming stars shining with almost sunlight brightness above them. It was to be a terrible year for many of them and not a few would leave their bones on the cruel veldt. None of them thought of this, however; the morrow and the battle filled their dreams.

At four o'clock on New Year's morning the bugle roused them, but they did not get away from Thornhill until after six when the sun was beginning to make itself felt. Only three or four hours and they would be in action. Secrecy was the main thing in their advance; the protecting kopjes, the brush and the grass sheltered them for the most part, but when they reached the sandy stretches it was feared that the cloud of dust raised my men and mules would alarm the Boers. Fortunately, however, a wind rose, and for once the soldiers welcomed the whirling pest that swept across the plains. The "dust-devils" sheltered them from any keen eyes that might be watching for friend or foe.

A little after nine o'clock, when the men were thoroughly fagged with the march and the heat and the dust, news was brought that the enemy had been located. They were at Sunnyside kopje, and after a march of several hours this hill loomed into view; and on its north end could be seen the tents of the rebels—white army tents of England.

Lieutenant Ryan reported that the veldt to the right was clear, and Major De Rougemont swept his guns on the trot to a convenient eminence, unlimbered, and at five minutes past eleven the first shot that the Royal Canadians had seen fired at the enemy went screeching towards the Boer laager. It was a range finder, but as accurate as if the range had been marked. Right over the camp it burst, and when the second followed the first, showing that it had been no chance shot the shrapnel sent the Boers scurrying to shelter. In five minutes five shells burst over the Boer encampment and soon all the enemy able to run, hobble, or crawl from the circle of their waggons, were on the lofty top of the overhanging kopje trying with their Martinis to get the range of the death dealing guns which had so promptly found them.

In the meantime the Royal Canadians were back on the veldt a short distance in the rear, crouching, kneeling, lying down; waiting impatiently for the command to advance into the fire-zone. The boys

CANADIANS SEIZING A KOPJE NEAR SUNNYSIDE. TORONTO COMPANY'S BAPTISM OF FIRE.

Colonel's Pilcher's brilliant raid to Douglas the Canadian Troops distinguished themselves by carrying a ridge which had been recognized as the Key to the Enemy's Laager. The C Company of the Royal Canadian Regiment, under Captain Barker, which consisted chiefly of Toronto men, formed the Infntry of Col. Pilcher's force. They came under fire for the first time, and behaved as cooly as if they had been accustomed to it all their lives.

SMART COLONIAL OFFICERS OF THE CANADIAN CONTINGENT AT THE FRONT.

The group here shown are Officers of the Canadian Infantry Contingent, and were with Lord Methuen's force. Some of them took part in Colonel Pilcher's

were hungry for a fight, and despite the empty water-bottles, the intense heat, the fatiguing march, were in holiday humor. It was their first great chance and they only thought of proving themselves men. As they lay there on the veldt over a mile away from the dark hill where the game they were hunting lay concealed they cracked jokes and sang dry snatches of songs brought from the Homeland.

The thunder of the guns, the ripping of the Maxims angered them; they wanted to have a hand in it too. But this miniature battle was being fought with true military insight. Colonel Pilcher was not going to sacrifice the men under him. That kopje must be taken before sundown, and if possible without loss of life. The guns must make it still hotter for the rebels, then he would try the sting of the rifle bullet, and at the end the bayonet. So the Canadians had to wait.

At last the suspense was broken; across the veldt from the guns a figure hurried. It was Reuter's correspondent, and when he came into hailing distance he shouted: "The Major wishes you Captain Barker to bring up your men at the double quick."

The hour for which they had been longing for the last month had come. Sections Two and Three were to advance to a kopje about twelve hundred yards from the enemies position; Section One as support took up ground about two hundred yards in the rear; and Section Four was to act as escort to the guns. Major De Rougemont led the men across the open plain in person.

Up till this time the Boers had been peppering away at the guns, peppering away with evident fright for their aim never troubled the gunners in the least. Now that they caught sight of the long line of khaki clad men doubling across to a sheltering ridge they opened fire upon them; and the Royal Canadians for the first time knew what it was to be under fire. The buzz of the bullets played about them singing a song of death; the thud of the angry bullets sounded at their feet, at their sides; but never a man was hit. It would indeed have required splendid marksmanship to bring them down; a man at a mile's distance is not an easy target, especially when that man is moving rapidly. The fates were with them, and although thousands of bullets splashed the brown dust of the veldt in front, in rear, and sang overhead, no chance bullet found a victim. Had they lost heart for a moment some would surely have fallen, but they did not. They had been ordered to extend in their advance and extend they did and kept their intervals of eight paces perfectly. Had they drawn together they would have made an easier mark; but however much these young soldiers might have felt the need of the sustaining touch of the next man, they showed no signs of it, but kept distance as well as if on a field day. In the days of Waterloo and the Crimea it was a case of united we stand, divided we fall; but now that had all changed; the Long Tom, the Mauser and the Lee-Enfield had made it a case of divided we stand.

At any rate when the Canadians reached the protecting kopje not a man had been hit. Chance, Providence, the bad marksmanship of the Boers, were all three in their favor. Not an infantry shot had yet been fired although the swish, swish of the enemy's bullets played around them. But now their turn had come.

Color-Sergeant Campbell fired the first shot; found the range, and a general well-directed fire began along the entire line. It was effective, and soon the singing of the bullets grew less frequent, and the less steady crackling of the invisible rifles in the enemy's stronghold told that they were either holding their fire and biding their time, or afraid to show themselves.

The fire had now ceased to be dangerous, and although an occasional thud and puff of dust told that some Boer still had the range, and the nerve to fire, no one ran any risk of being hit. But they did run serious risk from the sun. They were tortured with the heat; their tongues were like burned leather, and clove to the roofs of their mouths; their lips were parched and cracked. The hot stones were like burning iron to the touch and many felt they must soon succumb, when the welcome command was given that they must advance to another kopje some four or five hundred yards in front.

This was not as easy as it had been to occupy the first ridge, and so they moved forward with greater care, doubling when in the open but rushing to every shelter available; a bush, a rock, an ant hill—anything that would give them a moment's safety from the hot fire that was now poured upon them. At last the kopje was gained, and in the short rapid rushes, not a man had been hit. It was a gallant, well executed advance, and the whole of Section Three, twenty-three men in all, that had made it sat panting and exhausted for a moment before beginning their work of firing at their still unseen foe.

They had succeeded in getting to shelter and out of danger from the Boer marksmen, but another foe that had been with them since morning beat down fiercer than ever. The New Year sun baked and blistered them, and they sucked at the muddy dregs of their water bottles in vain for relief. Down at the base of the kopje they saw a Kaffir hut. Where human beings live water is never far distant, and so two of the privates, Tom Wallace, a son of Clarke Wallace, and Private Rae, volunteered to risk the dangerous descent. They managed to secure a small keg of water and brought it up the hill to their thirsty comrades. This put an end to the splendid extension that had been kept across the veldt under fire, and all crowded around the precious fluid. In their thirst they forgot their danger, but a sudden fusilade from the enemy's position told them they were observed, and before they could duck to cover a stream of bullets sang over their heads. It was a close call. There was nothing for it but to take shelter till the order to advance would be once more given.

It would be difficult to estimate the number of men who have been killed directly and indirectly in the South African war through thirst. Every letter from the front speaks of the insatiable thirst, and in almost every hot fight men have been struck down, either while crossing the fire zone to secure water for their comrades, or while exposing themselves to the enemy's fire in their efforts to quench a thirst more agonizing than a wound.

There was no time, however, to consider their need of water; that steep hill crackling with a treacherous rifle fire had to be taken, taken at the bayonet point; and so once more they rushed forward. Up a steep descent they went, then across the open for two hundred yards to a sheltering kopje. This distance was not made without danger. They were now near enough to serve as an easy mark for good shots, and the bullets rained among them like hail. A tunic was grazed, a helmet chipped, the dust flew in their faces as they dodged to this rock or that ant-hill, but never a man was struck. At last the kopje was reached ; they were in safety to wait and pant till the final charge on the enemy should be made.

In the meantime a very picturesque battle was going on. There away to the right the Royal Munsters were galloping across the open to cut off the escape of the Boers to the north ; on the left the Queenslanders were executing a splendid flank movement, creeping along the ridge of hills, slowly but surely drawing closer to the doomed foe. The trap was set, the outlets were being closed ; it was only a matter of minutes till the Boers must surrender or break through the tightening lines. Between the Canadians and Munsters the steady roar of the guns told that the well-placed shrapnel were still being sent across the mile of veldt ; while the fierce rending cracks of the Maxims told that the men from Toronto and Ottawa under Captain Bell were doing steady, effective work.

For four hours the "tick-tack" of the rifles, the boom of the guns, the rending rattle of the Maxims, the swish of shells, the singing of bullets, the shouts of men, kept the field a lively one indeed. Occasionally a bursting shell would find the hiding place of some Boer and make him expose himself for a moment as he sought some better shelter, and then the Canadians would pour upon him a storm of lead. Yet all this din and ammunition for all these hours only managed to strike some twenty men. It did not show that the aim was bad, but that South African war at long range had knocked M. Bloch's theories to pieces. Khaki and shelter more than counteracted the destructive force of the modern gun and the modern rifle.

The Canadians now at close range began a rapid, telling fire at the enemy. So well-aimed was it that soon the Boer fire grew slack and wild. They did not dare show themselves. For the last hour the Australians on the left were ready for the charge, and as the fire slackened began to double across toward the skulking enemy. At the same time Captain Barker's men got the order to fix bayonets. Forward they went at the double keeping well to cover, while the nervous fire of the Boers left them still unscathed.

The end had come; the Boers saw it and in despair threw down their rifles and raised the white flag. Into their position the soldiers rushed bringing them to their knees at the bayonet's point. Hot, thirsty, excited as the Canadians and Australians were the finish would have been a bloody one had not Colonel Ricardo prevented the men from using the cold steel. Many of the rebels knowing that they deserved but little mercy from the British were afraid to take their chance by remaining, and so threw themselves on their horses, and hatless, coatless, wild-eyed with fear, galloped away in the direction of Douglas.

The victory was complete, the rebel nest was broken up, six were killed, twelve wounded, and thirty-five taken prisoners and this excellent work done largely by amateurs at war with a loss of but two killed and three wounded. The Canadians had not a man injured—yes, one! He had been hit in the leg, but fearing the hospital and deeming it but a scratch did not report his mishap. Gallant work this, skilfully done.

And what a gang had been broken up! No wonder the people about Douglas had been in terror of their lives. Hamilton of the Globe who during the entire work of the first contingent did such effective service for his paper, and who was with Section Three during the whole day, thus describes them: "Slouching, round-shouldered, matted of beard and hair, beastly dull, and brutal as to eye." They seemed less than human in their animal grossness, rags, and filth. There were wounded men among them, however, and this touched the human feeling of the Canadians.

It was learned that in a gully at the foot of the kopje there was water. The thirsty men forgot everything else and rushed away to drink, and drink, and drink. But in their own necessity they showed that this first taste of war had not brutalized them. They thought of the wounded foe suffering a more agonizing thirst than the thirst of the dust and the sun—the thirst that comes as the blood drains from the heart, and tenderly went to their enemies to moisten their lips although the water was far from abundant.

The Boer laager was searched for loot, and some excellent saddles and bridles were found but little else of value. It was a well-supplied camp, with three fine waggons, a big water-cart, fourteen tents, a Kaffir wattled-hut, and a dozen splendid trek oxen.

The absolute unconsciousness of the Boers of the presence of the British force was shown by the utter surprise they must have received at the sudden boom of Major DeRougemont's gun and the simultaneous bursting over their heads of the screeching shrapnel. There had been no thought of danger. On their fires was evidence that they had been getting ready the noon-day meal. The fresh mutton half-cooked in some cases, was a welcome sight to men who had not eaten anything since early morning. After they had satisfied their hunger, they lay about for the most part to smoke, to rest, and to rejoice.

It may be thought that too much space has been given to a struggle in which the British loss was but two men killed and three wounded; but the number of casualities is no criterion of the importance of this fight. It was the first success of the British on the Western border for six weeks. It came at a time when the war cloud hung like a pall over London. Black news day after day; records of death, death were thrilling England from end to end. The finish of the struggle seemed a long way off; it looked as if the succession of Gibraltars that barred the way into the Transvaal would never be taken. This fight came like a burst of sunshine out of the black clouds. The kopjes could be won, won without much loss. The Colonials had shown the British Generals the true method of South African warfare. Skilful scouting, rapid leaps across country, fine flanking work during a well-planned frontal attack, would break the forces of the enemy and press them back and back from hill to hill till Pretoria was reached. The method adopted by Colonel Pilcher in this fight was the method that relieved Kimberley, that cornered Cronje with his four thousand men, that irresistibly swept the army on its road to Bloemfontein, that rushed Kroonstad, that

COLONEL PILCHER'S EXPEDITION TO DOUGLAS. THE COLONIAL TROOPS TAKING FORTY PRISONERS.

This little expedition from Belmont into the Douglas District west of Lord Methuen's position on the Modder River, proved entirely successful in breaking up a nest of rebellion. The Queensland Mounted Infantry and Canadians greatly distinguished themselves.

FORDING A RIVER.
The Royal Canadian Infantry crossing by the aid of a Life-line.

beat back the surprised foe before Johannsburg, that found the gates of Pretoria open and unguarded. It was a fine victory, at once showing how kopjes could be stormed and making General Methuen's line of communication comparatively safe.

The night of the fight the Canadians and the Mounted Infantry slept in the laager and in the morning made ready for the return journey. But this victory was not without its thorns. Private McLeod of the Mounted Infantry who had been fatally wounded, died during the night, and in the morning the Canadians stood by the grave of their brother Britisher from the sunny Southern seas. Major Bayly read the service over his grave, Last Post was blown by the bugler and a rough cross erected to his memory. Private Jones' body lay out on the veldt and two of his comrades who knew where it was went out and gave it a ruder burial—without bell or priest, without cross or stone.

This gloomy work performed the men were ordered to begin the march back, but not until they had thoroughly wrecked the Boer camp. Everything of value that could be borne away was packed in the waggons. Two of the Boer waggons were burned with other stuff and several thousand rounds of ammunition thrown into the fire. Then the men took the beautifully polished Martinis they would much have liked to keep, and raising them overhead smashed them against the rocks. Then they marched towards Douglas singing as they went while behind them they could hear the crackling of the bursting cartridge in the fire.

That evening after a march of twenty-one miles, hot and dusty as usual and expecting a fight, they reached Douglas. But there was no fight awaiting them. The alarm of their advance had been given and the terrified three hundred Boers who was garrisoning the town had fled, and instead of the Vierkleur of the Republics over the pretty little town waved the flag of England.

They were parched and dusty, dusty to the bone; but the Vaal River flowed past the town and in it they bathed till they were made over anew and ready for another fight or march. While they revelled in the cooling stream from the public square came the roar of exploding ammunition. It was the necessary destructive work of war, tens of thousands of cartridge were being destroyed; but it seemed to them like a gala day rejoicing over their victory.

The angry enemy were said to be in strong force and now in hot pursuit. It would not do to lose the results of this victory by having this little army overtaken on its way back to Belmont, and so accompanied by such of the loyal inhabitants, men, women and children, as did not dare to remain behind, a rush across country of forty-six miles was made by day and night with a speed that defied pursuit. On the way the Royal Canadians kept the women and children in good spirits and good humor by singing songs and playing on mouth organs.

They were hungry, spent, foot-sore; but the good work they had done not only buoyed up their own hearts, but enabled them to comfort the weak who were fleeing from their homes, their all.

Rumours of the pursuit of the approaching force had reached Belmont and several companies were sent out to cover the retreat if necessary. But they were not needed and served as a guard to escort the victors back to camp.

A hundred and two miles in five days, a long and fierce fight under a hot sun—not a bad baptism of fire for this gallant little band of Canadians.

CHAPTER X.

THE CONTINGENT AT PLAY.

THE victors on their return from Sunnyside expected an enthusiastic welcome. They were to be dissappointed. The remaining seven companies were exceedingly jealous of the honor done C Company. Naturally enough! Here they had been digging sand, tramping over sand, eating sand for two hot African months; enduring it all with the hope of getting under fire; the opportunity came and one company was singled out for the coveted work. In their anxiety for fight the soldiers forgot that the officers had to act to the best advantage, not only of the regiment but of the great campaign on which they had entered. It was not because the men in C Company were better men than those from British Columbia or Montreal, or the Maritime Provinces, but because they were better drilled. A thoroughly efficient soldier cannot be made in two months. C Company had been so long together, practically as a unit in Toronto, that in all South Africa there was no body of soldiers who marched better and used their heads to more purpose—a thing by the way the soldier in former wars was never expected to do. It was a compliment to the regiment that C Company should be placed on the firing line, while the Duke of Cornwall's Light Infantry were given what from the soldiers' point of view was the mere drudgery of battle without the glory.

No shouts welcomed the victors back from their trying march and fight; a solemn silence reigned over the little army at Belmont. Many indeed made light of the affair, and when they saw the stretchers empty, no man wounded; and learned that none had fallen out in the march, they even tried to convince themselves that their comrades had been under a hot fire only in their imaginations.

After this fight camp life became duller than ever, and but for the social instinct of the men it would have been unendurable. In the evening they would lie about in their tents while the earth was cooling down after the scorching heat of the day and chat of Canada or the progress of the war, tell stories, and sing songs. Sometimes some of them, unable to endure the heat of the tents, would lie out in the open, under the clear sky and the bright moon—a moon so luminous that they could read without difficulty by its light—and think and think of their friends overseas.

The monotony of drill and fatigue was relieved during these days by what seemed to the most of them sport, Maxim gun practice and rifle practice. Targets were erected with the kopjes for back ground and excellent work done. The regiment, however, had other methods of filling in time.

During Christmas week the instinct for play became very strong, and the friendly rivalry in the tug-of-war and the quoit competitions made them eager for more sport. It would be hard to find an English regiment at the front without the wherewith-all to play the national game of cricket, and here in the desert the Cornwalls were able to fish from their impedimenta wickets and balls. They found in the British Columbia men worthy antagonists. How contrary to all ideas of a cricket environment was this South African desert. Cricket suggests green grass, restful to the eye—green grass soft and juicy and cool from the perpetual watering it receives. How were they going to play cricket among these stones, on this dry, sandy, brown, yielding veldt. The men in Gibraltar on the hard rock of the fortress had found it possible; all it needed was the will and the way would show itself. Matting was spread for a crease, and a swift but not treacherous one it made. As might have been expected the Cornwalls were the winners, but only by a small margin.

Another sport much indulged in by the boys, and one played without umpire or referees, was tackling ostriches for their plumes. Ever since the Royal Canadians landed in South Africa they had not ceased to wonder at these ungainly birds that wandered singly or in stately flocks over the deserts. As they climbed the karroo in their crawling train, these birds like the cows and horses of their native land would sometimes race by their side. They would straighten themselves up, vibrate their extended wings, and skim over the plain with a speed that easily distanced the train, and not only did they maintain this speed for short bursts, but were as tireless as the engines, rushing along for hours without showing signs of fatigue.

From the moment the boys saw these birds they covetted the magnificent plumes that waved from wing and tail. There were not many things in South Africa they could send to Canada as souvenirs of their trip; but here was one, and every man in the regiment made up his mind to despatch across the ocean some of these feathers. They had plenty of opportunity. Stray flocks of ostriches and single birds, without owners for the greater part, now that the war had sent the Boers either to Cronje or Joubert or as prisoners to the Cape, wandered over the veldt and into their very lines.

In many respects the ostrich was more like a camel than a bird. Its great two-toed hoof-like claw with a thick pad beneath; its long, stout featherless legs, its eyes with overhanging brows and long lashes all gave it a marked resemblance to the ship-of-the-desert. Indeed if the camel's ungainly body could be trimmed up with a few feathers a somewhat gigantic and uncouth ostrich would be the product. Its strength and endurance too, and its stupidity are of a piece with the camel's. When enraged it not unfrequently turns viciously on its pursuers.

The birds standing when upright from seven to eight feet in height were no easy fowl to pluck. But the Canadians had to have feathers, no matter what danger they ran to get them. One adventure will serve to illustrate the sport almost every member of the contingent had with these grim, ungainly, gaunt, and monstrous birds.

A party was doing outpost duty near the Boer lines when they came on a flock of ostriches. The birds were moving slowly over the veldt browsing the tops of the dry shrubs or, as one of the boys remarked, stowing away an occasional bit of shell or cartridge case, for the ostrich does not stick at herbs or flesh, and is the only truly omnivorous creature alive. Whatever they were eating they were evidently enjoying it from the hoarse sonorous

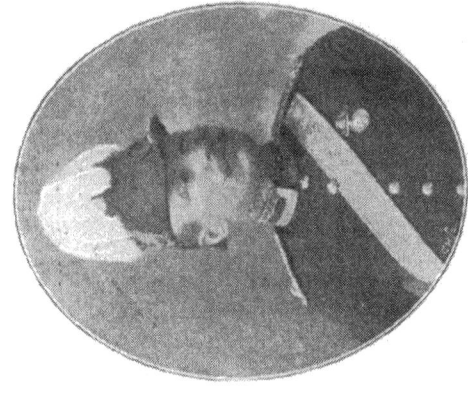

LIEUT.-COL. F. L. LESSARD.
Commanding Mounted Infantry of Second
Canadian Contingent

LIEUT.-COL. C. W. DRURY.
In Command of Canadian Field Artillery
in South Africa

MAJOR S. DENISON.
Canadian Officer on Lord Roberts's Staff.

LIEUT.-COL. BUCHAN.
Commanding the Royal Canadian Regiment of Infantry.

chuckling they were making. The boys eyed the birds and their feathers, and planned a campaign. First they coaxed them up quite close, and then made ready to tackle the victims. They were old football players, but the excellent rule of tackle low would not work in this case. They might as well try to tackle the wheels of a moving locomotive as those robust legs. If they did they would find themselves sprawling, probably senseless on the veldt. The only point of vantage seemed to be that long neck, scantily covered with thin down. So when they had wheedled the birds near enough, they dropped their rifles, made a wild dash into the flock and succeded in gripping one stalwart fellow about the throat, giving his neck a vigorous twist. Then came the tug-of-war. The ostrich resented this familiarity with his person and flapped and kicked and struggled, making it almost impossible to hold him. As the one who seized him first remarked, "The blamed thing was as strong as an ox." He was not vanquished without leaving his mark on his enemies, one of whom got a vicious kick that "came near putting him out of business." He was conquered, however, and in the end a few fine feathers were ruthlesely torn from him to be sent to far Canada. As soon as he was released he went flying across the veldt with angry stride to join his comrades who were now but a speck of dust on the horizon.

The officers saw that if the men were to be kept in good spirits they must have something more to amuse them than rifle practice, an occasional shot at a Boer patrol, or an adventure with ostriches, and so they planned a day's athletic sports for the garrison. The 17th of January was selected and on that day a general holiday was proclaimed. It was well to make it general as the number of entries took in almost every man in camp.

The sports began at ten in the morning and it was not until seven in the evening that they were concluded. To give some idea of the interest taken in these sports it is only necessary to note the number of entries in the hundred yards' dash, ninety-seven in all. The boys were evidently ready for either a double against the enemies position or a good retreat. The interest centered, however, not so much in the individual sports as in the tent-pitching contest and in the tug-of-war.

The members of C Company had proved themselves since coming to South Africa the most expert tent pitchers in the Canadian Regiment, and when Corporal Grant entered his squad, the other Companies felt they had no chance, and so they allowed Corporal Grant to fight it out with a squad from the Duke of Cornwall's Light Infantry. A time limit was set, and the squad having their tent nearest completion at the end of the stated time would be awarded the prize. A brilliant contest took place with the entire camp as spectators. Now Corporal Grant's men had the lead, now the Cornwall's looked like winners. Just as the Canadians were about to give the finishing touch to their work, over toppled their tent and they seemed to have lost. Nothing daunted, they erected it once more; and just before time was called the Cornwall's tent collapsed and the Canadians had the prize. The cheer that echoed among the kopjes showed how popular was the victory.

Great interest too was taken in the tug-of-war. Team after team succumbed and at last B Company from London and the Queenslanders were left in the finals. But the Queenslanders proved easy victors.

In the individual sports the Australians, too, won practically everything. They were a sturdy lot of athletes, strong and wiry and their successes were applauded in every case; no jealousy in this camp, no selling of races, no blaming referees. The entire day of sport was a struggle between the Colonials present; the British soldiers had practically no place in the contests, and it is to be feared that the Colonials thought themselves a superior race of beings. But this inferiority of the English soldiers as athletes should be no matter of surprise. The regiments of England were recruited very differently from the regiments of Canada and Australia. The Canadians were the pick of the nation; almost every second man having won for himself a name in some department of athletics. Out of the two hundred thousand men by this time scattered throughout South Africa, it would have been difficult to find a body of men so capable of giving a good account of themselves in the athletic arena as these soldiers from the Kangaroo state and the land of the Maple Leaf.

The friendly rivalry between the Australians and the Canadians made their contests somewhat serious affairs. There was another element in camp, the colored boys who were employed with the transports. Their race was infinitely more amusing than all the other contests. Down the dusty street they went tripping, jockeying, seizing hold of their opponents,—anything to win. The prize fell to the first man in, no matter how he got there; and a wily Kaffir boy of some fifty summers finished first

It was an excellent day's sport and broke the monotony of as weary a month as ever soldiers experienced. There was another sport, contrary to orders, especially after "Bobs" appeared on the scene, but nevertheless very much enjoyed. Occasionally patrols scouring the country about Belmont would come upon one of the widely scattered farmhouses that dot the veldt, and Kipling's little bit of rugged verse would be hummed as they eyed the low built homestead.

> "If you've ever stole a pheasant-egg be'ind the keeper's back,
> If you've ever snigged the washin' from the line,
> If you've ever crammed a gander in your bloomin' 'aversack,
> You will understand this little song 'o mine."

With the regular "Tommy" they could not comprehend

> "Why lootin' should be entered as a crime."

However, they commandeered an occasional square meal, and not a few chickens and ducks found their way into the Belmont lines. It was a little risky, but until "Bobs" came, making death, for a time at least, the penalty for looting, the worst that could follow was a few days' punishment with extra duties.

Early in February when a part of the regiment was marched to Graspan, they found their old friends the Highlanders anxious for a game of football, and although the Canadians were not adepts at the association game, they were glad of a chance for a little sport. But the Highlanders, skilled players, were too much for them and kept their goal keeper dancing about in the heat while they shot goal after goal.

But the best game they had in South Africa was on one hot afternoon in March when the officers of the Gordon Highlanders and the officers of the Royal Canadian Regiment tried their strength in a game of Rugby. Rugby suggests cold autumn days and muddy fields, but the scene at Bloemfontein was very different. A scorching day, the usual hundred in the shade; no turf on which to fall when tackled, but a field to which the term "gridiron" could be applied in every way. The teams, indeed, played on a great baked brick. It was a fine contest of two fifteen-minute halfs; but the weight and speed of the Canadians told; and Captain Barker, so well known as a football enthusiast and manager in the Dominion, steered his combination to victory. Lieutenant Marshall by brilliant play scored two tries, while the Highlanders failed to get the ball across the Canadian goal line.

The march to Paardeberg, that nine days' struggle before the Boer trenches, the privations of the advance on Bloemfontein, had in no way dimmed the ardour of the English, the Scotch and the Canadians for manly sports, which are after all mimic war. It has been said that a nation can be judged by her games. No other race has such manly sports as the Anglo-Saxon and they play them manfully and honorably; and as has been proved a thousand times, no other nation plays the game of war with the same dash and spirit and high sense of honor.

It will be a sorry day when England and her Colonies cease to play. This last great war has brought the Motherland very near to her children, but Wimbledon and Bisley, the cricket and football contests, have long been paving the way for this sudden springing to arms on behalf of the Empire that, in the words of Lord Salisbury, so took the world by surprise.

CHAPTER XI.

A WEARY MONTH.

Hope deferred maketh the heart sick; and if ever men were sick of waiting the soldiers of the First Contingent were. They had not come to South Africa to do garrison duty, but to fight, and for a time the chance of a fight grew more and more remote. Reports came to them of the fight-fighting under Gatacre and French, of the sturdy defense of Ladysmith, of the sorties from Mafeking and Kimberley, of Buller's desperate struggles along the Tugela. While these contests were taking place, while many gallant fellows had died for England, while on this field and that the Victoria Cross had been won, here they were cooped up in the Belmont "dust bin" doing a kind of police duty over a people who kept well out of sight. The camp was strongly entrenched, the kopjes were splendidly fortified; and there was nothing left for them to do but to walk up and down the grassless plain as outposts or patrols.

Camp duties no longer attracted them, the novelty of the soldier life had worn off. They had grown careless about their work and even neglected the rifle that they saw but little chance of using against an actual foe. Occasional rifle practice at distant objects on the dusty plain had lost its fascination. It is not to be wondered at that the men grew lax in their duties; several were even guilty of the unpardonable crime of sleeping on outpost duty. The regiment was sharply brought to time for this indifference, and extra guard mounting and sentry work was given them to do. The men took the punishment, but went about their duties with heavy countenances and often bitter words. The food, the heat, the dust, the inaction made many regret that they had ever left Canada. A number when they enlisted had made up their minds to remain in South Africa when they had wound up the war and make their fortunes as Beit and Rhodes had done; but the experience of December and January in Belmont had changed their point of view. They would not stay in Africa for all the gold of Johannesburg. What they wanted was one good stiff fight, and then a quick return to Canada.

The month of December was relieved by several expeditions not unlike the march to Sunnyside, but without the glorious ending that rewarded them on that occasion. The first was to Lubbe's Farm in the Orange Free State, and the Canadians had the honor of being the first considerable force that made a raid into the territory of the enemy; so far all the fighting had been done on British soil.

Jacobsdal was an exceedingly important town in the Orange Free State. It served as a base of supplies for the Boers who had so effectually stopped Methuen's advance on Kimberley. Over this district Commandant Lubbe reigned supreme in his cosy, shady, almost luxurious farmhouse not far from the British border. A raid on his habitation would be doing effective work for Methuen, especially if by any good chance the cammandant and some of his influential friends

MAJOR-GENERAL THOMAS BLAND STRANGE.

COLONEL WALKER POWELL.

could be made prisoners—a thing which almost happened.

The force this time was a good-sized one, in all four hundred and eighty-seven men and one hundred and eighty-eight horses. C Company had had its outing and so was left behind, while the two Maxims, A and B Companies and a part of H, a force of two hundred and ninety-three men from the Canadian regiment, paraded at six in the morning January 9, with a part of the Queensland Mounted Infantry under Colonel Ricardo, two guns of the Royal Horse Artillery, two companies of the Cornwalls, and twenty mounted men of the Munster Fusiliers. Surgeons, transport-officers, stretcher-bearers went along. It was in fact a veritable little army ready to give a good account of itself.

It was a cloudy day, but as the march was over a particularly sandy region it was an oppressively hot and thirsty one. Coats were thrown open to catch the light breeze, and the helmets, a weight to the heads, were carried for the most part on the bayonets. Nor was this a comfortable march; the bumping of the springless buck-waggons; the tramp, tramp of the men over the yielding plain that made the "seeming smouldering fire under their feet rise in clouds of choking sand,"—tried their powers of endurance.

If it was not a comfortable march, it was an exceedingly picturesque on; that long line of waggons, each drawn by ten mules, with an extra mule disconsolately jogging along at the side; those black Kaffir boys flicking the ears of the mules with their long whips and shouting their loud "eighs"; the tramping horses; the trundling guns; the steady march, march of the infantry—all gave life to a plain that seemed to have lain dead for ten thousand years. As the column went forward, to the front, to the right, to the left, the keen-eyed scouts examined every foot of ground. No chance to ambuscade this little force!

Stanley McKeown Brown of The Mail and Empire gives in one of his interesting letters, a most striking picture of the morning march towards Commandant Lubbe's farm.

"Hills and plains, kopje and veldt, past one on to the other; across the next and a small stretch of veldt is in front of you; sometimes the level land is half a mile, often the kopje is fifty feet high, but more frequently it reaches towards the heavens for four times that distance. No flowers, no trees, prickly bushes, hot sand, no change—nothing to startle you; the only thing that is magnificently grand is the sky, and that is always new. Each hour seems to work fresh wonders. But men on the march cannot push back their helmets and gaze at God's pictures in the sky. They must tramp on, and in this case on they went. The Mounted Australians darted a little faster, and with all eyes front we could see over rising ground the tops of tall, slender trees, nestled in the centre a windmill. This one green spot was Witdam Farm, the home of Commandant Lubbe, one of the Orange Free State Boer leaders."

The owner of the farm was at home, but he did not wait to welcome his unbidden guests. As soon as the Australian Mounted infantry appeared on the distant horizon, a party of Boers who were just about to sit down to dinner leaped on their horses and fled eastward. The Australians went in hot pursuit, but their jaded steeds were no match for the fresh mounts of the Boers and so no capture was effected.

The column had arrived at a convenient moment. At Sunnyside kopje Colonel Pilcher had appeared on the scene just as the enemy were making preparations for the noonday meal. The time was judged a little better on this occasion. The meal was prepared and on the table and Lubbe had generously left behind two grinning Kaffir servants to do the honors of the feast. The officers, nothing loath, "sat down and enjoyed," as only men who had been marching from early morning could enjoy, "the good-sized joints of veal and mutton, and heaping dishes of rice and barley, and the pots of tea and coffee."

The afternoon was spent in investigating the farm, picking up anything of value that could be found, smashing the rifles and destroying the goodly supply of ammunition that the Boers had left behind in their hasty flight. Late in the afternoon the Australians who had been keeping a watchful eye over the surrounding country brought in word that the enemy was in force in the vicinity. How big or how small a force the men cared nothing; a fight at last! Hastily the little army was disposed so as to resist attack to the best advantage. Artillery, Maxims, Mounted Infantry, Royal Canadians, all got ready for action when the scouts brought in the disappointing tidings that the enemy that had surrounded them was the Victoria Mounted Rifles. It was a close call; as an officer said, "Another ten minutes and the British would have been shelling the British."

Throughout this war there have been many such

close calls. Some of the Colonial and irregular mounted corps are in the distance so much like the Boers, who are all mounted, that time and again different divisions of the British force have been about to engage each other in deadly strife. Many of the rumors of Boer forces that disturbed the dull monotony of the Belmont camp were due to the diligent Colonials who patrolled every foot of the country lying along the Orange Free State border, and who made frequent flying incursions far into the enemy's territory.

The excitement of anticipated battle over, the force returned to the farm to thoroughly enjoy the evening meal. The fresh beef, newly killed for the men, the fowl for the officers, made an excellent break in the monotonous fare they had been having at Belmont. It was well to have made this forced march, if for nothing but these generous meals. The experience of the remainder of this outing is graphically described by Mr. Brown, the only Canadian correspondent that accompanied the expedition.

"No tents, and an order to stay at Lubbe's for the night, the men bivouacked. Great coats and a starry sky were their covering, sand and limestone served them as beds, and anything from a rock to a water-bottle sufficed for a pillow.

"The 'Rouse' blared out at four o'clock, before the sun had got up on the horizon, and with hasty preparations the flying column was able to proceed by half past six. The Belmont force went away in heavier order than they came, since they had with them some twenty horses, about twenty-five head of cattle, and the whole of the contents of Mr. Lubbe's house from the stove and stove pipes to the articles which he had hidden in the ground in the yard. An ox-team of fourteen lovely long-horned beasts was borrowed, together with an immense waggon, well-racked to carry to camp what had been taken from the home of the Boer incitor.

"The return home was made by a shorter course to the north-west, and though we once missed the road which delayed the journey somewhat, we were back in Belmont shortly after noon, having made practically no stops except to pick up a few chickens at a farm house whose occupants are out in the deep hills with the Boers."

They did not get back, however, without a further alarm, and once more they were drawn up in order of battle only to find that the threatening force was the 9th Lancers on an outing from Modder River.

On the day of their return to camp Lord Roberts and Lord Kitchener arrived at Cape Town. Over two months before, on October 31, Sir Redvers Buller had reached South Africa, and amid the salvos of the populace set to work at once "to finish the war." He knew he had no easy task before him; but his coming "relieved the tension" of the Britishers in South Africa and the prophets began to foretell the speedy downfall of the Boer cause. He failed utterly, and the people clamoured loudly for Lord Roberts, Roberts of Kabul and Kandahar. It was evident that the greatest military genius of England was demanded, not so much on account of the enemy's numerical strength, as by the difficult nature of the scene of the conflict. Buller has lost for the present much of his popularity as a general—not with his soldiers but with the public at large—but when this conflict is over and the three factors that have made his path into the Transvaal a difficult one are calmly considered, his old renown will return with increased lustre. The slowness of the war office in getting sufficient men to South Africa; the inadequate knowledge they possessed of the topography of Natal; the folly of sending practically nothing but infantry and inefficient artillery to cope with mounted men and the finest of modern long range guns—these were the first difficulties that faced the British leader. Then the urgent cry that was daily flashed across the heavens from Ladysmith for immediate relief, and the clamor of the English world to make haste to the beleagured town, forced Buller's hand at a time when the thing needful was to play a waiting game. Then, too, there were the difficult kopjes that he had to force his away among, every one a fortress as easily defended as Gibraltar or Quebec. Under the circumstances no man ever did better work than Redvers Buller, and but for his strenuous efforts, his untiring watchfulness, his crossing and recrossing the Tugela that gained for him the title of the "Ferryman," Ladysmith would surely have fallen, and Roberts would have found the relief of Kimberley a much more difficult matter.

He bore the heat and the brunt of the day, Roberts and Kitchener came in the evening to win the victory and reap the glory. Napier in his "Peninsular War" says: "In the beginning of each war England has to seek in blood the knowledge necessary to insure success; and, like the fiends progress towards Eden, her conquering course is through chaos followed by death." Sir Redvers Buller's experiments were necessary to teach Roberts how the foe had to be fought; and the

British blood that reddened the Tugela was not shed in vain. Napier's words were true of the Crimean war, of the Indian Mutiny, and never more so than of the South African war; but it was hard to have to be the general to create the knowledge necessary for a successful campaign.

"We have been taught a lesson," said a great English journal, "But not one that need make us uneasy, and certainly not one to cause despair. We have been taught that this matter is grim earnest and that we must away with vain boasting; shut our teeth and go steadily through with it. It is a great mercy that the lesson came so soon and so completely. We shall not forget."

This was written just before Lord Roberts landed in Cape Town. With his appearance on the scene of conflict, the public became less feverish. His attractive personality, his experience seemed to set all minds at rest. The war if not shortly finished would have its whole course changed. Victories instead of defeats were now to be expected. But for a month the questions went up, "What is 'Bobs' doing?" "Where is Kitchener?" Had the reputation of the people's idol and the reputation of his great Chief-of-Staff been swallowed up by that "grave of reputations," South Africa. To none was Lord Roberts' arrival in Cape Town of greater interest than to the Canadians at Belmont. When they heard of his landing they began to look forward to speedy action. The fact that he had not hurried to the Natal frontier made them hope that his first move would be against the besiegers of Kimberley. As the days lengthened into weeks and no move was made they too began to lose faith.

Lord Roberts, however, heeded not the complaints

and clamourings of the press and the public, nor the interfering of the War Office. He had a free hand. This war, from the number of men under him and the character of the country through which he had to fight, the greatest he had entered upon in his fifty years of service needed the most careful preparatory work. Ladysmith, Kimberley, Mafeking, would have patiently to endure siege until the time came for him to strike, and then he would move forward with an irresistible impetuosity that would prove to an astonished world that for endurance and dash there are no troops like the British troops, and that, as ever before in British history, the great need had found the great man. Roberts is at once a Marlborough and a pocket Wellington with a dash of the "Little Corporal" thrown in.

While he was organizing his forces, studying the country, patiently waiting for additional forces, having thousands of horses—the thing most needed in a modern war—brought from the ends of the earth, the Canadians groaned wearily in their hot camp. The two expeditions into the enemy's territory had taught them what war meant, but had not quenched their ardor. The rapid exhausting march to Sunnyside on half rations and the fight in the blazing heat, the dash into the Orange Free State only made them the more eager for some such battle as Magersfontein or the fierce conflicts that were daily being waged about Ladysmith. These two outings, too, taught them the difficulties with which their leaders had to contend. Horses were a necessity to a successful advance, and yet the horses of the Queensland Mounted Infantry, two hundred and eighty in all, were rendered unfit for service by

LIEUT.-COL. HENRY CASSADY ROGERS.

MAJOR GEORGE STEWART.

these two forced marches. They died by the dozen and those that survived were so weakened that it was found necessary to send them down to the district about Orange River where pasture could be obtained ; and so the Canadians lost the companionship of the Queenslanders, to whom through their friendly rivalry they had become very much attached.

On the 21st of January another expedition of twenty-six officers and four hundred and eighty-six men, including A Company, six officers and one hundred and twenty-six men, went out towards Thornhill where they bivouacked for the night. The patrols several times came in contact with the enemy's outposts and a part of the Victoria Mounted Infantry was skilfully drawn into ambush by the Boers and one of their number had his arm shattered by two shots, but succeeded in escaping. In such force were the enemy about Thornhill that Colonel Rochfort-Boyd, the new station commandant who had taken Colonel Pilcher's place when that popular officer was given command of the Mounted Infantry at the Modder, ordered A Company to fall back upon Richmond where G Company was stationed. For three weeks these companies remained at Richmond where they built a fine fort and did the usual drudgery and trying tasks of soldiers in a position liable to an attack.

In the meantime an enemy more deadly than the Boer had visited their camp. On January 20 the order book contained the following sentence : "In view of the several recent cases of enteric fever (typhoid) the greatest possible care must be taken in respect to camp sanitation." This was the beginning of the end. The regiment that was to stand the rigors of a march that scarcely has a parallel in history, as trying fighting as ever fell to the lot of soldiers, was to have its strength sapped, to be literally smashed to pieces by this deadly fever. Two were to be taken while they were still encamped at Belmont; and this was but the beginning of a continuous record of death. There is little wonder that fever visited this camp. The scarcity of water made cleanliness impossible, and encamped as they were on a battlefield strewn with ghastly memorials of the fight, they were fortunate to escape a plague.

The brightest day in this weary month was the one on which the issue of chocolate was made to the regiment. This chocolate was the personal gift of Her Most Gracious Majesty to her troops in South Africa, and the soldiers treasured the boxes that contained it as in the olden days a Raleigh or a Sidney would some gift from Good Queen Bess. The age of chivalry dead! These chocolate boxes alone were needed to show what a part Queen Victoria's name has played in this momentous campaign. One letter from Private C. Jackson to his father will suffice to show the esteem in which the gift was held.

"I have just received a box of chocolate, Her Majesty's present to the South African soldiers, which just arrived to-day. It is very nice, in fact almost too good to keep here, there is such a demand for them by the officers and everybody else, as mementos. In fact I have been offered £5 for mine, and at the Cape as much as £10 is being paid, so you will readily understand why I am sending mine home. Somebody might take a fancy to it as they did to my match safe. Take good care of it until I return, which I expect will be in a few months."

"Until I return!" Poor Jackson! He was one of the first to give his life for his Queen in that fierce Sunday fight at Paardeberg.

Things began to look a little more like war towards the end of January. Major-General Hector Macdonald passed through Belmont on his way to the Modder to take command of the Highland Brigade. "Fighting Mac's" presence suggested war. A further evidence of the coming conflict was the crowded state of the line from Cape Town to the Modder. A continuous stream of men poured northward; evidently a large army was being mobilized by Roberts. With the forces, supplies were rushed to the front, supplies apparently sufficient to feed a nation. The Canadians began to wonder when their turn would come. That the eye of the great field-marshal was on them was shown by the signal honor done the regiment in the appointment of Major Septimus J. Denison to the staff of Lord Roberts. The letter to Major Denison from Neville Chamberlain, private-secretary to Lord Roberts, announcing the appointment gave further evidence of the high estimation in which the Royal Canadians were held. "Lord Roberts desires me to add," he writes, "that it gives him much pleasure to avail himself of your services, as a representative of the magnificent body of troops sent from the Dominion of Canada to serve in South Africa."

A few days after this appointment was made three companies were marched north to Graspan only to be promptly ordered back to Belmont. It was a forward movement, however, and the hearts of the men rejoiced; battle was in the air. On February 8 all doubt as to the meaning of the trains loaded with men and supplies that had been steadily toiling towards Kimberley for days was ended by the appearance of Lord Roberts and Lord Kitchener at Belmont Station. They stopped for but a few minutes, only long enough to inspect the station and the station guard.

What a contrast there was between the little Field-Marshal and his tall, square shouldered Chief-of-Staff. But it was not hard to understand why this little old-young man of sixty-eight had been chosen to save England's good name. His quick eye, that seemed to lose nothing, his nervous restless energy, the sympathy that beamed from his face, the stern determination that showed itself in his firm lips, all made it evident why "little Bobs" was the biggest soldier in the Empire. And what a weight he was carrying, a weight that must have pressed with peculiar heaviness upon him every time he saw those strong, ambitious young men who were ready uncomplainingly to follow him to the death as they would have followed no other leader living. Over by the Tugela lay his brave young son, dead, as he when young had hoped to die, in the hour of duty; dead, winning the British soldiers' highest honor, the Victoria Cross, the thing he himself valued before all his other decorations. Whatever he felt he showed no sign of feeling; only perhaps in no war has this great-hearted general showed such solicitude for his men as in the South African war —doubtless in every wounded, suffering soldier he saw something of his son. It is adversity that brings out true greatness, and Roberts' splendid response to the nation's call in an hour of crushing sorrow shows the strength of the will of this soldier who has fought his way to the highest renown on the most difficult battlefields of the Empire,—in India, in Afghan, in Abyssinia, in Burmah. He had hoped nineteen years before to have put an end to England's difficulties in South Africa, and now in his declining years the work he had been sent to do when Colley fell at Majuba once more was his and there was going to be no retreat this time. Next to the Queen's chocolate box, the soldiers of the Canadian regiment valued most this first glimpse of their Commander-in-Chief.

Kitchener attracted attention but not in the same way. He has been called the "Man of Ice and Iron," and alongside of his sympathetic leader, his cold, strong face looked it. A fighting machine, who in the Soudan utterly destroyed the Khalifa's forces with a slaughter unparalleled in modern war. But if the men felt that they could follow Roberts anywhere, they felt too that Kitchener's organizing genius was needed for the march to Pretoria. Of him it had been said in his Soudan campaign: "It appears to be the Sirdar's policy to advance deliberately step by step; to make his position secure after each step before venturing on another; to run no unnecessary risks, but, at the right moment, to strike hard with unexpected suddenness, and follow up the blow with energy." This sentence is as true of his work in South Africa as it was in the Soudan; every advance from Cape Town to Pretoria has been an illustration of this deliberate, machine-like method.

When these two great soldiers left Belmont the Canadians breathed easier; it was only a matter of days till they would follow them up the line. On the 9th they found that they had been brigaded in the 19th Brigade with their old and tried friends the 2nd Duke of Cornwall's Light Infantry, the 2nd Shropshires, and the 1st Gordon Highlanders, with Colonel Smith-Dorrien as their commanding officer. On the followin day Colonel Smith-Dorrien arrived in camp, inspected the Canadians and found them worthy of the reputation they had gained in South Africa.

In mimic war had they defended and captured every kopje within ten miles of Belmont; they had grown weary of repelling and routing large forces of imaginary foes, and they now wished to try themselves with bullets singing about them and shells bursting in their ranks. They were soon to have their wish.

CHAPTER XII.

THE MARCH TO PAARDEBERG.

THE forward movement was to begin at once. The first intimation that the Canadians had that they were to be hurried to the front was a telegram of February 3, which reached the camp at ten o'clock at night, "Canadians to move to-morrow to Modder."

It was a brief despatch but the one for which they had been waiting for two months. It found the "Maple Leaf Camp" in a somewhat scattered condition. A and G Companies were at Richmond on the Douglas road where they had been for three weeks; D and F were up the line five miles guarding the track. One company was ordered to remain at Belmont—H was chosen; and so only three companies, B, C, and E, were able to respond to the urgent telegram.

The soldiers left Belmont without any regret. The nine weeks of heat, monotonous work, and dirt had been too much for them; but their chance had come at last. Tents were struck at three in the afternoon; and as if to assure them that they had seen the last of Belmont everything pertaining to the camp was taken along with them, and all unnecessary lumber left behind. The nine mile march to Graspan was a hot one, but the welcome they received from their old friends the Highlanders, who led them into camp with the pipes, and the Munsters made up for the tramp.

How different was this camp from Belmont. Plenty of water here; they could drink without stinting themselves, wash when they felt like it, and swim in the big tank at their pleasure. They began to feel now as though they were at the front. Past them whirled troops, and big guns; past them rolled cavalry and mounted infantry all getting ready to sweep the enemy from before the gates of Kimberley. They were, however, to experience a bitter blow.

Scarcely had the three companies got nicely settled in their new quarters when the command came that they were to be once more marched to Belmont. Dusty, scorching, thirsty Belmont—how they hated the name!

But shortly after their return the regiment became a unit once more. A couple of days after Roberts and Kitchener had passed through all the eight companies were assembled and awaiting the word that was to make them join the northward-flocking troops. On the 12th the long hoped for message came, and the Canadians got ready to join that moving world of men and horses and cattle that was sweeping with irresistible force on the doomed Boers. At four o'clock they left the camp which they hoped never to see again, entrained and moved north to Graspan where they bivouacked for the night.

The strength of the contingent had somewhat diminished; two, Farley and Purcell, had been laid to rest during the past week, a number of others were sick so that only eight hundred and ninety-five of all ranks were able to undertake the trying

LIEUT.-COL. CHARLES EDWARD MONTIZAMBERT.

MAJOR J. C. McCORKILL, B.C.L.

march after the enemy. Their trials began that first night at Graspan. Hot when they entered camp, the air cooled as they lay wrapped in their great coats, a wintry chill was on the earth before morning, and they shivered with chattering teeth till reveille roused them at three in the morning, weary and tired, for the day's march.

There was an enormous army to be provided for, about forty thousand men in all and twenty thousand horses, and this host was to move with a celerity that would paralyze the Boer forces. Each man had to carry with him the means of sustenance for two days, and so emergency rations and two days' rations—twelve hardtack as hard as the stones of the kopjes—were issued, and then began a march of five days that will live in British history. Over dusty plain, across dry veldt, past gloomy kopje they tramped through the heat to Ramdam, only between twelve and fifteen miles, but they felt as if they had marched a hundred. The dust of a moving host of men, the clouds of dust made by the innumerable oxen, mules and horses that accompanied the advancing army, filled the air. Far about them the transport waggons stretched, far in the rear they toiled, creaking and groaning on their axles to the accompaniment of the neighing and braying and bellowing of oxen, and asses, and horses, and the loud harsh cries of the negro drivers. Yet vast as was this army and innumerable as were the oxen and waggons how small they seemed under the pure hot sky and on that great brown plain; like a fleet of ships on the pathless ocean, they were lost in the immensity of the environment.

The march was a trying one. The men staggered

along through the blazing heat, now one now another falling from the ranks through sore feet or exhaustion or chilled with the deadly enteric. Over fifty men of the 19th Brigade dropped out and at Ramdam Colonel Otter was forced to leave fourteen men behind as unfit to advance.

All this week thirst played havoc with the soldiers; any one of them would have given ten dollars for a single refreshing drink. Several times they passed fields of melons on their line of march. They eyed the tempting fruit thirstily but dare not leave the ranks to pick them. Sometimes the negroes on the transports—and what negro African or American could resist a melon—would manage to leave their high seats, secure these prizes, and greedily devour them, throwing away the green, moist rind. The men with lips parched and cracked, were glad to pick these skins out of the dust to moisten their lips and cool their tongues. What a thirst was this! When they reached Ramdam they hoped for water, but here they found nothing but a green slimy pool with creeping things in it. The horses turned away in disgust sniffing at it scornfully; but the men bent over and drank. Had they been told it was poisoned they still would have drunk. One of them in writing to his mother said of it, "The water was muddy and bad, in fact so bad that you had to hold your nose while you drank, but drink we had to, we were so thirsty."

Once more they bivouacked in the open. There was now no doubt about the work they were on: war was evident, a march such as this could only end in battle and sudden victory or disastrous defeat. Up the next morning before daylight; off at five in company with the Highland Brigade, and after a march of twelve miles as hot and trying as the one of the day before, they reached Watervaal drift on the Riet river in the early afternoon. Tired and footsore as they were they found a heavy task awaiting them. The big naval 4.7 guns were at the river and a fatigue party of two hundred men was detailed to get them across. It was a big undertaking, but after about three hours pulling, hauling, and shoving, these monster weapons that were to do such excellent service on the road to Pretoria were safely across the stream. The work was well done; in fact whatever the Canadians undertook in this campaign from building sidings to charging an army in the trenches, they did with a spirit that gained them among the regulars the name of the Royal Dare Devils. This work finished, at six o'clock the whole battalion crossed the stream "dead tired," to use the words of Colonel Otter.

At Watervaal drift Field-Marshal Lord Roberts met the brigade and tired as the Canadians were with much marching and privations, hungry and thirsty, shoes broken, khaki uniforms shrunken and ragged—his presence seemed to put new life into them and they marched past him with a carriage that called from him words of most enthusiastic praise on their physique and appearance—and "Bobs" is not given to praising where it is not merited.

Still no real rest! In the open they slept once more, up at daylight, and off, this time as the advance guard of the brigade and they set a pace with their long wiry legs that made the regulars groan to keep up. But the march was telling on the regiment, here seven more men had to be left behind as unfit to proceed. This was but a short march, a break in the week. Between eight and nine o'clock they halted at Wegdraal drift on the Riet after doing nine miles and the whole battalion was kept busy doing outpost duty for the brigade.

On that day Cronje left his trenches at Magersfontein. For over two months with splendid military skill and a courage that Lord Methuen was the first to praise, he had on the one hand kept Kimberley in a state of siege and on the other checked an army of double his strength in its career of victory. For two months he had called down on himself the mingled hate and admiration of the English world, and in the hour of defeat he was to win still further renown. He feared nothing from Methuen, but he learned with uneasiness of the vast army that was being gathered together about Graspan and Honeynest Kloof. With his force he could not capture Kimberley, but he would await developments.

Luckily for the British he waited just twenty-four hours too long. Had he left Magersfontein on the 14th instead of the 15th in all probability Roberts would never have overtaken him, and the Transvaal would have had its most reliable general till the end of the struggle.

On the 15th of February he saw that the movement was evidently against his position; he could not hold out and so with the five thousand Boers under his command he slipped quietly out of his strongly entrenched position and started a race with the British who were trying to outflank him.

That the rapidity of Roberts' move had taken the Boers by surprise was evident from the state of their encampment. Shortly after they had evacuated their position, some of the British soldiers entered their trenches and found a strange assortment of camping material and supplies. Bags of mealies, mealie flour, rice, saddles, blankets, pots, pans, the enameled plates they ate from, and in many cases their precious tin trunks. There was no time to pack up these things, if they wished to escape with their lives the lighter they went the better. And what a filthy hole they left behind them. It is amazing that they were not all swept away by a plague of their own making. The dirt, the filth was appalling; the air was filled with a sickening odour; foul carrion lay about their trenches; heaps of supplies were covered with the undressed hides of lately slain oxen—all these things attracted black swarms of flies. They must have been more than hardy to live in such a place as this for weeks; only men half savage could have existed in all this filth. Yet these men time and again had proved themselves as humane as the best of their enemies.

There was no time for the British to moralize on the filth or admire the skill with which the Boers had entrenched themselves. Just a passing glimpse at the earth torn and discolored by the deadly lyddite, and a feeling that their "slim" enemy through their engineering skill had suffered but small loss.

In the meantime Major-General French, the hero of Elands Laagte, was dashing forward towards Kimberley, sweeping from his path the few Boers who remained among the intervening hills to bar his progress. No time to save man or horse; troopers fell from the ranks, wounded and exhausted horses rolled over on the plain and gasped with stiffening limbs, but the whirlwind of war waited not till the green trees surrounding the Diamond City came into view. "The long, weary weeks of anxiety and hardship; the disappointment of Magersfontein, and the heartsickness of deferred hope were alike forgotten. Kimberley was relieved and the remainder of the march might as well have been a review." Ten thousand men and forty-two guns had been rushed forward with a rapidity probably without a parallel in war; and Kimberley was relieved.

When the besieged read the signal of the relieving column, "This is General French coming to the relief of Kimberley," they doubted the glad message. The four months of constant shelling made them look on the Boer attack as a permanent part of their daily life. This signal was surely a trick to throw them off their guard. But reassuring messages came, and when they realized that it was General French and his gallant brigades, the men leaped from the trenches, manned the walls, and the women and children crawled from the depths of the diamond mines to welcome their deliverers.

In the meantime the 19th Brigade was steadily advancing. Jacobsdal, the Boer base of supplies for the force at Magersfontein, was but five miles away from the bivouac on the Riet. A sharp, short fight had taken place at this spot; the Boers had resisted the advance, but the column in front of the Canadians had scattered them as chaff before the wind. The Canadians reached Jacobsdal at ten in the morning and rested for the day.

It was a homely little village surrounded by a stone wall, a Dopper church the only building of any importance. This church was now turned into a hospital where sick and wounded Boer and British soldiers were being cared for, and well cared for too. The town was somewhat deserted, every man capable of bearing a rifle had left, and only the women and children and a few old men could be seen in the streets and houses. Their scowling faces, their sullen demeanor showed how intensely they hated the "rooineks."

During the afternoon news was brought into Jacobsdal that General Cronje was in full retreat from Magersfontein and that he was being hotly pursued. Evidently he was making for Bloemfontein, but so perfect had Kitchener's organization been that everyone knew he would soon be run to ground. In the dead of night he had left the trenches that had served him so well for so many weeks and begun a retreat as masterly under the circumstances as was the English advance. Under him were less than five thousand men; on his trail came a force of forty thousand of the best equipped, officered, and organized British troops that ever went into battle. A correspondent of the Daily Chronicle gives a stirring and sympathetic description of this retreat,—a retreat almost successful despite the heavy odds.

"At dawn on Friday the retreating Boer army was seen from the British naval gun station on Klip drift kopje, trekking eastward across the Britsh front at a distance of five thousand yards. Our guns opened upon them, and a force of mounted infantry, crossing the river, made a dashing charge in the attempt to cut off the head of the enemy's column. But in half an hour their whole force had gained shelter under a line of kopjes.

"Meanwhile two of our batteries had come up and the Oxford 'Buffs,' West Ridings, and Gloucesters. Our infantry crossed the drift, and for three hours were engaged with the enemy, while our batteries shelled his position. The mounted infantry kept hard at work.

"Unable to stand our shell fire, the enemy retired, disputing every inch of the way, and took up a second position on the kopjes to the eastward. It was a magnificent spectacle to see the Boer army thus at bay. Their rear guard, two thousand strong, fought us, while the main body trekked further east, and then brought their guns into action while the rear guard retired.

"The action lasted through the day. Our infantry fought splendidly; but the enemy held his ground under the continued bombardment. Later on the Boer commandant ventured on a bold stroke. Leaving two thousand of his men under cover, he withdrew the rest from his main position, and headed for Klip Kraal drift six miles to the east.

"This movement was soon discovered. Our mounted infantry came back across the drift, and marched along the south bank to endeavor to head off the enemy. When they reached the neighborhood of Klip Kraal drift, night had fallen, and half the Boers were already across to the south side. Our infantry harassed their movements.

"Meanwhile, the Boer rear guard, having covered the crossing of the main body, retired slowly, and successfully passed the drift. The rear guard fought desperately, and as it fell back to the river it was harassed on the flank and rear by the British.

"Having thus passed the Modder under cover of darkness the Boers trekked through the night in the direction of Bloemfontein."

There was no escape; General Kelly-Kenny and "Fighting Mac" were hard after Cronje spreading out to his right and his left, soon he would find

MAJOR JOHN DALEY.

MAJOR ALEXANDER GEO. HESSLEIN

himself hemmed in on all sides with retreat irretrievably cut off. For weeks the British public and press had been cursing this man, the "brutal" leader of "half-savage" men, but the news of his masterly retreat made him as popular in England as almost any of their own generals. There is nothing an Englishman loves so much as a worthy foe, and in "The Lion of the Transvaal" they had found one. With his small force he had out-generaled Methuen; he was giving Roberts and Kitchener the hardest march of their military careers.

For four days the Canadians had been hurrying forward with only the vaguest idea as to their destination. When they left Graspan they understood that they were to take part in the great flanking movement which was to entrap the Boer forces; but it was not until Friday night that they knew definitely the work they were bent on performing. They were asking no questions however: they had willingly become a part of that great fighting machine the British army.

They left Jacobsdal a little before five o'clock on the afternoon of Friday and began a trying night march that lasted until three in the morning. About nine at night while tramping through the darkness they saw gleaming far ahead of them the searchlight of Kimberley. Then they knew whither they were bound. But Kimberley had already been relieved; French was there and the hungry city was delirious with joy. There was other work for them to do, more trying work than a wild gallop across the veldt to a city from before whose gates the terrified enemy had fled.

This march was not without its exciting incidents. While the great body of the Boers were fleeing before the British advance, some hung on the rear of the forces and on one occasion attacked the British transport waggons. The waggons had been creaking over the plains trying to keep up with the rapid forward movement but lagged behind. A commando of Boers swept down on them, and a warm fight which lasted all morning was kept up about the invaluable transports. To save them Roberts would have had to check his advance. This would never do. Cronje must not escape, no matter what the cost; and so he at last ordered the waggons and their fine trek-oxen to be abandoned. This was a great loss to an army already on half rations, but to let the enemy slip through his hands would have been a still greater calamity. So the rush forward continued. At daylight on Saturday the Canadians reached Klip drift, rested until five in the afternoon, and after a very scanty meal began a night march across the veldt to Paardeberg.

On this night the British Mounted Infantry had come up with the rear guard of Cronje's army and had forced them back upon the main body; there was now no escape; it was only a matter of hours till the Boers would be completely surrounded,— and the Canadians were to be in at the death. Through the night they marched, these eager hunters of men, plodding in the yielding sand, stumbling over the rocks of the kopjes, forcing their way through the prickly shrubs; hungry, footsore, thirsty. Along the way they left traces of the terrible race they were in: dead horses, mules and oxen dotted the plain at intervals. Occasionally a soldier unable to proceed farther, tottering, staggering, struggling to keep up with his fellows, would leave his place in the ranks and fall spent on the plain. But the regiment could not stop to help the exhausted. To-morrow they would be reported missing, and if not picked up by the stretcher-bearers, if they had good luck they might be carried on their way by the transport; or rested might be able to join some other regiment and continue the march. War is cruel but in nothing is it crueller than in the march before battle; then neither horses nor men can be considered.

A bit of the description of this march by one who accompanied the British convoy is well worth reading.

"When night came, and the cattle were toiling painfully along over rough ground, there was much thunder and sheet lightning, but, fortunately, no rain. After the heat of the day the air struck one as delightfully cool, albeit the temperature was probably as high as that experienced in England during average summer weather. Every now and then you are compelled to pause, owing to some accident to waggon or ox, and neither was of infrequent occurrence during this particular journey. In the former case the damage was promptly made good, and in the latter the animal was outspanned and left to die on the route. So far as horses, mules, and oxen are concerned, the entire way between Modder River and Bloemfontein has proved a veritable Calvary. In some countries natives direct their course across the desert by following the bleached bones of man and beast which mark the route; but in the present case there will be no land marks of that description to assist the traveler. Truth to tell, the stench of the rotting cattle on either side has become so appalling during our hot autumn, and the spectacle of birds of prey feasting upon the remains so revolting, that Kaffirs have been engaged for the purpose of burying the unfortunate animals."

It was well for the Canadians that this first great march found them fresh and strong. Later in the campaign when they were worn out with toil, their nerves shattered from privations, their strength sapped with the deadly germs of fever, such a march as this to Paardeberg would have caused them to fall out by the dozen.

At two in the morning as they toiled forward they could hear far ahead of them the roar of great guns. As they caught the music of distant battle strength seemed to return and their pace was quickened. Between five and six the treble of the crackling rifle was mingled with the base of the artillery, and they knew that a battle was in progress. Exhausted as they were, they had but one wish, to get into it. The firing increased and so excited were the men that some even neglected to take the coffee and biscuits that were issued to them, rushing along the river to get a glimpse of the fray. They had covered twenty-three miles during the night, and as they drew near their halting place in the early dawn they could hardly keep their eyes open; but the presence of actual war, a big engagement, thoroughly aroused the sleepiest among them, and, when, before they had finished their hardtack and coffee, the assemble sounded, they forgot their privations, their exhaustion, their aching feet and clutched their rifles with determined hands. A "mouthful of army rum" was given to the soldiers to brace their nerves and steady them for the work.

Cronje had a strong position a short distance

away; a well-sheltered position and the 19th Brigade was to be an important factor in forcing him to surrender. Highlanders, Shropshires, and Canadians were to be at once hurried forward against the enemy's line.

The Canadians were to have nine days of hard fighting, and they were to begin their battles with a bit of work that tried the nerves of the boldest. The Modder that rushed by muddy and deep and swift had to be forded. Usually the Modder in February is an almost dry stream, but the Boers had broken the dam farther up and a full flood of water swept along. The Canadians crossed at two points. At one spot a rope was strung over the river and by it the men pulled themselves safely through the treacherous waters that swept their feet from under them; farther up where the water was shallower but as swift, they locked arms and four abreast to keep from being swept away, crossed the turbulent stream. Without a serious mishap the entire Canadian regiment reached the further bank and prepared to play their part in the orchestra of battle that was dinning in their front, to their left, and to their right.

CHAPTER XIII.

THE FIRST BATTLE.

THE river was crossed, and the men with their clothes hanging about them like lead scrambled up to the dusty plain. The excitement of the swift stream, the cooling water, the feeling that they were now on the battlefield made them forget their hunger and the weary night march. Laughing and joking they tried to shake the water from their bulging knees, but the close-fitting puttees kept it from running out. Some danced about in their efforts to get rid of it, while others cut holes in their trousers. Captain Arnold, who was so soon to be struck down with a mortal wound, laughingly said as he gazed at his dripping men, " There is nothing for it, boys, but to stand on your heads,—" and some of them in the spirit of fun actually took him at his word and the water ran out at their shoulders. Soldiers these that would have delighted the hearts of Mulvaney, Ortheris, and Learoyd. They knew what they were going into; the battlefields of Graspan and Magersfontein were familiar to them; the wounded soldiers brought past their camp by the score from the front told them what they might expect; and yet they prepared to advance into the deadly firing line with as light hearts as they would have gone into a gala-day review.

Already the distant crackling of the rifle-fire told

them that a part of their brigade was engaged. The enemy had got sight of the Highlanders and an occasional burst of dust rose from the bullets falling in their advancing line. Cronje was speaking with well-aimed rifles. He would not surrender and was beginning the most desperate fight of his life. He was in a trap, a hopeless trap, with every outlet closed. Kitchener had done his work well; from North, South, East, and West batteries of artillery, naval guns, Howitzers, brigades of infantry, fronted him. He had kept Kimberley invested for weeks; his little well-entrenched army had stopped the advance of Methuen's strong force, and held him defiantly at bay. Now he was caught, caught without hope of escape, yet he would not surrender. Reinforcements might arrive, darkness, a storm, might give him a chance of slipping through the tight drawn lines of men and guns. His retreat had filled the besieging force with admiration, and now his determined stand in the bed of the Modder gave him a new right to his title, "The Lion of the Transvaal." A lion at bay—one worth capturing, but his captors would have to suffer.

For nearly a mile he was ensconsed in the deep river bed on either side of the Modder. He had chosen his ground well; the thickly-wooded banks afforded him excellent shelter and at the same time fine positions in which to place his keen-sighted sharp-shooters. Dongas deep and safe, natural trenches running from the river, made him additionally secure. Added to these natural protections he had constructed an almost impregnable system of trenches in the river bank. Even the terrible shell fire to which he was to be subjected

THE CANADIANS CROSSING PAARDEBERG DRIFT ON THE MODDER.

The right hand men held a rope, the others joined hands and stumbled across. The Canadians, it will be remembered, acted with great gallantry in the final attack on Cronje, who might have held out longer but for the terrible fire poured on him from their trenches.

PHYSICIAN AND STORY-TELLER: DR. CONAN DOYLE ATTENDING
WOUNDED CANADIANS IN THE LANGMAN HOSPITAL.

THE FIRST BATTLE. 237

could make but little impression on such a well-chosen position, so splendidly defended.

On such a position, against such a man, the Canadians began to advance as soon as they had shaken some of the water from their clothes. The regiment was in luck. A kopje in front protected their advance as they slowly deployed to the left. On the right was the Duke of Cornwall's Light Infantry, and on the left the Gordons, and a little farther off the Shropshire Light Infantry. As they advanced the "tick-tack" of the rifles from the enemies' trenches and the trees came with strange music to their unaccustomed ears. A Company led by about fifty yards, C followed close behind, D and E acted as their support, while B, F, H, and G were held in reserve. Major Buchan commanded the firing-line, while Colonel Otter was with the supports. Slowly the men moved forward, the officers ten yards in advance of the companies, keeping well out of sight of the enemy under the protection of the hill in front. Occasionally a bullet would strike the dust at their feet or go singing with angry hiss overhead—a bullet evidently aimed at the Highlanders, who were within the enemy's vision.

At 9.30 the firing line got into the open, and the bullets began to fall, at first like the big drops that foretell the fierce storm, and then thick and fast and threatening. The men had been advancing in extended order with only two paces between them, but this was soon increased to five. The bullets sang and screeched overhead, but no man was hit, the ground still serving as a shelter.

Soon, however, one stray bullet found its mark. Private Findlay was the first to be struck, the first of the Canadians to fall in battle. He had been advancing fearlessly, joking with his nearest comrades, when the messenger of death found him out. Shot through the heart; his dying cry, "O my God!" which reached his captain's ear, told his last thought.

Greater care had now to be taken in the advance; Magersfontein and Enslin had taught the officers a lesson. Every rise in the ground, the ant-hills scattered here and there over the veldt were taken advantage of as the line advanced with short, sharp rushes of thirty paces at a time. As the fire became hot the men were halted to rest and commanded to lie still and hold their fire for a time.

It was scorching work, stretched out on their stomachs on the plain. Their clothes by this time were dry and the hot sun streaming down on the unsheltered plain scorched their backs and blistered the soles of their feet. The enemy, too, evidently had the range marked, and fired volleys into the extended line with deadly accuracy.

The Canadians through the Sunnyside affair had lost respect for the much vaunted Boer markmenship. But Cronje had with him a different race of men from the cowering rebels of the Douglas district. In his command were the sons of the Voortrekkers who had fought their way into the Transvaal half a century before with incredible adventures against savage beasts and savager men. Some of the very Voortrekkers themselves were there; grey-bearded men, who for fifty years had had the rifle as their constant companion. The men in the firing-line, and indeed in the supports too, soon learned to respect the enemy's fire and did not dare show themselves.

The line had advanced in extended order, keeping their intervals splendidly till within from five to eight hundred yards of the enemy's trenches and the sheltering trees along the Modder. Till this time they had held their fire, but now they began a steady fusilade. During the morning A Company got out of ammunition, and C Company joined them, and kept up a heavy fusilade to cover the deficiency. The hollows and the ant-hills served as excellent protection, but still an occasional man was struck.

How unsatisfactory it was throwing bullets into space. The enemy did not show themselves and only the puffs of smoke from the Martinis or the momentary flash of the smokeless powder told where they lay concealed. Sometimes the trembling in a treetop, the swaying of the branches, gave a suggestion of the presence of a "sniper" and served to direct the fire. But for the most part the men knew that they were merely keeping down the enemy's fire by their steady rifle practice.

It required no mean amount of courage to lie there patiently on that bullet-searched plain. It needed pluck, pluck of the highest order. The long discipline at Belmont, the steady fixing of the mind for those weary weeks on future action had made the Canadian soldiers veterans. Baden-Powell in his excellent little book, "Aids to Scouting," says:

"Many people will tell you that pluck is not a thing that can be taught a man; it is either born in him or he has not got it at all.

"But I think that, like many other things, it is almost always in a man, though in some cases, it wants developing and bringing out. The pluck required of a scout is of a very high order.

"A man who takes part in a Balaclava charge is talked of as a hero, but he goes in with his comrades all round him and officers directing; he cannot well turn back."

The courage demanded in this battle was practically the pluck here described. Each man was depending on himself, without feeling the touch of the soldier to his left and right. The air was full of death from an almost invisible fire from an entirely invisible foe. Nothing easier than when safe shelter was found to maintain it without running any risk from the enemy's fire. Why expose themselves! Their comrades were too busy keeping cover and endeavoring to pick off the foe to observe what the next man was doing, and the officers were too thinly scattered along the widely extended line to take note of individual cases of cowardice. There were none to note. To a man the Canadians behaved like heroes; A and C Companies, despite the hail of bullets that sang about them, kept up a steady fire. The firing-line had to be strengthened however; first D Company was advanced into it, then E, and part of B, while the remainder of B and F and G Companies acted as supports. H was held in reserve but it too knew that it was in battle, for although sixteen hundred yards from the Boer position three or four men were struck during the day.

Never were soldiers more thoroughly tried than those in the firing-line of the Royal Canadian Regiment on February 18th. At times the air seemed alive with singing bullets, and the soldiers' only safety lay in clinging close to the dry plain.

Some who had not the protection of hollows or ant-hills scooped themselves holes in the sand where they could lie with comparative safety. At times some Boer marksmen got knowledge of a definite hiding place and then showered bullets towards it till it was untenable. A rush was out of the question; to stand upright, to attempt to double to another shelter would have meant instant death, yet the position had to be left; and occasionally squirming figures could be seen crawling forward—never back—on their stomachs, creeping through the dust as they dug their hands and feet into the sand. Occasionally someone more bold, almost foolhardy, would leap from his shelter and dash forward from ten to thirty paces, and he was lucky indeed if he escaped the deadly aim of the watchful enemy.

By this time the long line was somewhat scattered and not a few of the Shropshires and Highlanders on the left and right were mingled with the extended Canadians. Nor were the soldiers the only ones in the firing-line. Several of the correspondents stuck gallantly to the very edge of danger and death. Pencil in hand they sweltered through the heat of the day and by their dauntless courage did not a little to inspire the fighters around them. Here too were the chaplains, and particularly that noble self-sacrificing priest Father O'Leary, who has time and time again in this war proved himself worthy of the Victoria Cross. Than he there was no braver soldier in South Africa; wherever a wounded man needed succor, he was there; where a dying lad needed to be shrived there he was to be found. Out of the firing-line he could not keep, and his escapes were miraculous. Dangers, privations, hardships effected him but lightly; his only thought was for the men he had come to Africa to sustain and comfort in the hour of danger and sickness, and the only commander he heeded was duty. He was courting death in the firing-line that bloody Sunday in February, but death passed him by; and yet how close it came.

"Behind an ant-hill I lay prone," he wrote to his brother, "sharing the tiny shelter with one of the Black Watch. Finding that there was not room for two, I decided on making a dash for a little mound some fifty yards forward. As I raised myself on my hands and knees preparatory to a dash, I remember him calling out, 'My God, Sir, take care; Godspeed you!' Just then a volley was directed at us, too late for me, but, alas, for him. Next morning at early dawn I found him behind our friendly ant-hill just as I had left him, but pierced through the heart and body by the bullets that perhaps had been intended for me. Do you know that a feeling of guilt came over me as I gazed on my poor comrade of an hour, but still had I remained a minute longer this letter would never have been written."

This letter splendidly exemplifies the reason why Father O'Leary is dear to every man of the Canadian Regiment.

All through the morning the hot sun blazed over head, scorching the bodies of the men and parching their tongues; all through the morning that unceasing fire made them keep close cover. The dust from the smitten ant-hills flew about them, bursts of dust like the exploding of innumerable puff-balls

THE FIRST BATTLE. 243

sprinkled the plain and an occasional groan or cry of pain told that someone had been hit.

If the Boers kept up a steady fire from their entrenched positions the Highlanders, the Shropshires, and Canadians as steadily returned it. Several times during the day the cry was passed along the line "Stop firing on the left!" The soldiers on the right were being hit on the flank and rear apparently by the Canadian fire. But in the dongas and watercourses on the left rear of the Canadians the Boers had a strong position; and owing to their smokeless powder and the uproar of the battlefield were able to sweep the flank of the Canadian Regiment. For some time their position was not discovered, but by noon their fire was effectually beaten down. Captain Bell and his gallant little squad had managed despite the deep water and rapidly rushing stream, to bring a Maxim gun across the Modder, and under a heavy, well-directed rifle-fire, succeeded in taking up a position on a piece of rising ground on the left of the line a thousand yards from the enemy's trenches. From their position they did most effective work. The fire of the enemy in the treacherous dongas was soon beaten down, and at intervals all through the day they poured shells into the Boer trenches.

While this sharp fighting was going on deeds of bravery were being performed on the field that well deserved the Victoria Cross. If a soldier was hit he always found his nearest comrade ready to dress his wound and help him to a sheltered spot, or to the hospital tent a mile or so in the rear. Several times soldiers doing this noble work were struck themselves as they fearlessly returned to the battlefield. Through the lines succouring the wounded passed the gallant fellows who had volunteered as stretcher-bearers, Curphy, who afterwards died at Bloemfontein with enteric fever; Page, who gave his life later in this siege did work that glorifies the butchery of battle, did service that called down the praises of their commander—but there were so many heroes on that day that it is unjust to individualize. Chief among them, however, was Surgeon-Captain Fiset. He was everywhere, fearlessly doing his work of mercy, and the fact that he was busy with the wounded did not save him. Indeed he seemed to draw the Boer fire. At length gallant Captain Arnold was struck down with a mortal wound. The stretcher-bearers attempted to carry him from the field, but such a leaden hail played about his stretcher that they too fell. Under this fire Surgeon-Captain Fiset dressed his wound as best he could and then himself acted as stretcher-bearer to help remove him out of the range of the deadly rifles. His work done, back he went to the field to help others.

While the stretcher-bearers were doing these gallant deeds of mercy, equally as brave were the ammunition carriers. All day they crossed and re-crossed the deadly line, fearlessly keeping the bandoliers of their comrades in arms supplied. Private Kennedy of C Company, who later in the day was wounded no fewer than seven times, was especially mentioned for his gallantry in leading an ammunition-mule right up to the firing-line. The mule was killed but for the time being he escaped.

The men fighting the battle could guard themselves to some extent, but the stretcher-bearers

THE REV. P. M. O'LEARY,
Chaplain of the Contingent.

THE CORNWALLS, ASSISTED BY THE CANADIANS, DRIVING THE BOERS FROM THE RIVER BANK IN CONNECTION WITH THE CAPTURE OF CRONJE

and the ammunition men had to courageously expose themselves as they moved from front to rear and made the return trip. After once safely passing out of the storm of bullets that "buzzed about them like a million flies," it must have required almost superhuman courage to once more face the deadly range. But the men had the fine example of their officers to keep up their courage. Major Buchan in the firing-line and Colonel Otter with the supports, the captains of the companies and their lieutenants, all acted as though war had been the pastime of their lives. Lieutenant Ogilvy moved from point to point about the field bearing Colonel Otter's orders much as he would have moved about on a review day.

There were strange sights, too, on this battlefield. Some of the soldiers had had nothing to eat since the previous afternoon. They were utterly exhausted from hunger and thirst and the long night march, and in the lull of the firing it was not uncommon to see one of them opening his haversack and munching at a piece of bread, or trying to force a little dry biscuit down his parched throat. Occasionally, too, a diary would be produced and the events of the trying week, and particularly of the previous night's march and the excitement of fording the river, set down. Cameras even were produced and striking pictures of the firing-line taken. One of these camera fiends had his helmet, his tunic, and his instrument struck while taking a picture. Had these boys no sense of fear! It was little wonder that the regulars looked at their dare-devil dash with amazement.

The day grew hotter but the fight slackened but little. The exhausting march to Paardeberg, the need of food, the heat, were telling on the men. Some of them were growing dizzy and faint, when above the roar of the battle the thunder boomed across the sky and great cooling drops of rain fell. It was a blessed relief. The men caught the rain in their hands and moistened their cracked lips and parched tongues, and their burning bodies grew cool under the refreshing storm. But it had come from the antarctic world; the breath of an iceberg was in its wings and from panting and suffocating with the heat the soldiers shivered under the chilling storm. When it passed, many of them refreshed and rested fell asleep where they lay and several were struck as they slept.

There could be no better evidence of what the Canadians had endured than this. A man must indeed be worn out when he can sleep with death singing its song about his couch. One instance will serve to show how exhausted these men must have been.

Private Sippi of London was wounded in the foot, but when the disastrous charge of the day was made he wished to be in it. Unable to keep up with the line he took off his shoe, dressed, with the field dressing every soldier carries in his haversack, a painful wound, then crept into the shadow of a bush and slept. Wounded under fire and yet able to sleep: these men were either utterly played out, or not as other men.

The day was drawing to a close and still the trees and the river bank were alive with Boer riflemen. If a head was raised or an arm was moved, if a wounded man changed his position on the plain, the bullets rained thick and fast. The officers were losing patience, and the men were ready for anything that would relieve the nervous strain of lying exposed on the open veldt.

At four o'clock Colonel Allworth of the Cornwalls told Colonel Otter that "he had been sent to finish this business, and proposed doing so with the bayonet." He brought up to the firing-line first one company of the Cornwalls, then two others; and when the line was thus thoroughly enforced, offering five pound to the first man in the enemy's trenches, gave the command to charge. Bugler Williams leaped on an ant-hill and while the bullets rained about him the clarion notes of the charge, so welcome to the Saxon ear, rang out. The tired, exhausted line woke up and swept forward at the double, stumbling, falling, mowed down like grain before the reaper. Forward, forward, through a hell of bullets; at last they could stand it no longer. The Cornwalls' Colonel was killed with five bullets, the "recall" was sounded and his men broke and retreated. The Canadians were too near to the enemy to retreat. One gallant fellow who had outstripped the others was indeed found next morning riddled with bullets, at the very trenches' edge. Retreat would have meant terrible havoc in their ranks and so they fell prone on the plain behind a ridge scattered over a wide stretch of any where from one hundred to five hundred yards from their invisible foe. At this close range no help could be given to the wounded and the dead had to lie where they fell. Until darkness they lay on that ghastly plain searched by the deadly rifle-fire. Many of the wounded as they writhed in agony were struck a second time. It was a horrible ordeal for the young soldiers, and yet but the beginning of nine days of as severe fighting as ever tested men.

The charge was as magnificent as the charge of the Light Brigade, but it should never have been made. As has since been proved the British knew absolutely nothing of the character of the Boers' position. They might as well have tried to carry Gibraltar at the bayonet's point as Cronje's position. The soldier dearly loves the spectacular in war, and nothing is so magnificently inspiring or picturesque as a bayonet charge; but whatever it may have been in the days of the "thin red line," it has a place in modern war only on the rarest occasions. Of all the blunders of this war this at Paardeberg is perhaps the most unpardonable. Magersfontein has its excuses, but Paardeberg has none. However, the mistakes of England's leaders have been the glory of the English soldier; and this charge gave Canada a permanent place in British history. "The Men of Paardeberg" will stand out in bold characters on the future pages of the story of the Empire. But there was a terrible butcher's bill for the renown gained. Seventy-five per cent. of all who fell on that black Sabbath met the fatal blow in this mad charge.

There was nothing the Canadian could do but lie where they fell till darkness came. The Boers gave them no chance of retreating as an unceasing storm of well-directed bullets played along the entire line.

If the Canadians suffered the Boers must have suffered too. From the big guns and the Howitzers shells fell all day long into the bushes and the trenches. Occasionally the men watching the fight from cover could see the sickly green fumes from the lyddite as the shells burst right in the midst of the Boer position. Nor did the fire slacken as the day went on, but as if to avenge the fallen after the

THE FIRST BATTLE.

fatal charge the shells fell with greater accuracy and frequency. The laager long since untenable took fire, and mid the bursting of shells, the burning of transport waggons and camp supplies, the furious crackling of thousands of rifles, the day went out and darkness fell upon the earth, and the Canadians exhausted in body and spirit retreated to their camp leaving the dead and wounded where they had fallen. No wonder many of them said on that night of desolation, " We have seen enough of war."

CHAPER XIV.

A WEEK OF WAR AND DEATH.

THE Royal Canadians had gone into the battle of Paardeberg with the feeling that war was a great game in which they were playing their part. They laughed and they joked as the enemy's bullets sang around them, but at first they had no thought of being struck. They had seen the wounded men brought down from Magersfontein, they had looked into the faces of men who had been slain on the battlefield, and they had trembled then; but it never seemed to occur to them that it might be their turn now. As this day drew to a close and from all sides they could hear the groans and cries of the wounded, the pitiful calls for the surgeons and stretcher-bearers, the stern reality of the fight took hold of them and when darkness fell they were glad to escape to their lines.

As they retreated how ghastly was the plain they passed over. During the day so busily had each man been employed either keeping to cover or returning the enemy's fire that they did not fully realize how dreadful had been the slaughter; but as they stumbled back to their bivouac through the darkness with an occasional bullet from the ever-watchful Boers singing about them, they saw the battlefield thickly dotted with the dead and the dying. In the blackness among the ant-hills the bodies lay like the thickly strewn stones of a kopje.

The day had been hard enough to try men of steel and by nightfall, utterly exhausted, they stole back to the river they had crossed with such rejoicing twelve hours before. Half the regiment had not come in; many were dead, many were wounded, some after the "recall" from the fatal charge had fallen asleep in the shelter of the bushes or even on the open field, and many more were standing by wounded fellow-soldiers trying desperately to get them to the field-hospital. As the men came in and looked about for their comrades, as they heard of this friend and that companion who had fallen under the deadly rifle-fire, their nerves unstrung by their terrible experience, they broke down and wept like children or sat in sullen silence with breaking hearts. Life friendships had been rudely snapped in an instant by death; and this was but the beginning.

To add to the gloom, after the heat of the day the night was cold and the survivors sat huddled about their fires or slept in the open with nothing but the hard earth under them and the sky for a covering. The transports had not yet reached them, and for the most part they were without blankets, having on an average one for every three or four men. It was not until ten o'clock that night that they were able to get a meal. A biscuit and hastily swallowed mouthful of coffee or tea at six in the morning; a plunge across a turbulent stream; a twelve hours fight, first in a blazing sun, and then in a rainstorm that chilled them to the marrow; a wild mad charge; hours on the plain with death at their elbows; and nothing to eat or drink since

SURGEON-CAPTAIN FISET.

LIEUT.-COL. JOHN MACPHERSON.

daybreak—this was indeed a day to make them veterans.

Some of the hardier among them, or some who had comrades who had not yet come in, bravely volunteered to go out and search the plain for the wounded. Back they went on their humane work, a work as trying as the battle of the day. G. W. Steevens in "From Cape Town to Ladysmith," makes the following comment on war: "In war, they say—and it is true—men grow calloused; an afternoon of shooting and the loss of your brother hurts you less than a week before did a thorn in your dog's foot." The Canadians had not yet grown callous, and it is to be doubted if the rapid succession of engagements they passed through in their march to Pretoria made them indifferent to the death of a comrade.

On this gloomy Sunday night their hearts ached as they groped their way over the plain to find first this body and that cold in death. Past succour many of these recumbent figures, and so they left them to seek others who lay where they had fallen tortured with wounds and thirst. The moon was now high over head and the plain was almost as bright as day. It was dangerous to show one's self, as the crack of the rifle still came from the trees from which the Boers had done such deadly work during the day, and the angry ping of the bullets sang over the dead and among the living. The ambulance corps were doing heroic work under this chill moon. Fearlessly they passed about the field of slaughter picking up the wounded and bearing them to the rear. Like angels of mercy on the background of an inferno their lights gleamed. The Boers saw them, knew the work they were on, and yet they kept up a steady fire at their moving lanterns. The Divine hand was surely guarding these men on their brave and humane work; for not a man was hit during the night. Many of the wounded, however, lay close to the enemy's position and in the bright moonlight it would have been foolhardy to risk attempting to bring them in; and so the brave fellows who had fallen in that last charge for the most part had to lie where they fell till morning broke.

Over this field went the men of the Black Watch, Gordons, Cornwalls, Shropshires, Canadians, all searching for their comrades. Occasionally a soldier would be seen dragging his way towards the rear, trying to keep back the groan of pain and asking appealingly where his regiment was. At times they would come upon a cluster of wounded men closely huddled together; men of all the regiments of the heroic 19th Brigade unable to drag themselves from the field had come to each other for mutual companionship. It would be easier to die with their comrades of this well-fought fight about them; or in the chill of the African night they might keep each other warm. Here a soldier was found prone on his face, under him lay his diary, open, splashed with his life's blood; he had just been penning a sentence that his mother and sisters were to read when the war was over and he was back at the Canadian fireside. There lay a lad, scarcely of manhood's years, by an ant-hill, an unlit cigarette crushed in his stiffened fingers. His rifle a few feet away told the story of his death. He had recklessly exposed himself going to a comrade for a smoke to sooth his exhausted brain and nerves, and death had found him out.

Grim lessons were taught the Canadians on that Sunday. Over ten per cent. of their regiment had been struck, many through their inexperience and reckless bravery. They lost none of their courage, but for the future they practised the tactics of their wily enemy and never exposed themselves unless it was absolutely necessary. When the roll was called and they could count the cost, it was found that eighteen were killed, sixty-three wounded, and two missing.

Next morning it was discovered that Cronje had left his position and retreated up the Modder a few miles to a stronger spot and one in which he would be able to make a more dogged resistance. He at once entrenched his troops in a system of trenches from which they could laugh at even the deadly lyddite. He was surrounded, brought to bay, all escape cut off, only the most remote possibility of reinforcements reaching him,—yet he would not yield.

Monday was a day of comparative rest for the Canadians. The transports that had slowly toiled after them from Graspan had not yet reached Paardeberg; blankets were needed, food was very scarce, and the regiment waited for supplies. They were kept busy however, from early morning. That ghastly field had to be cleared and so the day was spent picking up the wounded who had survived the night and carrying in the dead, some of whom had died during the darkness. A big trench was dug and all the dead of the regiment were laid to rest together.

When the news of this fight reached Canada a feeling of pride thrilled through the Dominion. Much had been expected of the contingent; it had surpassed expectations. At first it was thought by some that many of the reports were colored by the correspondents, but from every quarter came the same enthusiastic despatches; for endurance and dash the Royal Canadian Regiment was without a superior in the British Army.

It was feared that the enemy might try to slip through the lines at night and a most careful watch was kept. On Monday at five in the afternoon the regiment was advanced to within three miles of Cronje's lines where they acted as outposts. Few of the Boers, however, attempted to escape. It was too hazardous, and Burnham, the famous scout, who moved over the field on either side of the river, creeping up night after night to the very trenches of the enemy, reported but three or four desertions a night, most of whom were captured by the British; on one night, however, a considerable force seems to have escaped unobserved.

On Tuesday the bombardment began again in earnest. If Paardeberg had given Cronje a strong position Wolveskraal offered him better natural protection. He had occupied about two miles of the river-bed, which was here a ditch about one hundred and fifty feet wide and fifty feet deep. Both banks of the stream were deeply wooded; in such a position only a storm of shot and shell could have any effect. The storm broke, and the Canadians played their part as effectively as on the previous Sunday.

The outposts were advanced to within two thousand yards of the Boer laager. The Canadians occupied the centre and were supported by the Shropshire Light Infantry on the right, the Gordons on the left. They advanced until the firing-line

A WEEK OF WAR AND DEATH. 261

was one thousand yards from the enemy's position and there they lay all day subjected to a trying fire, but they returned it with interest. The enemy once more kept themselves invisible, and there was less reckless exposure in the Canadian firing-line than in the first battle. Still the boys never shirked their work, and, crouched behind a protecting ridge, they kept up a steady fire that served as excellent support to the naval guns which poured shells into the laager from early morning till night, and to the troops who were constructing a strong line of trenches within five hundred yards of the enemy.

Several times our soldiers had their courage thoroughly tested on this day. The Boers determined to kill their fire and so trained on them their Maxim automatic gun. This gun has as many names as any noted criminal. It is known in the newspapers as the Vickers-Maxim, the Maxim-Nordenfelt, the Hotchkiss, or even the Gatling; but by the soldiers it has been christened the "Putt-Putt," the "Pom-Pom," the "Diarhosen Dick," and "The Bloomin' Door-Knocker." Its bark is fortunately a great deal worse than its bite, but it would indeed be a brave regiment that could face its music for the first time without a tremor. Five times that day its ripping roars were heard, and five times its shells burst close to the Canadian firing-line. On several occasions the boys wavered, but only for a moment; along the extended line the officers fearlessly went, and Colonel Otter, who has never needlessly exposed himself, but who has never been found wanting in the hour of danger, passed from company to company to encourage his men. It poured shells into the Canadian line but not a man was hit, however, the noise of it and the rapidity with which it vomited forth shells when it had once found the range did much to keep down the Canadian fire.

All day the bombardment continued; every few minutes clouds of dust and sickly green smoke would rise a hundred feet in the air as the lyddite burst in the Boer laager. Pity at times seized the besiegers, but they could not let up in their deadly work; even the women and children who they knew were in the doomed encampment moved their hearts but for a moment.

A paragraph of the account written for the Times gives an excellent idea of the work of destruction done by the British guns.

"Tuesday, the 20th, was marked by the severest bombardment of the investment, and a Boer doctor describes the position as awful. Nothing could be done but crouch in the trenches and wait till dusk prevented further attack, while waggon after waggon in the laager caught fire and burnt away into a heap of scrap-iron amid a pile of wood-ashes. The desolation produced was fearful, and it soon became impossible to make any reply. The losses inflicted upon the horses were the turning point of the siege. So enormous a proportion (estimated by some at seventy-five per cent. of the total number present) of the horses, for which no protection could be made, were lost, that any dash for freedom by night was impossible, and the condition of the laager rapidly became so foul that that alone, apart from the want of food, would have compelled an early surrender."

At six o'clock that evening the men heard the bugle calling them to their bivouac. It had been a hot day as usual, and they had been on the field from early morning with but a biscuit to munch at and without water to drink. An attempt was made to bring a water-cart up to the firing-line, but without success as the Boers promptly turned on it their "pom-pom." Thoroughly fagged, those who were not on duty threw themselves on the ground and slept despite the penetrating chill of the African night. So carefully had the work of the day been done that there were none killed in this hard day's fighting and only four were wounded; and all these in the reserves at about 1600 yards from the enemy's trenches.

News of Cronje's determined resistance flashed around the world. Some called him brutally obstinate in his stubborn resistance, sacrificing his men to no purpose. To no purpose! He checked the advance of the British on Bloemfontein and gave his fellow-countrymen time to study the situation and plan a retreat; and he tired the English force that had beset him, utterly played them out, sapped the strength of the living and thinned the ranks; a force greater than his own was destroyed directly or indirectly by his dogged stand. For the most part the English world watched his resistance with enthusiasm. They even neglected to read the swelling lists of the dead in their eagerness to learn of his courageous opposition to "Bobs" and Kitchener and forty-thousand of England's best troops. Of him the Daily News said, and it voiced the feeling of the Anglo-Saxon world: "In a position covering only a mile square, hemmed in on all sides, circled with a chain of fire from rifle, Maxim, and Howitzer, played on by deadly lyddite, bursting in its own sickly green light, his hastily built trenches enfiladed by a stream of lead sweeping down the river from the north bank, General Cronje still elects to fight. It is magnificent courage." Or as one of the Canadian boys put it at the close of a letter home describing this siege: "He is a determined man."

Still there was no let up in the fight. At night the occasional roar of the guns told that the British were keeping the Boers awake. They, however, were going to make no more rash charges on Cronje's position. They had calmly settled down to force him to surrender by the destructive fire of their artillery, or to starve him out.

On Wednesday the Canadians had a comparative rest. Rations were still scarce but a little fresh meat was a relief from the hardtack. On this day they shifted camp and during the night did outpost duty. On Thursday they felt fresher than they had been since leaving Graspan and that afternoon hailed with pleasure the order to march from the camp in force to assist in cutting off a large body of Boers supposed to be coming to Cronje's relief. They caught sight of no enemy however. General French and his cavalry were sweeping the country round about and only a very strong army could have cut its way through the British lines. So far they had been suffering from thirst, heat and hunger; the hunger was to continue, but for the rest of the week instead of the scorching sun they were to have the other extreme. Scarcely had they taken up their position on a kopje overlooking the surrounding country than a furious rain-storm beat up, soaking the men. Steadily through the afternoon it poured and when darkness came it was still raining. There was no shelter save among the rocks, and the soldiers lay on the sodden ground

CANADIANS AT CAPETOWN.
The men from St. Thomas.

SECOND CANADIAN CONTINGENT.

Royal Canadian Artillery. "D" and "E" battery ready to start for the Prieska Region.

hungry and shivering; a scant issue of rum at night drove the chills away for the moment. But for one burst of sunshine the next day was as gloomy and threatening, and at night rain again came down in torrents. The scanty supply of rubber sheets and the deficiency of blankets compelled the Canadians practically to lie on the bare, wet ground exposed to the tempestuous weather.

While the regiment was engaged in this arduous duty on the kopje, in the bivouac at the Modder there was deep sorrow. Captain Arnold whose company was the first to ford the stream on Sunday, and who had led his men into the firing line with such courage was fighting desperately for life. The surgeons could not save him, however, and he passed away five days after receiving his fatal wound, and that same day he was buried in the African veldt within sight of the battlefield on which he had so nobly fallen.

The Boers in the meantime were suffering terribly. The fierce shell-fire of Tuesday had played havoc with their laager. The men escaped severe punishment by burrowing in their trenches, but, as has already been said, the rain of shell slaughtered their unprotected horses and oxen. Their encampment began to look like a gigantic slaughter-house. Even if an opening should now present itself in the cordon of the besieging host, they could not avail themselves of the chance of an escape. Their horses and oxen dead, they could but fight to the death. Vainly they strained their eyes for sight of the signal that would give them news of a relieving force, but no such signal came; everywhere on the plain and kopjes they caught glimpses of the artillery, the cavalry, and the khaki clad infantry of the British.

The horses and cattle in the circle of the waggons, wrecked with shot and shell, began to decompose and Cronje sent a messenger to Lord Roberts to ask for a day's armistice to bury the slaughtered beasts and the dead Boers who lay among the cattle; but the British general feared that it was merely a bit of Boer slyness. They were playing for time. An armistice would give them a chance to still further fortify their position or perhaps give time for a relieving host to assemble to try to drive the British from Paardeberg. The request was refused, although a safe-conduct to the women and children in the Boer laager was offered. Through a mistake on the part of the interpreter Lord Roberts was led to believe that Cronje was prepared to surrender, but the Boer general indignantly resented the suggestion. He would not even accept the safe-conduct for the women and children but would fight till his position was taken by storm.

The British officers and soldiers could not but admire such courage. His march from Magersfontein had been as trying as theirs, more so in fact; for during nearly the whole of the journey he had to keep up a hard fight with the hotly pursuing enemy; the heat and the rain, the thirst and the privations he too was enduring; day and night into the narrow limits of his position a stream of shells was being steadily poured. There was no safety anywhere save in the trenches, and there the Boers sat chewing at times their scanty stock of biltong or stealing to the river to get fresh supplies of the nauseating water of the muddy Modder.

They could not bury their dead cattle, and after the armistice was refused, cursing the English as wretchedly inhuman—and so they must have appeared to the imprisoned Boers—they tried as best they could to drag the rotting carrion that was creating an unbearable stench to leeward of their position. Still the shells fell with deadly accuracy into their stronghold and still the slaughter went on. To free themselves from the plague the dead carcasses were creating, they resorted to a method that in the end wrought greater havoc in the ranks of the British than the fire of all their "pom-pom's" and Mausers. The stream that rushed by them, at times shallow and narrow, at other times, when swollen with rain, deep and broad, would help clear their camp. To it they dragged the putrifying carcasses and sent them whirling down to the bivouac of the 19th. Brigade. A suffocating stench filled all the air. In the morning the Canadians awoke to find dead horses and oxen aground on the river bank, or stranded on the shallows or rocks in mid-stream. Disgusting as the task was there was nothing for it but to plunge into the water and send these horrible objects on their downward course. The Modder was their only source of water supply, and now it was made poisonous by these carcasses. Still they had to drink, and this water, laden with germs of enteric, spread a plague through the British army. The thousands of men who at one time filled the hospitals at Bloemfontein for the most part owed their suffering to this week of hardship before the Boer four thousand.

There was no escape from the hardships however. The Canadians tried it, but shift their camp as they would their trials were only increased with each day. On Saturday they were recalled from their arduous duty on the kopjes, where they had been watching lest Boer forces might either escape from the laager or break through to its relief. Small parties had assaulted the British lines from the direction of Kamelfontein, Osfontein, and Poplar Farm, but with none of these had the Canadians come in contact. They were to end their week of fighting and watching with a day of rest.

They were marched back to their first camping ground at Paardeberg drift. It looked as though they might have some rest at last and they needed it sadly. The contingent had left Belmont on the twelfth 895 strong; on this day, between those slain in battle, wounded, exhausted by the march, struck down with fever, only 708 officers and men answered to the roll-call. Practically a third of the force that had left Canada had been placed *hors de combat.* During the day a warm sun at intervals broke through the clouds, a good night was promised and the soldiers prepared to enjoy it; but another disappointment awaited them. Once more it rained and the hard clay on which they had bivouacked soon became a great pool. Drenched and soaked they got but little sleep, and next morning they were in a lamentable plight. Their uniforms were shrunken, their accoutrements ruined, and they themselves aching in every limb from their exposure.

On Sunday the swollen river rushed passed, a fierce, turbulent stream. It was then that they saw how effective had been the steady cannonading of the week. Past them whirled the bodies of horses and oxen and slain men ; a continuous host of dead creatures swept by. How hopeless, they thought, must be the plight of the Boers; and still they resisted.

Sunday, the Sunday after the battle of Paardeberg, was a genuine day of rest and they needed it. Bright and warm for the most part, the night was cool and refreshing and they awoke rested and strengthened. They were still on half-rations, getting but two meals, and scant ones at that, a day. But they were not complaining; the officers endured the hardships with the men. Even "Bobs" suffered with the rest. It was said that at this time "when rations were running low, he called his men around him and told them that what was good enough for them was good enough for him, and so he lived on the ordinary soldiers' rations. It was not an uncommon sight to see him seated on a biscuit-box outside his tent eating the same food as the men around him."

The Canadians needed the repose of this Sabbath to strengthen and to nerve them for a great task to which they were about to be assigned. The final blow was to be struck, and to them would be the honors of the fight. They had been tried in their first fight at Paardeberg; they were now to be proved.

CHAPTER XV.

THE SURRENDER OF CRONJE.

STILL Cronje would not yield; from his trenches he laughed at shrapnel and lyddite and heeded the rifle-fire no more than he would have heeded the barking of so many dogs. True his laager was untenable, his horses and cattle were slain; but he still had a two-fold hope. Small commandos had been attacking the British cordon, and he daily expected Joubert from about Ladysmith with a force of nearly ten thousand men, if they once appeared he would endeavor to cut his way through the exhausted British army. Moreover he was of the opinion that Roberts could not support an army so far from his base of supplies. Cronje thought, and he was not far wrong, that the British for the successful conduct of their advance needed close contact with a railway system.

So, despite his losses, despite the rain that drenched his camp, he mounted the steps of his waggon, while the lyddite shells and shrapnel burst around him, and fearlessly scanned the country with his field-glasses. Disappointed he would return to his trenches to sustain the courage of his men and comfort the women and children. He had still some days in which he could resist the storm of shot and shell, and then if he had to yield he would yield with the consciousness that he had done all man could do for the honor of his country. His men were suffering but for the most part uncomplainingly; some of the Free Staters were hoping for a speedy raising of the siege or for surrender, but the bulk of his four thousand were Transvaalers, who believed in, worshipped, and relied on Commandant Cronje much as the British troops did on Roberts. What he did was right. If he ordered them to follow him through the lines of the British they would follow him ; if he commanded them to cling to their position and fight till the last man had fallen as did the Spartans at Thermopylae they would obey him.

Each day of the siege, however, their chances of escape or relief grew more and more remote. Small parties had tried to creep through the lines, and about mid-week a considerable force under Commandant De Beers on their best horses had succeeded in stealing out during the night ; but all hope of further escape was cut off by the destructive fire of the fifty British guns. Despite the fact that an ammunition waggon had caught fire and exploded they still had plenty of cartridges in their trenches on both sides of the river for a prolonged resistance, but in all things else they were deficient. They had but little ammunition for their artillery, indeed they did not need much, for they had with them but four twelve-pounder Krupp guns, one Maxim, and a Vikers-Maxim. What had become of the guns with which they resisted Methuen's advance still remains a mystery. No doubt some of them were buried, but most of them must have been trekked north with a rapidity that astonished the British and the world. Their "pom-pom," which had played such an important part early

MAJOR ROBERT CARTWRIGHT.

CAPT. F. L. CARTWRIGHT.

in the week, was silenced. A Howitzer lyddite-shell had fallen on it wrecking the gun and killing eight men, who were buried where they fell.

The putrid water of the Modder, too, was their only source of supply; and, through the havoc wrought in their waggons, the end of the week of bombardment found them with but four days' supplies of food. The British were on half-rations, and even quarter-rations, but they could communicate with the outside world; but the Boers saw absolute starvation staring them in the face.

The next week opened with renewed energy on the part of the beleaguering army. Their fire had been effective, but they would make it still more so. A captive-balloon, which defied the shot and shell of the Boers, was sent up and every detail of Wolveskraal laager noted. The trenches were studied, the accurate position of the Krupp guns marked, the battered red house which had been Cronje's headquarters, and the wrecked and burnt circle of waggons were observed, and the gun-fire went on with more deadly accuracy than ever.

This was on the 26th of February, the morrow would be Majuba day. Nineteen years before the British arms under an able leader had suffered a defeat from this nation of shepherds and hunters, a defeat the most humiliating in the history of British wars. Some of the very men who had inflicted this defeat were penned up in front of Roberts' army; and in his force were men who had shed bitter tears on that disgraceful day, and since had waited and waited for a chance to wipe out the disgrace. Chief among them was Brigadier-General Hector MacDonald. He had courted death on that day as a lieutenant in the Gordans, fighting with a bravery that won him the admiration of his foes. While his company broke and fled he had faced the enemy single-handed, as a reward the chivalric General Joubert had returned to him his sword. He had been spared to see the Boers routed, corralled. Majuba Day was approaching and a great reverse, a reverse that was to change the whole progress of the war and shape events that in the end would bring the republics under the British flag was about to crush Cronje's army, the flower of the Transvaal and of the Orange Free State. "Thus the whirligig of time brings in his revenges."

Though "Fighting Mac" was not to be in at the surrender—a wounded foot had temporally sent him to the hospital—he could not refrain from writing to the Field-Marshal, reminding him of the fatal day whose memory still rankled in the breast of every English soldier. To force Cronje to surrender on that day would be a crowning feat of arms which would send the British world wild with rejoicing.

For a moment it is necessary to roll back the veil of years and consider the victory of Majuba Hill. FitzPatrick, no sympathizer with the Boer, in his "Taansvaal from Within." gives an account of this fight that can be accepted as not at any rate overrating the fighting qualites of the Transvaalers.

"On February 27 came Majuba, when Sir George Colley designed to retrieve his fortunes and strike an effective blow without the aid of his second-in-command, Sir Evelyn Wood, whom he had sent to hurry up reinforcements. The scaling of the mountain at night was a fine performance. The neglect to take the rocket apparatus or mountain

THE SURRENDER OF CRONJE.

guns, or to fortify the position in any way, or even to acquaint the members of the force with the nature of the position which they had taken up in the dark, and the failure to use the bayonet, were the principal causes of disaster. The Boers attacked in force a position which should have been absolutely impregnable, held as it was by a force of 554 soldiers. The Boer force is not known, but probably consisted of upwards of 1000 men, since Christian Joubert after the fight offered to take a portion of the men numbering, as he said, some 500 to attack a small British laager on one of the spurs of the mountain. The splendid feat of taking the hilltop, however, was accomplished by a small storming party of less than 200 men, the balance of the Boer forces covering the approach of their comrades by an accurate and incessant long-range fire. The result, as is known was terrible disaster: 92 killed and 134 wounded, and a number taken prisoners, represented the British loss, whilst the Boers lost one killed and five wounded. No attempt had been made to occupy positions below the crown of the hill which commanded the approaches, and the Boers were able to creep up under good cover from place to place by the exercise of their admirable tactics. It is impossible to detract from the performance of the Boers, and a glance at the position leaves one more astonished than ever that a successful attack could ever have been made upon it. The Boers displayed on this day the finest fighting qualites. The generalship of their fighting commandant, Nikolas Smit, was of the highest order. The cleverness of the attack and the personal bravery and audacity of the storming party are beyond praise."

Then England made terms of peace. She had been beaten by the Boers, "when they were on the top of the hill and we were at the bottom, and when we were on the top of the hill and they were at the bottom." Making peace while the disgrace of defeat rested on their arms made the ignorant farmers think England a weak nation, and by her action she prepared the way for the bloody and costly war which has called forth the entire land strength of the Empire.

Lieutenant Hector MacDonald was in the final disastrous scene of 1881. Sir Frederick Roberts had been sent to retrieve the blunders of the leaders who were calling down on England the ridicule of Europe, only to learn that peace, from his point of view an ignominious peace, had been concluded. Now Brigadier-General Hector MacDonald wrote to Field-Marshal Lord Roberts of Kandahar urging that the disgrace of Majuba Day 1881, be wiped out in a glorious victory on Majuba Day 1900. Sir Henry Colville sent in an equally earnest plea. But Lord Roberts, much as he wished it, faltered. He remembered Magersfontein and Colenso, Chieveley and the Tugela, and his own heavy losses in the first battle of Paardeberg. It was costly work this trying to drive the stubborn Boers from their trenches; better to wait than needlessly throw his men on the "pom-pom" and the Mauser. If we can believe the Times correspondent, "the insistance of Canada broke down his reluctance, and the men of the oldest colony were sent in the small hours of Tuesday morning to redeem the blot on the name of the Mother-Country." Whatever the reasons, General Roberts decided that a determined attack should be made on the Boer position at dawn on Majuba Day; and the Royal Canadian Regiment of Infantry was to have the place of honor in the attack.

From the time the announcement was made till the men were ordered into the trenches some 600 yards from the nearest Boer trench, they went about their task with silent seriousness. No more joking and laughing on the eve of battle. That heap of stones with its circle of shells at Paardeberg told them what war meant. The work now assigned them could not but mean death and wounds to many. Cronje would not surrender without a struggle. Their task would be a trying one and so they were ordered to take what rest they could before beginning it.

The attack was to begin at two in the morning. It was a beauitful night, the clear African sky shone with innumerable brilliantly gleaming stars, "the moon was on the wane, just a thin rim of it was left." The air was cool and bracing and stimulating. Six companies of the regiment lay in the trenches which had been constructed while they were busy on Tuesday keeping down the enemy's fire. C Company was on the extreme left and G and H by the wooded river bank on the right. In the trenches were 480 men and officers nervously awaiting the order to advance. A Company had a position across the river, while B was placed in reserve at the bivouac.

At two o'clock in the morning the Gordons occupied the trenches and the Canadians were ordered to move forward. Out of the trenches they "scrambled like monkeys" and began to advance in two ranks. The front rank was the firing-line and moved forward through the uncanny darkness with rifles loaded and bayonets fixed ready either to drop on the plain and begin firing or to charge into the enemy's stronghold. They hoped for the latter; a bayonet charge has a terrible fascination for the young soldier. It was the intention of Lord Roberts to have the Canadians reach if possible a point within 100 yards of the enemy and there throw up a new line of entrenchments; so the rear rank had their rifles swung over their backs and carried picks and shovels in their hands. They were reinforced by fifty of the Royal Engineers under whose direction they acted. Lieutenant-Colonel Buchan was on the left of the Canadians, Major Pelletier on the right, and Colonel Otter on the left-rear.

Slowly the men advanced through the darkness at intervals of less than a yard, each holding the coat sleeve of the man on his left. When they had advanced for about 500 yards through the small bushes that dotted the plain it was found that the flank had outstripped the main body, and so a brief halt was made to correct the alignment. Here several soldiers caught glimpses of stealthy figures moving in their front; no doubt Boer watchers who were hurrying to cover to warn their friends of the advancing line. Once more the advance began; this time with every effort to maintain absolute silence, but the crackling scrub and some empty meat tins that the Boers had strung in front of their position served to alarm the enemy, if their sentries had not already done so.

Instantly a line of fire sputtered in their very faces. The firing-line was between fifty and twenty-five paces from the enemy, and the closeness and suddenness of the fusilade stunned them for a moment. The cries and groans of their comrades brought them to themselves, flat on their faces they fell and began vigorously to return the close fire. Like a continuous bursting of gigantic fire-crackers the rifles snapped before them; no head was seen but so close were they that the light from the continuous fire revealed the polished weapons and at times the arms and hands that held them. For about fifteen minutes, and it seemed like fifteen hours, a stream of lead swept over them and tore the earth about them, occasionally finding a victim. They were not idle. Steadily, effectively, they sent back bullet for bullet, and so well directed was their fire that the enemy's fusilade became less dangerous. They no longer thought of aiming at that brave line of prone figures on the open plain, they dare not show themselves in their trenches but raising their rifles high overhead fired at random. For the most part the hot fire prevented the rear rank from constructing trenches. They too lay on the plain and in several instances illustrated the uses of a shield in modern warfare by holding their shovels in front of their heads, in one case a shovel turned no less than three bullets. About a mile away on the left the Canadians' old friends the Shropshire Light Infantry began to pour volleys into the Boer laager; and the crackling and volleying, the whizzing of the bullets through the darkness, the spitting flashes from the rifles, the groans of the wounded, made the night a pandemonium.

In the midst of this uproar of battle, someone on the left gave the command, "Retire and bring in your wounded." Along the line to the right the message sped and soon the whole of the regiment with the exception of G and H companies were speeding to the trenches they had left, "making record time," to use the language of more than one in the retreat. Who gave the command will probably never be known; perhaps he lies buried in the South African veldt for his blunder, for blunder it was, as in retiring lives were lost and men wounded who would otherwise have gone through this battle uninjured. Those barking rifles and pursuing bullets lent speed to their feet and they waited not till they tumbled pell-mell into the trenches where the Highlanders stood with fixed bayonets. In the darkness of the morning they were mistaken for Boers and several were wounded by the fatal mistake.

Brave deeds were done, too, in this retreat; one, and there were several like it, is worthy of more than passing note. Private Charles Donaldson was retiring with the rest when he came upon Corporal Thomas who had been mortally wounded in the first sudden volley. Donaldson had joined in the retreat but the cries of his comrade-in-arms made him halt. He nobly supported the wounded man from the field despite the fact that the agonizing cries of pain were drawing the Boer fire. Several times as the bullets flew thick and threatening about him he was tempted to leave his comrade, but in the end carried him to the trenches where the surgeons and stretcher-bearers were busy with the wounded. It is not every time that the prize is deserved that it is given; here was a deed worthy of the Victoria Cross but in the darkness no officer's eye could see the courage of it.

In the meantime G and H companies which had not heard the command to retire held their position, and while the front rank blazed away

LIEUT.-COL. CHARLES JOHN MacDONALD.

LIEUT.-COL. ALEXANDER WILLIAM ANSTRUTHER.

through the bushes that gave them fair cover the rear rank threw up an excellent trench. Into this trench the entire companies leaped. They were within sixty-five yards of the crackling Mausers. Their dead lay still nearer. How close they had come to charging the enemy in their very trenches; and how narrowly they had escaped another Magersfontein. Only the darkness, the intervals, and the promptness with which they had thrown themselves on the ground saved them from having their entire line cut down. The Boers had no search-light this time to turn night into day. Once in the trenches these soldiers from the Maritime Provinces under the direction of Captains Stairs and Macdonnel kept up a steady well-directed fire on the bursts of flame from the rifles in their front. They did not know that the other companies had retired and they wondered at the strange silence on their left. The guns on account of their position were unable to shell the Boers, and only the distant but effective volleys of the Shropshires joined with their uninterrupted fire. Till daylight the Canadians kept the Boers, now thoroughly alarmed, from showing themselves above their trenches, and the firing of the enemy which had been very wild, with dawn almost altogether ceased.

Cronje saw that the end had come. The trench of the Canadians was at right angles with his line of rifle-pits, and the marksmen could from their shelter sweep his entire position. He might still hold out; but with the captive-balloon directing the fire of the guns, with his trenches enfiladed by the splendid marksmen with the maple leaf on their helmets, it could only be with great loss of life. Unable to secure water, food running low, the stench of the dead animals permeating his camp, a hot fire sweeping through his ranks—all these things made him determine to surrender and so he raised the white flag.

At first no attention was paid to it. The Boers had so frequently abused the white flag that the Canadians were not going to be caught by the barbarous trick; and so they kept up their fire for another hour. At six o'clock the Boers began to pass into the British lines and seeing that they did indeed intend to surrender the "cease fire" rang out, and the Canadians on "The Dawn of Majuba Day" sent up a mighty cheer. The chance had been given them, and although through a cruel mistake four companies had retreated, the remaining two had done their work so well that to them was the honor of giving the final stroke to the nine days of battle that were the great turning point in the South African War. The Free State would be British territory in a few days and the irrestible advance could now continue till the forts of Pretoria were manned by English troops.

Cronje had surrendered. The following is an account of the meeting between the great fighting General of the Transvaal and the Commander-in-Chief of the Britsh forces:

"A group of horsemen then approached. On General Prettyman's right rode an elderly man clad in a rough, short overcoat, a wide brimmed hat, ordinary tweed trousers and brown shoes. It was the redoubtable Cronje. His face was almost burned black, and his curly beard was tinged with grey.

"Lord Roberts walked to and fro in front of the cart until the Boer General arrived, when the

British commander advanced gravely and kindly saluted the Boer commander. He then motioned General Cronje to a seat in the chair which had been brought for his accommodation, and the two officers conversed through an interpreter.

"Cronje's face was absolutely impassive when he approached Lord Roberts, exhibiting no sign of his inner feelings. Lord Roberts was surrounded by his staff when General Prettyman addressing the Field Marshal said:

"'Commandant Cronje, Sir.'

"The Commandant touched his hat in salute, and Lord Roberts saluted in return. The whole group then dismounted and Lord Roberts stepped forward and shook hands with the Boer commander.

"'You made a gallant defence, Sir,' was the first salution of Lord Roberts to the vanquished Boer leader.

"General Cronje after this breakfasted with the British officers."

No event in Lord Roberts' military career gave him greater pleasure than this timely forcing of the Boer position. His despatch in the early morning of the day of surrender shows the pride he had in his brilliant achievement. "I hope that Her Majesty's Government will consider that this is very satisfactory, occurring as it does on the anniversary of Majuba."

At first it was thought that Canada's part in this great event had been exaggerated, but the detailed report of Lord Roberts written at eleven o'clock on the morning of surrender shows that the eulogies heaped on the entire regiment and particularily on G and H companies which so admirably kept the enemy in play while the trenches were being dug, were deserved in every particular.

"At 3 a. m. to-day a most dashing advance was made by the Canadian Regiment and some engineers, supported by the 1st Gordon Highlanders and 2nd Shropshires, resulting in our gaining a point some 600 yards nearer the enemy, and within about 80 yards of his trenches, where our men entrenched themselves and maintained their position till morning, a gallant deed worthy of our Colonial comrades, and which, I am glad to say, was attended by comparatively slight loss.

"This apparently clinched matters, for, at daylight to-day, a letter signed by General Cronje, in which he stated that he surrendered unconditionally, was brought to our outposts under a flag of truce.

"In my reply I told General Cronje he must present himself at my camp and that his forces must come out of their laager after laying down their arms. By 7 a. m. I received General Cronje and despatched a telegram to you announcing the fact.

"In the course of conversation he asked for kind treatment at our hands, and also that his wife, grandson, private-secretary, adjutant and servants might accompany him wherever he might be sent. I reassured him and told him that his request would be complied with. I informed him that a general officer would be sent with him to Cape Town to insure his being treated with proper respect en route. He will start this afternoon under charge of Major-General Prettyman, who will hand him over to the general commanding at Cape Town.

"The prisoners, who number about 3000, will be

THE SURRENDER OF CRONJE.

formed into commandos under our own officers. They will also leave here to-day reaching Modder River to-morrow, when they will be railed to Cape Town in detachments. Roberts."

There was much more in this victory than the mere relief of Kimberley and the capture of a few thousand Boers. Till this time there was great danger of a general rising of the Dutch in Cape Colony and Natal on behalf of their kith and kin in the republics, but the capture of the hero of Potchefstroom and Doornkop, the man recognized as the greatest fighting general in South Africa since the days of Nikolas Smit, for a time completely demoralized the enemies of England.

Paardeberg was the beginning of the end; steadily by forced marches the British swept onwards to Pretoria, driving back from kopje and hill the forces of the enemy that tried to bar their progress. In these marches and in this fighting the Royal Canadians did their part as nobly as at Paardeberg.

The news of the good work done by the regiment caused great rejoicing in the Dominion, and for a moment the people forgot the price paid. About thirty were dead and over ninety wounded. In the last brilliant charge seven were killed and thirty wounded and a pall hung over the rejoicing of the regiment as the seven gallant fellows were laid to rest on the morning of their victory in the plain on which they fell.

CHAPTER XVI.

REST AFTER BATTLE.

CRONJE had surrendered; the terrible tension of the nine days of privations and fighting was removed and this very fact seemed to rest the men. After the formal surrender the prisoners were marched from the laager.

They were a mixed crowd composed of 2592 Transvaalers, 1327 Free Staters, 49 Scandinavians, 45 Artillerists, and 200 Sappers. Several commandants, a number of field cornets and other officers were in the crowd, chief among whom was Major Albrecht of the Orange Free State Artillery, who under Cronje had directed the magnificent retreat from Magersfontein and planned the fine defences at Wolveskrall.

It was a motley concourse, a strange rabble, the artillerists of the Free State, a splendid body of men, alone were in uniform, but their uniforms were now dirty and tattered. The rest of the Boers for the most part were clad like the peasants of any rural district, "with short coats, loud-patterned trousers, narrow-brimmed light-brown soft felt hats." From their stronghold they marched with eyes fixed on the ground, gloomy, sullen. Here were grey bearded men with their snowy unkempt locks hanging about their stooped and rounded shoulders, holding in their memories Majuba Day 1881 and wishing that death had met them on this fatal morning: there were lads, boys of fifteen and sixteen, who had been made hardened soldiers by the struggles at Belmont, at Enslin, at Modder, by the weeks of military work at Magersfontein, by the march to Paardeberg, and the terrible bombardment in their last stronghold. There were among the prisoners four generations; the feeble, but determined old men, who had trekked across the Vaal to escape British rule with their sires in the thirties, and the smooth-faced boys to whom even so late an event as Majuba Hill was but a heroic tale of their people. Out of the laager, too, marched some forty or fifty women and children; homely hard-faced women these, who, like the Spartan women of old, could say to their sons and their husbands "with your shields or on them." All of the latter had escape injury, save one little girl who had her finger slightly wounded. Most noteworthy among them was the wife of General Cronje, a stern-featured woman who carried herself erect by the side of her husband, bent with years and toil, and cast defiant glances to left and right.

All now seemed sullenly content with their misfortune and marched with faces as impassive as their stubborn commanders. It had not been so when the news that Cronje had surrendered spread through their entrenchments. The bitter tears were shed and stern curses uttered. The Free Staters were no doubt tired of war; but the Transvaalers, and particularly the "Old Guard of Potchefstroon" who had swept Majuba Hill with their deadly fire and so skilfully entrapped Jameson and his men when on their ill-starred raid,

LIEUT.-COL. J. BELL FORSYTH.

LIEUT.-COL. LEON P. VOHL.

would have died to a man rather than surrender to the "rooineks."

There was, however, keen disappointment in the British ranks when they saw the ragged, dirty horde they had captured. The bravery of the Boers in so long resisting shrapnel and lyddite had given the English soldiers an exaggerated notion of their appearance. They were prepared to see an army of stalwart fighting men marched into their lines. What a disappointment!

"A drove of tramps, carrying bundles of rags and such rubbish as tramps collect. A regiment of Weary Willies and Tired Tims, with ragged beards and smashed slouch hats, and tin cans and empty beef tins dangling by strings from their brace buttons. Some carried sauce pans slung over their shoulders, some carried tea kettles; one or two walked with green umbrellas."

This is as an onlooker saw them. There were, however, many Boers of noble type here; doctors and lawyers from the Free State and the Transvaal, and farmers with countless flocks and numerous servants, but almost any casual observer would have got a similar impression. And what else could have been expected. Earth is cruel, and unless the spirit keeps reaching upwards the body and mind will assuredly be dragged downwards. These Boers as James Bryce has said "started with a seventeenth century standard and deteriorated for 300 years."

The tattered and brutalized body of peasants instead of rousing hate should have stirred pity. They were marched across the river and on the day of their surrender set out under a strong guard for Modder. Cronje, his wife, grandson, and immediate attendants were sent some hours in advance of the others.

The Lion of the Transvaal, this hunter of beasts and of men, was caught and would soon be confined on the little island rock where the Atlantic beats eternally. Rough, uncouth, without ambition, cruel it may be, courageous without doubt, he had come through probably his last fight and his country for which he had fought so well was lost to him forever. As dumb as the sphinx of the North African wilderness, he sat puffing great clouds of smoke as he was driven across the veldt he loved. On his face there was no sign of feeling; nothing to show how keenly he must have felt the loss of his army, and the blow that had been given the Boer cause. Intensely religious as he was, he no doubt felt as he went into captivity as did the Israelites of old. The Philistines had conquered but the chosen of Jehovah would return in Jehovah's good time to claim their own. Like the Jews of old the Boers' stubborn isolation and arrogance had left them without a country.

When the Boers had all passed out of the laager the British entered it. What a sight of desolation and destruction was revealed! It was like the ruins of a fire-swept town in which many living things had been caught in the whirlwind of death. The ground was torn by the fierce shell-fire, and great blotches of greenish-yellow color told how every part of the enclosure had been searched by the suffocating lyddite. The great circle of waggons and Cape-carts was smashed and torn and burnt; some were a mere heap of ashes and iron, the tops of others, torn with shrapnel, were hanging over on the ground like the sails of a dismantled vessel after a storm; none had escaped the fierce fire, all bore marks of bullet or shell. The odor of death was in the air; within the circle of waggons and indeed all along the plain, lay the dead carcasses of horses and oxen and sheep. The river was full of them, and here and there were flocks of vultures, who, now that the firing had ceased, swooped down on this field of death. They were heavy, lazy birds, gorged with the rich harvest of death that they had been pursuing from Belmont to Paardeberg.

What surprised the British most was the comparatively few dead Boers that were found within the laager. No doubt many bodies had been thrown into the river, many had been buried, but the fierceness of their fire and the narrow limits of the Boers' quarters made them expect ghastly heaps of dead. They had been sending reports that the death list of the Boers would amount to thousands, but as only 170 wounded were discovered, the number of killed must indeed have been small, when compared with the British loss. The Boers have invariably lied about their casualties in this campaign, but at Paardeberg their losses were probably not one fifth as great as those of the English.

The reason of this was not far to seek. On both sides of the river they had a system of trenches so skilfully made that they astonished even such old campaigners as Roberts and Kitchener. The trenches were "quite bomb-proof, being constructed something like a bottle, narrow at the top and opening out below, say two feet at top, four feet and five feet at the bottom; not in one long line but in a succession of pits from six feet to eighteen feet long and about four feet six inches deep." Many of the trenches, no doubt the ones in which the women and children took shelter when the laager became untenable, were built merely for protection. These were "long underground tunnels with but a small square opening or shaft at either end."

Perhaps the greatest disappointment the soldiers experienced was in the small number of the guns captured. The British had been losing guns in this campaign, and the Canadians had hoped that the capture of this army would make up the loss; but there were only six guns in the laager—a "pom-pom," wrecked by a shell, a Maxim and four Krupp guns. All showed that they had felt the fire of the British. For the present all were useless; the Boers, probably after the decision to surrender had been arrived at, had removed the breech parts and either buried them or threw them into the river. Plenty of Mauser and Martini ammunition was found, and, as if to bear out the stories of explosive bullets, a waggon loaded with these barbarous missiles.

Before ten o'clock the entire 19th Brigade was in the Boer laager and Lord Roberts at his own request inspected the Royal Canadians and complimented them on the fine work they had done.

However the men were getting used to praise and they were thinking more now of the substantial meal. Those lost transports kept them on a couple of biscuits a day, supplemented by occasional "bony chunks of beef or goat boiled, but innocent of any flavoring, and thrust into the pot almost while the breath was still in the animal's body." On this diet they had endured long marches, sleepless nights, and fought through two whole days of scorching heat and one night of fierce battle. Here was food at last, and in the loot of the camp they would be able to have a feast. They found a good deal of mealy flour and the frying pans were soon sizzling over many fires as the men made "slapjacks." It was the first chance since leaving Graspan that they had had of obtaining a satisfying meal, and as a result the sick list next morning was a large one, especially among those who had used Kaffir soap instead of grease in their cooking.

That night the regiment slept in the Boer laager, and despite the desolation and stench rested well. For a time at least battle was at an end; they need not fear the clarion note of the call to arms which a few days before they had been so eager to hear. They were utterly exhausted, dirty, ragged, hollow-eyed; they looked at the Boer prisoners and they looked at each other and thought themselves not unlike the men they so cordially despised. On some the privations and nervous strain had been particularly trying, and it was not uncommon to find mere boys with their hair turning grey.

When the strain of fighting was removed the day after the surrender was far from being a light one. Two companies did the inevitable outpost duty, while the remainder were busy collecting stores and ammunition in the laager. There was but little of value. There were great quantities of Mauser and Martini cartridges and some fairly good carts and waggons, but little else. It was surprising the number of old-fashioned Martini rifles that were used by the Boers, but as Bennet Burleigh points out, the Burghers preferred the arm to which they had been accustomed.

While busy at this work they were almost suffocated by the stench from the dead horses, oxen, sheep and goats that were decomposing rapidly in the hot sun and contaminating the river, their only source of water supply. Bury the animals they could not; there were too many for that; to stay in the infected atmosphere and drink the putrid water of the Modder which scarcity of fuel prevented them from boiling, would inevitably smite them with a deadly plague—indeed it had already done so. For these reasons the regiment was moved about two miles farther up the river to Osfontein where the whole division were in one camp for the first time in the campaign. Here they were to rest for five days. Scarcity of food continued, heavy rains beat down upon them, and their tents for three nights were practically afloat. Horses and oxen and mules died all along their line of march and by the score about their camp. So many carcasses lay rotting in the sun that the men of the contingent with grim humor changed the name of their resting place to "Deadosfontein."

The men were glad of the rest, such as it was, of the week after Majuda Day; but they were longing too, to get away from Osfontein. The violent thunder-storms, the camp at times a great pool; shivering about the fire to keep dry and warm—all made them long to be off once more. Bloemfontein was to be occupied in a few days, the Boers were said to be in force in front; but Roberts and Kitchener and French would drive the enemy before them with the same irresistible dash that they had swooped down upon Paardeberg. Though their khaki uniforms were ragged and shrunken, their shoes broken and falling to pieces, though the regiment's strength had been reduced by 150 in the last three weeks, they rejoiced when on March 5 they received orders to advance towards Bloemfontein. The sooner the march began the sooner they would be through with this war and with South Africa.

GEORGE STERLING RYERSON, M.D., C.M.

MAJOR HENRI BEAUFORT VIDAL.

CHAPTER XVII.

WITH THE SICK AND WOUNDED.

So far deeds of daring in the field and of endurance on the march have been recorded. There is another side of war which is rarely considered when cabinets and statesmen, and the daily press are stubbornly or ignorantly calling for the arbitrament of the sword. A visit to the field of battle, to the operating room of a field-hospital, to the crowded wards where fever stricken patients toss in their burning agony or cry out in delirium would surely make men less keen to go to war. Fever and wounds take the gilt edge from the glory of war—and yet they at the same time make it glorious. The "ministering angels," men and women, who follow in the wake of an army, attending the wounded under fire, braving the foul contagion of a plague-stricken camp are as truly heroes as the men to whom triumphal arches are raised and who return with the plaudits of the multitude.

The line of battle is under fire, to right and left men are struck; a bone in the arm is shattered and the rifle falls useless on the plain; a leg is broken and the victim unable to rise tries to drag himself out of the fire zone. His blood is ebbing fast and as it ebbs a thirst fiercer than the thirst of the desert is upon him; death seems to be standing by his side and a cold prespiration breaks out on his body. The cry goes up for the surgeon, but the surgeon is busy on some other part of the thinly-extended line. A comrade takes from his haversack his field dressing, crawls through the sand and tenderly binds, with inexperienced hands, the wound or broken limb. But perhaps the deadly missile has torn its way into the very vitals of the soldier. Pain, too great to be borne, makes him cry out in agony and those nearest feel that it may be their turn next.

Through the murderous fire pass the Army Hospital Corps bearing the wounded to the hospital in the rear. Sometimes a rude temporary dressing serves, but often it is impossible to remove the wounded till their wounds are carefully dressed, and under a trying fire—for in this war the Geneva Cross instead of protecting seems only to have attracted the enemy's aim—the surgeons and stretcher-bearers did their noble work. On that bloody Sunday at Paardeberg back and forth they went bearing their burdens, moistening the lips and brows of comrades, binding up wounds; in some cases giving their lives for their fellowmen. The soldier who died in the charge on the trenches' edge with the lust of blood in his heart is not as truly heroic as the man who, with calm deliberation, stays by the wounded till they are moved to a place of safety. There are those who say that no nation ever attained greatness without war: true, but it is not the war spirit that has made nations great, but the peace spirit. The lasting glory is to the men who by war have sought peace, to the men whom the sufferings caused by war have made more humane. "War is hell," and the field hospital, were it not for the nurses, stretcher-bearers, and surgeons, would be but a ward in the inferno.

About the operating tent there is the sickening odor of ether and chloroform. On the whole, however, in this war the hospital has not been such a ghastly place. The Boers have depended entirely on their shell-fire and their rifles, and in the first fights the Canadians suffered nothing from shell fire. For the most part the wounds were made by the swift-speeding Mauser bullets, small and long, that made a clean wound. Once dressed the wound gave but little pain, and the injured men in the presence of their fellows braced their wills to endure without showing signs of feeling. Stoics these; no writhing, no groaning, no complaining— only an occasional fierce cry of agony from some poor fellow hurt unto death.

Among these wounded men went Captain-Surgeon Fiset, tender of hand, sympathetic of eye and voice. They had long since learned to love him; in their camps at De Aar, at Orange River, at Belmont he had not only been a physician to their bodies, but to their spirits as well. But it was not till Paardeberg that his true worth was proved. On that day he exposed himself a dozen times to a fierce fire while dressing wounds or helping bear soldiers from the field. That the death rate from fever and wounds had been so low among the Canadians is largely due to his unflagging zeal.

Before this time a number of Canadians had been placed on the sick-list and were at several of the hospitals, but after this it was no easy matter to keep track of the regiment's invalids. The majority were at Bloemfontein, but wounded and sick men were to be found at Kimberley, at Honeynest Kloof, at Orange River, at De Aar, at Naaupoort, at Rondebosch, at Deilfontein, at Victoria West, at Wynberg, and later in the campaign all along the line from Bloemfontein to Pretoria. Enteric was the chief cause; but dysentery, pneumonia, veldt fever, and rheumatism did their work too.

The men who were brought to Wynberg were indeed fortunate. It was a veritable fairyland. The road between it and Rondebosch "is ornamented by planted woods of oak, stone, pine, and poplar, whose foliage forms a striking contrast to that of the silver tree which forms natural woods along the sides of the mountains."

If the air and the scenery were such as to put new life and vigor into the sick and wounded, the treatment they received was equally good. Tender hands were ready to do their bidding, and on two days in the week visitors flocked to the wards with gifts and kindly words.

Were there no hospital hardships then? or did our contingent escape the suffering and abuse and neglect so lately brought to the attention of the world by Mr. Burdett-Coutts. On the whole the Canadians did fare better than the older regiments. In a sense they were a large family, and Colonel Otter, Lieutenant-Colonel Ryerson and Surgeon-Captain Fiset were ever watchful for their comfort and health. At the beginning of the war it was almost a pleasure to be sick; but as the campaign went on all that changed, and especially after the epidemic of typhoid had visited the troops at Bloemfontein. All the hospitals in South Africa became crowded, and while in the vicinity of Cape Town and in Kimberley the patients were almost too well cared for, those in the hospitals on the

Great Karroo and along the line of march to Pretoria were often sadly neglected. From the Canadian soldiers came but few complaints. They had gone to South Africa to fight, and they soon learned to recognize that war was cruel, and so they stood the forced marches, the starvation, the neglect when sick, as the inevitable accompaniments of war. Those who had been invalided up to the time of Paardeberg had not much they could complain of, but many of the sold'ers who experienced hospital life later in the campaign suffered greatly.

The great majority of the Canadians had their hospital experience at Bloemfontein. The long march, with but scanty food, to that city, the forced marches they were afterwards compelled to take, shattered many iron constitutions; but the greater part of their troubles began at Paardeberg. The "liquid filth" of the Modder, the nauseating draughts they got at the wayside stagnant pools bred enteric in the regiment. They fell under its grip not by individuals but by scores. The other regiments fared no better, and soon the beautiful and healthy city of Bloemfontein became a city of hospitals, echoing with the sound of the muffled drum and the slow tramp of soldiers carrying their dead comrades, rudely wrapped in blankets, to the grave. Hourly the sounds of "Last Post" echoed through the wards crowded with suffering men.

The Free State offices, the places of worship, and the Raadzaal were filled with sick and wounded. The beautiful grounds of the Rambler's Club was white with the tents of Langman's Hospital, and the breezy outskirts of the city were dotted with a hundred hospital tents. In these outlying tents were many Canadians, and—there is no use of mincing matters—here they endured great suffering. Smitten down with fever they were in many cases carried into these tents, their heads aching, their bodies chilled, and there left very much to themselves. The heat too was oppressive and many of them must have said as did the lad at Orange River when burning with fever, "If I could only get a breath of pure Canadian air and snow instead of this terrible sand, I would pull through all right."

Here is the experience of one of our soldiers gleaned from his letters to his brothers and sisters. Chilled and aching with the fever he tried to go about his duties but at length had to give in. He was carried to one of the hospitals outside of Bloemfontein and laid on the ground in a tent with twenty others. The heat and the flies tortured him during the day, and he shivered despite his fever in the cold of the African night. The medical attendance was thoroughly bad; each day a new doctor would visit the tent and the treatment of the previous day would often be changed. The hard ground, as the first fierce attack of fever left him, made him "one sore," but there was no kindly hand to alleviate his sufferings. All this time his thoughts were by the blue St. Lawrence.

"I dream," he said, "I am home nearly every night, and waken to find myself in this measly old hospital."

Those who were sent to Kimberley fared much better than those about Bloemfontein. The people of Kimberley had but very lately suffered privations from war and they knew how to help others. The only wonder is that many of the sick and wounded were not killed by their kindness. However Lieutenant-Colonel Ryerson, M. D., of the

Canadian Red Cross Society was on the spot; and next to Colonel Otter no man of the First Contingent deserves greater praise. As far as his human limitation would allow him he kept a careful watch over the men of the regiment, and was familiar with the condition of the sick and wounded in all the hospitals from Wynberg to Kroonstad.

Lord Roberts had a word for his excellent work. After praising the various medical corps at Kimberley in one of his reports, he added that but for their good work, " and the energy and zeal of Lieutenant-Colonel Ryerson, M. D., and the Canadian Red Cross Society, the condition of the sick and wounded would have been very different from what I found it on my visit there last month."

As time went on some few of the invalids were permitted to return to the front, but for the most part their health was too much shattered to continue in the campaign, and so they were sent over the long hot miles between South Africa and England to gather strength in such fine retreats as Woolwich, Torquay and Shorncliffe, where they might grow strong for future fighting and hardships, or robust enough to return to their friends in Canada. And they did return, some lame for life, some with constitutions shattered, some with hair whitened by what they had endured; but all happy in the knowledge that they had done their work well, and that they had brought their country prominently before the world and helped to firmly base the scattered British Empire.

CHAPTER XVIII.

TO BLOEMFONTEIN.

THE Canadians were rejoiced to be once more on their way to Pretoria. Osfontein with its rotting carrion, poor water supply, and heavy rains had not given them much real rest. They had stood it well however, and as they sat about the puddles in their tents "quacked like ducks and cracked jokes about regattas."

The forward movement began again on March 6 with a tramp of only six miles to Koodœsrandt Drift. Here the battalion bivouacked for the day and grew expectant of the morrow. Another big battle was promised them. The enemy were in force in their front and were confident of being able to check Lord Roberts in his march to the Orange Free State Capitol. General Delarey and General Christian De Wet, who has since proved himself an unrivalled leader in guerilla warfare, were in command of the Boer troops. How large or how small the force was, was not known; but it was known that they occupied a very strong position at Poplar Grove, and that it would be no easy task to force them from the kopjes or turn their flank.

The soldiers had a very exaggerated idea of the strength of the enemy. They no doubt expected that a fierce resistance would be made to their entry into Blœmfontein and reports spread through the

THE FIRST CONTINGENT DEPARTING FROM QUEBEC.

NORTHWEST MOUNTED POLICE.

British army that the kopjes in front were crowded with Long-Toms, Krupp guns, and Creusots; and that on the morrow they would very probably have to face, not the fire of the Mausers, to which they had become accustomed and which they could protect themselves from to some extent, but a fierce shell-fire such as the British had thrown into the Boer laager at Paardeberg, and they would be without the impregnable trenches that saved their enemies in that bombardment. However any kind of fighting would be better than the monotony of heat and cold, hardtack and dirty water.

On the morrow the "rouse" sounded at three o'clock and by four they were ready to play their part in the battle Lord Roberts had planned. They were to do important work, but not as conspicuous or dangerous as against Cronje. They advanced from Koodoosrand Drift for about three miles as the rear regiment of the 19th Brigade. They were now within range of the threatening hills. At any moment a shell might come screeching through the intervening miles and drop into their midst. The command was given to extend, and the whole regiment continued its advance towards Leeuw Kop at intervals of from eight to ten paces. The Canadians were still supports, and, while the Shropshires were making a reconnaissance, rested for several hours.

So far a silent battle had been going on. The Boers were waiting, and the British cavalry, artillery, and infantry were manoeuvering along their thinly extended line, some ten miles in extent.

At eleven o'clock the music of war began. A Boer gun spoke from Leeuw Kop. It was not directed at the infantry regiments but at the naval twelve-pounder guns. Her "Majesty's Jollies" became interested, and while the infantry brigades waited and manoeuvered a very picturesque artillery duel took place between the heavy guns. The Boer guns were well manned, and their shells fell with deadly accuracy about the sailors; but their ammunition was evidently defective for the shells did not burst. Had they done so the splendid marksmanship with which they were directed would certainly have silenced the British guns early in the action. The British fire, on the other hand, after the range was found was most effective. Clouds of dust and smoke and flying fragments of rocks told that the shells were bursting right in the Boer position. The fire from Leeuw Kop grew less dangerous and at last for a time their Long-Toms failed to speak. But only for a time. Once more the boom of the cannon was heard and the 4.7 men were almost instantly under an accurate fire. Half a dozen shells in rapid succession searched their ranks and for hours one of their guns spoke no more. It was seen that the naval guns were in serious danger and they were ordered to retire.

Meanwhile the cavalry and the infantry were endeavoring to turn the flank of the enemy, who were neither so numerous nor so well entrenched as was at first supposed. De Wet had before him the fate of Cronje. He saw the long line of the British brigades slowly but surely surrounding his position, and not wishing to spend the rest of the summer on St. Helena, commanded the retreat of his entire force; and his men left the field of battle with the same haste that marked Cronje's flight from Magersfontein.

His retreat however was conducted with masterly skill. Rifle-fire had played no part in this day's struggle and the Boer guns kept the British at a distance of 4000 yards in their rear. So ended this day of fighting, and another important step was taken towards ending the war. The enemy's forces were flying before Roberts' troops and even Presidents Kruger and Steyn, who had been confident of ultimate success with the aid of the God of Battles and the intervention of some foreign power, became dismayed.

The day of the battle of Poplar Grove had been as trying on the Canadians as any day since they left Graspan. The heat was oppressive, and they had to march without water or food till late in the afternoon. True they did pass some swampy places during the day, muddy and slimy and trodden with the hoofs of horses and oxen; here they drank, drank from pools in which the carcases of dead animals were floating. They had started out as the rear of the brigade, but when the halt was called in the late afternoon the "long-legged Canadians" were leading. That night they bivouacked at Slaagskraal at the foot of the kopjes that had thundred during the day with the enemy's guns.

Next day they were too tired to advance, and rested where they were to talk over their successes, to anticipate the speedy fall of Bloemfontein, and the rapid close of the war.

Ladysmith had been relieved on February 28. With Kimberley relieved, with Cronje and his army captured, with the Boers scattered along the Tugela, with Lord Roberts triumphantly sweeping the enemy's force from before him in his march on Bloemfontein, the stubborn little Republics that had put up a fight which had astonished the world, and taxed the strength of the British Empire, would surely sue for peace. The Presidents saw they were beaten, that for the future their fight would be a running one, and that nothing could keep the British out of Pretoria, and so they meditated terms, and on March 5 sent a message to the British Government as the initial step towards a cessation of hostilities.

And such a message! They wanted to maintain "the incontestible independence of both Republics." They were still sure that the "Triune God who lighted the unextinguishable fire of love of freedom in the hearts of ourselves and of our fathers will not forsake us, and will accomplish His work in us and in our descendants." Still they would have felt more comfortable if Lord Roberts was not pursuing them. The whole message was a tremendous piece of folly, only equaled by Kruger's Ultimatum which precipitated the war in October, and closed with a sentence that could only irritate the British Government and people. They would have spoken before, forsooth, but they were afraid they "might hurt the feelings and honor of the British people. But now," they said, "that the prestige of the British Empire may be considered to be assured by the capture of one of our forces by Her Majesty's troops, and that we have thereby been forced to evacuate other positions which our forces had occupied, that difficulty is over, and we can no longer hesitate to clearly inform your Government and people, why we are fighting and on what condition we are ready to restore peace."

They got their answer short and sharp. Roberts continued his advance, and while he was thundering on his road to their capitals they were driven to despair and even to tears by the message of "The Marquis of Salisbury to the Presidents of the South African Republic and Orange Free State," which closed with the emphatic and unmistakable words: "Her Majesty's Government can only answer your Honor's telegram by saying that they are not prepared to assent to the independence either of the South African Republic or the Orange Free State."

The troops were rapidly nearing Bloemfontein and the independence of the Free State would be permanently settled in less than a week.

On March 9 the Canadians crossed the Modder at Poplar Grove Drift on pontoons, bivouacked there for the night to prepare for another trying tramp. Once more the mobile enemy had entrenched themselves at Abraham's Kraal some eighteen miles away. They were said to be in force and still determined to keep the British out of Bloemfontein. French with his cavalry had galloped on ahead sparing neither man nor horse; he soon had the country clear of the enemy. The artillery was trundling after him, while the 6th Brigade was on hand to take part in the expected battle.

Roused next morning while the chill was still on the earth the 19th Brigade began their march a little after five o'clock. The Canadians this time set the pace. They were anxious to get to the scene of battle, and so strongly did they march that Brigadier-General Smith-Dorrien, who had complimented them a day or two before on the excellent work they had done since leaving Graspan, had to send orders to them to slacken their pace; and the slower-gaited Highlanders, Shropshires, and Cornwalls cursed them, as only the regular "Tommy" can curse, for their unusual display of energy.

Late that afternoon the whole hot and tired brigade began to quicken their step. The music of battle was before them; a stubborn fight was under way between Abraham's Kraal and Dreifontein. The Boers were being pressed back and back; but they were not giving way without a struggle. When the Canadians, leading the 19th Brigade, were within seven or eight hundred yards of the fighting regiments of the 6th Brigade an impetuous bayonet charge was made at the Boers' most important position and they broke and fled; and the last fight on the road to Bloemfontein had been fought. This had been an expensive battle to both armies. The British had 300 casualties, and as the Boers left 210 dead on the field they must have suffered much more severely. Four of their guns, too, were captured besides a number of prisoners.

The 19th Brigade had now advanced about fifty miles since leaving Osfontein, and they had not done this without great suffering. Men staggered along footsore and exhausted, hardly able to stand, yet by mere force of will keeping up with their comrades. Frequently, however, they would fall unconscious along the line of march to be picked up by the ambulance corps in the rear. For the most part, however, the Canadian soldiers struggled manfully on after their regiment and managed to join it at the nightly bivouac. They had no difficulty in following the trail of the army; as on the road to Paardeberg, dead horses lined the route, and living ones too.

It was indeed a sad sight, this army of starved men and beasts toiling through a deserted country.

Every farm house was empty of inhabitants. The Boers had fled before this force as before a red pestilence. The "rooineks" whom they had despised had come like a swarm of locusts.

The rest of the journey to Bloemfontein was for the Canadian regiment uneventful, excepting for the usual round of hardships. After leaving Dreifontein they made a day's march through the heat to Aasvogel. Only ten miles, but in that short distance about a hundred men fell out. However these were made of the right stuff, and turned up at the bivouac later. From Aasvogel they tramped to Venters Vlei, sixteen miles, once more outstripping their transports. The end was in sight; but one more heavy tramp and they would be at the railway within seven miles of Bloemfontein. Rest was near at hand.

They were in rags; between the heat and the rain their shoes were falling to pieces. Indeed some were actually barefooted, some had bound their puttees about their bruised and swollen feet, others had bound them up in pieces of sheep skin; but all did their best to keep up with the regiment. The capture of the Orange Free State capital they thought would be the end of the war, and they wished to be with their comrades in the last great battle, and to have a share in the triumphal entry. There was to be no last great battle. The defeats at Poplar Grove and Abraham's Kraal had scattered the Boers. A panic had seized them, and the divided commandos did not wait for further fighting, but percipitately fled from their laagers.

That dashing cavalry officer, General French, was galloping with his mounted men in the van of Lord Roberts' army, driving the frightened Boers from their positions, capturing prisoners and generally spreading dismay among the enemy. Horses and troopers might tumble on the veldt, but there must be no time given the Boers to recover from the blows that had been struck. The forces that had been about Ladysmith might be hurried to Bloemfontein. They must be given no time for concentration. Bloemfontein if possible must be entered without a battle. While the artillery, infantry, and transports were laboriously toiling over the dusty veldt French had taken every important position, and on the evening of March 12 had driven the enemy from all the kopjes barring his way to Bloemfontein. "Before the Boers realized the situation he was outside the railway running from Bloemfontein to the south. They were still rubbing their eyes when he had seized the station with the rolling stock, fought his way to two commanding kopjes, and had Bloemfontein under his thumb, waiting for Lord Roberts to come up."

This work had not been done without heavy loss. Hundreds of horses as a matter of course fell in this march, but the casualties in the British forces, chiefly among French's men, in the final rush on Bloemfontein amounted to almost 400.

On the morning of the formal surrender, March 13, Lord Roberts made his triumphal entry into Bloemfontein. Despite the jaded appearance of the men and the horses it was a magnificent spectacle. For over a mile stretched the line of soldiers, and as he advanced towards the Presidency he was hailed by the acclamations of a thankful people. Nor were these cheers and plaudits the utterances of a cringing and hypocritical populace. Bloemfontein is a small town with but a population of only 3500

MAJOR GEORGE WILLIAMSON.

LIEUT.-COL. ROBERT THOMPSON BANTING.

whites, and of this population at least 2000 are either British or of British descent. If the British had been forced to lay seige to the town many British subjects and sympathizers must have fallen in the struggle. At the market square the climax of the jubilation was reached and the martial music joined with the cheers of the people who had just escaped the horrors of a seige. At the Government buildings Lord Roberts took possession of the Orange Free State in the name of Her Majesty Queen Victoria, and when the Union Jack with a shamrock in the corner was hoisted over the Presidency that vast army shook the city with their shouts. It was a great day, and many not only in Bloemfontein but in every part of the world thought that the war was practically at an end.

The Canadians had not shared in this day of triumph. While the people of Bloemfontein and the soldiers were shouting themselves hoarse, they were staggering on, hungry and hot, from Venters Vlei to Ferreira Spruit siding, and after doing over eleven miles halted to learn that the cavalry force had entered Bloemfontein without opposition. The relief to the men was almost as great as was Cronje's surrender.

That evening a sound they had not heard for a month broke upon their ears—the whistle of a train. It was like a voice out of the past. When the cars manned with trainmen found in the British ranks rumbled into the station they cheered it enthusiastically, and then, despite the heavy rain, slept. Most of them thought that now the campaign was about ended. They had had enough of war and would be glad when they received orders to return home. Not that they regretted having enlisted ; but the toil, the privations, and the filth had taken all the glory out of war. On the 15th of the month they moved towards Bloemfontein and went into a permanent camp on the west side of the town.

They had suffered much during the last month, but as they marched into their new quarters they seemed, in a country where all the troops were fagged, an exceptionally robust and fit regiment.

A big army cannot move with the steady rapidity of a small force. A well established base was an absolute necessity, and so the troops had to wait while provisions and supplies were heaped up for miles along the track on the outskirts of Bloemfontein ; but chiefly they had to wait while horses were procured. French had done wonderful work, but he had only done it by leaving his troops practically without mounts. So for over a month an army of almost fifty thousand men were forced for the most part to wait and watch.

The British world meanwhile was echoing with their praises, and even the European war critics grudgingly applauded the work done. Their march from Graspan to Bloemfontein would remain as one of the great marches of history, and in it no body of men acquitted themselves better than did the Royal Canadians.

PART TWO.

FROM BLOEMFONTEIN TO CANADA
VIA PRETORIA.

PART TWO.

CHAPTER I.

A SECOND CALL TO ARMS.

CANADA is not without its cynics, and when the First Contingent sailed from Quebec there were many who were of the opinion that the soldiers had not taken the war seriously, and that the great attraction had been the novelty of the trip to South Africa. In October but few in this country supposed for a moment that the war would be a long one; and what seemed initial victories on the part of the British made many think that when England had an army of from sixty to eighty thousand troops properly organized and concentrated the march to Pretoria would be a holiday procession. The adventurous young spirits would have an excellent outing—so said "The Man in the Street."

But the Sardinian was not out of sight of land before a change came over public opinion. The Boers were showing fighting qualities of a high order, and were outwitting and out manœuvring the English generals. The soldiers from the Dominion were likely to see a good deal more of Africa than Cape Town. A hard campaign was evidently before them. Had they known this would they have been so ready to enlist?

The answer was soon given. The disaster at

Nicholson's Nek where two British regiments were captured, and the isolation of Ladysmith showed that England needed the assistance of her colonies. The readiness of the young men of Canada to enlist in the First Contingent led the Government to believe that another contingent could easily be raised, and so on November 2 offered the Colonial Office a second force for service in the South African war. However the War Office required Magersfontein and the reverses of the Tugela to wake it from its lethargy and the offer, for the time being, was refused. The events of the next month proved to England how lamentably weak she was in two important branches of the service. Infantry corps she had in abundance, but her artillery was deficient and her mounted force was wholly inadequate to cope with the mobile commandos of the Republics. Her generals had on account of their lack of horses been unable to take advantage of the few victories they had gained, and had been forced to allow the Boers to break away with comparatively light loss and with their guns. Methuen and Buller had been checked in their advance not so much through their fondness for frontal attacks as because the forces under them would permit of no other kind of fighting. They had either to sit down before the enemy's trenches or take them at the bayonet's point. They tried the latter, and as a result the bayonet will no longer be used in battle between civilized powers. To turn the flank of the Boer entrenched positions before Kimberley and Ladysmith a large force of cavalry was an absolute necessity.

On December 18 the Dominion Cabinet met to discuss the advisability of sending a second contin-

A SECOND CALL TO ARMS. 333

gent, and after due deliberation gave the following statement to the public:

"The Imperial Government has at last cabled its acceptance of the offer of the Canadian Government made on November 2 last, of a second contingent. A Cabinet Council was held this morning and instructions given the Militia Department to prepare this second contingent to go forward at the earliest possible moment. A cable to this effect has been sent to the War Office."

Scarcely had this statement been printed when the Militia Department was deluged with letters and telegrams from every part of the Dominion. Even before the character of the troops required had been announced hundreds had volunteered for service. Many who had not volunteered in October because they thought that England had no real need of them and that the war would be of short duration—probably concluded before the Sardinian could reach the Cape—now that a long and hard struggle was before the Empire made haste to try for a place in this second force.

On December 21 an announcement of the character of the contingent to be raised was made. It was to consist of three squadrons of mounted rifles, and three battalions of artillery. A Squadron of Mounted Rifles was to be enrolled in Ontario, Quebec, and the Maritime Provinces; B Squadron at Winnipeg, Portage La Prairie, Verden, Brandon, Yorkton, Regina and Moose Jaw; C Squadron at Prince Albert, Battleford, Moosomin, Qu'Appelle, Lethbridge, Fort McLeod, Medicine Hat and Maple Creek. The artillery was to be enrolled in Eastern Canada and Winnipeg; C Battery concentrating at Kingston, D Battery at Ottawa, and E Battery at

Quebec. On December 27 the list of officers was published together with the fact that the Government had decided to add a fourth squadron of Mounted Rifles.

Lieutenant-Colonel Francois Louis Lessard was in command of the 1st Battalion (A and B Squadrons). The choice was a good one. He had had twenty years military experience, having entered the Quebec Garrison Artillery as a 2nd lieutenant in 1880 and having since been closely connected with the military institutions of this country. Commissioner L. W. Herchmer of the North-West Mounted Police had command of the 2nd Battalion (C and D Squadrons). Since boyhood he had been a soldier, having been gazetted ensign in Her Majesty's 46th Foot in 1858, when but eighteen years old. With this regiment he served in India and on leaving the Imperial service had come to Canada. He had since been connected with civil and military institutions on the western plains, and was well fitted to handle the hardy dare-devils who rushed to enlist in the Canadian Mounted Rifles.

While the mounted infantry were being enrolled principally from plainsmen and the Mounted Police, the Government was actively enlisting men for the three battalions of Royal Canadian Artillery. Lieutenant-Colonel C. W. Drury, who was already in Africa with the First Contingent, was to be commander-in-chief. Major J. A. Hudon was to command C Battery, Major W. G. Hurdman D Battery, and Major G. H. Ogilvie E Battery.

On January 20, Colonel Herchmer's battalion was reviewed at Ottawa. Mr. Norman Patterson in the Canadian Magazine for March gives the following description of this review:

No. 1 TROOP, D SQUADRON, C.M.R.

No. 3 TROOP, D SQUADRON, C.M.R.

A SECOND CALL TO ARMS.

"Of the 325 officers and men under Colonel Herchmer 130 were policemen or ex-policemen. The rest were ranchers from the Territories. The The whole body was drawn up in a hollow square in front of the broad flight of steps leading up to the main building on Parliament Hill. On the top of these well-known stone steps were grouped Sir Wilfrid Laurier, Sir Louis Davies, Hon. Clifford Sifton, Hon. R. W. Scott and the officers of the Ottawa corps. Shortly afterwards, escorted by a dozen troopers, the Governor-General rode up in a sleigh, accompanied by Lady Minto and two of the inevitable A.D.C's. The Governor-General inspected the three lines of men, and Her Excellency presented three silk guidons which she herself had embroidered for them, saying, 'I know I am giving these guidons into very safe keeping.'"

On these guidons was worked the motto of the Elliot clan, "Wha daur meddle wi me."

His Excellency, Lord Minto, then bade them Godspeed.

While this farewell was being given in Ottawa to the Western men, Halifax was *en fete*. On that day D and E Batteries were embarked on board the Laurentian. There were 365 men of all ranks, and twenty times that number of people had come in from every part of Canada to see them off. They were the first regiment of Canadian artillery ever sent to take part in a foreign war. The First Contingent was still sweltering at Belmont; Paardeberg had not been fought, and these batteries hoped that their guns would yet clear a way for the infantry.

A week later Halifax was once more gaily decked with bunting, noisy with the shouts of the populace, and sonorous with the music of military bands. On

Saturday the 27th, Colonel Herchmer's men from the West were embarked on board the Pomeranian; and that same afternoon amid the shrieking of a fleet of tugs and excursion boats they were accompanied for a few miles on their way to South Africa.

Meanwhile C Battery and the First Battalion of Mounted Rifles chafed under delay. It was not until February 21 that arrangements were completed for their transportation.

Canada, a peace nation, had evidently become a military power. Even greater enthusiasm than had been displayed when the First Contingent left for the war was shown at every point at which the soldiers stopped on their way to Halifax, and at the point of departure it was almost impossible to control the multitude that surged in the streets, at the Armouries, and on the docks.

As the Milwaukee drew out from the wharf the thousands broke out into Auld Lang Syne and Rule Britannia, while the loyal Soldiers of the Queen replied from their crowded deck with God Save The Queen.

While the Government of Canada had been busy organizing the Mounted Rifles and Artillery and seeking transport, and no doubt wondering what the people of the Dominion would say when the war bill of two or three millions would have to be faced, Lord Strathcona, the Canadian High Commissioner, had quietly determined to offer to equip and support at his own expense an ideal body of men for service in South Africa. With that shrewd insight that has won for him fabulous wealth, the highest honors in the gift of the Queen, and the most coveted office in the gift of his country, he saw the character of the troops England needed most;

A SECOND CALL TO ARMS.

and he knew, too, that the place to procure these troops was in the western and north-western plains of Canada with which he was so thoroughly familiar. A regiment of scouts was a much needed thing in a war with a nation of scouts and spies.

The offer of Lord Strathcona was accepted by the War Office and the Minister of Militia for Canada was given a free hand to raise this regiment. It was decided to enlist 531 in all, consisting of 25 officers, 36 non-commissioned officers, and 470 troopers. These troops were to be raised in Western Canada, two squadrons in the Territories, and one in British Columbia.

The Minister of Militia was fortunate in being able to secure the service of Lieutenant-Colonel Steele of the North-West Mounted Police for this special regiment. He was at Halifax at the time as second in command of the 2nd Battalion of the Canadian Mounted Rifles, but was at once recalled to Ottawa to take charge of the organization and enlistment of the Strathcona's.

By the 1st of March almost the entire number of men required were enlisted and quartered at the Exhibition Grounds at Ottawa. Hundreds had offered their services, but the tests to which they were subjected were severe, and only men of perfect physique, fine horsemanship and, as far as possible, experience were accepted. The horses selected for the troops were hardy little western mounts between fourteen and fifteen hands, tough and wiry, accustomed to the hardships of the plains, and no doubt well-fitted for the arduous South African veldt and climate.

When the guidons were presented at Ottawa on March 8, 5000 people crowded Parliament Square.

The Strathcona's were to carry these banners "as Talismans in the hour of danger." At this farewell Sir Wilfrid Laurier and Sir Charles Tupper were both present. The former said, as he looked over this magnificent body of men, and there was not a dissenting mind in the assembled throng, that: "Lord Strathcona was one of these men who honored mankind;" while Sir Charles Tupper, thinking of the excellent work done by the Canadians of the First Contingent, rightly prophesied that these horsemen would take their stand, "side by side with the other gallant soldiers," and by their endurance and gallantry "maintain that high position that the Canadian troops had attained."

On March 15, this body of luxuriously equipped troops rolled into Halifax on beautifully-appointed Pullmans and first-class coaches. With them came 100 brave fellows, who had gallantly come forward to join the Special Service Battalion recruited to fill the gaps made in the First Contingent by Mauser bullets and enteric.

On the following day they bade good-bye to Halifax. An enormous crowd had come to the city to see them off. The streets were packed with strangers all wearing the colors of the Strathcona's. The final inspection at the Armouries was made by General Lord Seymour, and the General never looked upon a finer body of soldiers. The other contingents had been the pick of Canada, but this was the pick of the plains. The men in it were hardy, daring; for the most part experienced scouts, and all finished riders. There was something more than strength and dash about them, they had that look of natural intelligence that beams from the faces of sailors and plainsmen, of men whose books are the skies and the prairies. In the ranks, too, were men of refinement and blood. It is only necessary to point out that as a private in the ranks was the grand-nephew of the General who gave them their final inspection; and there were many other men of equally good families.

That afternoon they embarked. Their transport the Monterey gay with bunting, and with the motto of Lord Strathcona and this regiment, "Perseverance," flying at the mast-head, drew out into the stream. She lay at anchor during the misty and rainy night and on the morning of the 18th steamed away for South Africa.

CHAPTER II.

THE ARTILLERY, MOUNTED RIFLES, AND STRATHCONA'S ON THE DEEP.

The day on which D and E Batteries boarded the Laurentian ended cool and wet and dismal. Evidently a storm was brewing and as the vessel was in a somewhat topsy turvy condition through the haste of embarkation, the captatn very wisely decided to lie at anchor till the wind that was rapidly rising to a hurricane had spent itself. Had he gone to sea that night it is much to be feared that men, horses, sheep (there were 110 on board), and guns would have been mingled together in strange confusion.

Next morning the winter sun was shining brightly over the roughened waters of the harbour, and as the fury of the storm had abated the Laurentian weighed anchor, and while the Sunday morning calm still rested on the sleepy city glided past the forts of the harbour on the way to Cape Town.

Although the wind had fallen somewhat the big Atlantic seas still chased each other like heaving mountains as the steamer ploughed her way through them. In the olden days when she was the Polynesian, she had been christened the "Rolling Polly," and as she pitched and tossed, tumbling the landsmen about, she proved that the change in her name had not changed her character. Occasionally big seas came pounding on board and as the scuppers were stopped with the refuse occasioned by the hurried embarkation, tons of water were soon swirling among the horses and sheep. There was a call for men to look after the animals and clear the scuppers, but very few could respond. Sea-sickness had gripped them and they lay in their hammocks and about the decks careless whether the ship floated or sank.

The voyage was a pleasant one on the whole and after their first attack of sea-sickness the men had splendid health. The horses suffered a good deal, however, and by the time they reached Cape Town twenty-six had died and the rest were so thin and used up as to be unfit for service till rested. The mortality among the horses would have been much greater had it not been for that ideal officer of irregular troops Lieutenant "Gat" Howard, who was acting as ship's-quarter-master, and who seemed to have every detail of a soldier's life at his finger's end, from caring for a sick horse to galloping a machine-gun into action.

There was one stop on the journey. Major Hurdman was anxious to send the Government information that would help them in transporting the troops on the Milwaukee and the Monterey, and so on the last day of January the Laurentian ran into the harbor of San Vincent, Cape Verde Islands. This fine harbour presented a busy scene. A fleet of vessels lay there, most of them connected in one way or another with the South African war, and were resting on their way to or from the Cape. The big, graceful, ocean greyhound City of Rome with her 2300 British volunteers on board, and the

English cruiser Cambria attracted the most attention. All glasses on board the vessels already at anchor were turned on the Laurentian as she steamed into the harbour. A long boat was manned by the Cambria's men and a lieutenant and crew of blue-jackets pulled along side of the Canadian steamer with long picturesque sweeps.

Four hours after they had come to anchor they were once more steaming on their southern journey. Some of the soldiers had been anxious to get on shore, but they had to rest content with the distant glimpse of this oasis in the wilderness of salt sea.

By this time the men of the batteries had become thoroughly acquainted. They were like one great family. Of course there were dissatisfied members in the family who growled about their food and their duties. There were very few of these, however, and the complaints were mainly because the Government had very wisely decided that no intoxicating liquor should be sold on board. Some of the seasoned gunners and drivers, accustomed to their daily draughts of beer, did not take kindly to condensed sea-water.

The time was wiled away as on the Sardinian with concerts and athletic contests, but it was heavy on their hands; and they were glad indeed when on February 17 the Laurentian rolled into Table Bay.

Joyful news awaited them. Kimberley had been relieved two days before; the morning papers were full of the account of French's dash on the besieged city, and of the retreat of Cronje with Roberts and Kitchener in hot pursuit. The First Contingent had at last been moved forward to the fighting-line,

THE CANADIAN CONTINGENT READY TO EMBARK ON BOARD THE "MILWAUKEE."

DR. BORDEN, MINISTER OF MILITIA AND MEMBERS OF THE ASSEMBLY AT LUNCH ON BOARD THE S.S. "MONTEREY."

and it was expected that they would help run Cronje to earth.

Next day the batteries disembarked and were marched to the famous camping ground at Green Point Common. They had not long to wait for news of their fellow-countrymen with Roberts. In a couple of days word came that Cronje had been surrounded. Even while they were marching through Cape Town to their camp the Royal Canadians were in the midst of a fierce fight, and as tents were being pitched, were lying on the plain after the fatal charge waiting till darkness came and they could slip back to their bivouacs. It was good to be a Canadian that week in Cape Town. The men from the Land of the Maple Leaf commanded a respect that was given to no other regiments.

Colonel Drury was now in command of the batteries, and had a busy week sorting and distributing stores, inspecting remounts to take the place of the 26 horses that had died on the voyage and generally whipping the battery into shape for immediate service.

The voyages of the Pomeranian and the Milwaukee were but repetitions of the trip of the Laurentian; heavy weather, sea-sickness, dying horses, sports, band concerts, and drill alone broke the monotony of the voyage. The Pomeranian arrived in South Africa on Majuba Day, and the Mounted Rifles thrilled with pride when they learned the heroic part the First Contingent had played during the past nine days, and particularly when they read the account of the final charge and the heroic stand in the trenches that forced the Boers to raise the white flag.

Nearly three weeks elapsed before the Milwaukee brought C Battery and the First Battalion of Mounted Rifles into Cape Town. By that time Bloemfontein had capitulated. Ladysmith was long since relieved, and the Canadians at Green Point Camp thought they might now have to return without seeing active service.

The Monterey was the last of the transports bearing troops to South Africa to leave Halifax. Compared with the other vessels she was a palace. Everything possible had been done to make the men comfortable; but when the inevitable heavy weather of the North Atlantic struck them, their luxurious quarters availed them nothing. The hardy plainsmen, who professed to fear neither man nor devil, when sea-sickness seized them regretted that they had ever left the prairies. The vessel pitched badly; with 647 men and 599 horses above the water-line it could not be otherwise.

She had scarcely got out of sight of land when the western horses began to die. A plague of pneumonia had spread among them. It was hard to account for it, but doubtless these horses accustomed to the high, dry atmosphere of the prairies were the worst possible to stand the winter ocean-voyage. Daily they died by the score, and when the vessel had reached the warmer latitudes the dorsal fins of numerous sharks could be seen cutting the water in the wake of the ship, waiting for the carcases. By the time the Cape was reached 163 horses had perished. One of the troopers as he helped dump his own mount into the ocean said: "I guess we'll be Strathcona's Foot by the time we get to South Africa."

There was one serious mishap on board during

the voyage. On the other vessels on several occasions the fire-call had been sounded to test the men, but on the Monterey the bugle rang out a genuine call. A fire at sea, especially on a crowded vessel, is a horrible thing to contemplate. Usually a panic follows the alarm. But there was no panic on the Monterey, every man went about his work as calmly as if going on parade. While the axes and buckets were being employed to extinguish the fire Colonel Steele stood among his men directing them. At the slightest sound his commanding voice rang out: "Steady there, men. No talking. Keep silence there," and on the instant not a word was spoken.

On April 10, the ship after a very speedy voyage cast anchor at Cape Town, and the Strathcona's wondered when they would get into battle.

CHAPTER III.

THE "REBEL CHASERS FROM AMERICA."

An order had been given to move D and E Batteries towards the front and then countermanded and the men began to dread the fate which had befallen some of the other corps—a protracted stay at Cape Town.

Camp duties were very wearing, and only those who had to break in their balky remounts appreciated the stay at Green Point. On February 27 the Pomeranian arrived with the Second Battalion of Mounted Rifles under Colonel Herchmer, and made a more striking impression on the citizens of Cape Town and the military authorities than either the First Contingent or the Artillery. They were just the men for a special bit of work General Kitchener had in mind, and it soon became rumoured that both the Mounted Rifles and D and E Batteries were to be given a chance to prove themselves.

In giving an account of the work done by the First Contingent the rebellious state of the country northwest of Belmont was dealt with. The Sunnyside affair somewhat lessened the strength of the rebels, but throughout the entire region from Belmont Station to Victoria West Road Station, and far into the Karroo on the West there was a hot bed of rebellion. At the beginning of the war this region had been in an uncertain condition, but after Cronje's successful resistance to General Methuen at Magersfontein and the victories of General Joubert at the Tugela, large sections of the people broke out into open rebellion, driving the loyal inhabitants out of the districts of Britstown, Prieska, and Kenhart, bordering on Carnarvon, looting and destroying property. These rebels were probably the worst class taking part in the war; many of them were half-breeds; Zulu and Kaffir blood was in their veins, and they were capable of almost any savagery.

The relief of Kimberley and Ladysmith, the capture of Cronje's men, Robert's hurried advance with his vast army and the capitulation of Bloemfontein had intimidated the more intelligent and they had returned to their farms; but there were still thousands of rebels scattered throughout this wide district,—ignorant farmers and shepherds who stubbornly refused to believe in the British successes. Besides they felt perfectly safe in their remote wildernesses. Many of them had never seen a railway; and the wide stretches of alkali desert made them think that it would be impossible for a considerable force to march into their country.

It was planned by Kitchener to send two columns one from De Aar and the other from Victoria West. The Victoria West column was to be commanded by Sir Charles Parsons, and was to consist of about 1200 men and an equal number of horses. It was a volunteer column made up of New Zealanders, West Australians, Canadians, and Imperial Yeomanry. The Canadians were numerically the strongest body, constituting more than half of the column besides contributing the 12-pounder guns and the two Vickers-Maxims.

The force was moved forward in sections, and as it reached the Victoria West Road Station it was detrained. D Battery was the first to move, and encamped on the veldt with no worse enemies than lizards and hard-shelled, alligator-like beetles to disturb their slumbers. Outposts had, of course, to be placed on the surrounding kopjes, "sniping" at sentries had been going on, and this new duty, peering out into the darkness for foes, expecting each moment to hear the crack of a rifle, tried the nerves of some of the men. On March 12, D Battery and a squadron of the Mounted Rifles under Major Hurdman were toiling along the dusty road leading to Carnarvon. That afternoon the balance of the Mounted Rifles under Colonel Herchmer followed in their tracks, and on the following day E Battery under Colonel Drury brought up the rear.

The rebels were reported to be some 3000 strong with two guns somewhere in the vicinity of Van Wyks Vlei.

The first great halting place in the road was Carnarvon. The march to that place was very uneventful; the inhabitants on the road from Victoria West all knew of the recent successes of the British and were either exceedingly loyalist, excepting in their charges for food, or dumbly neutral. At Carnarvon, which the entire column reached by the 19th, they received an enthusiastic reception.

The British flag was much in evidence. The houses and public offices were gay with bunting, and the women of the district had prepared "gallons of tea and mountains of cake" for this thirsty and hungry army. Here the soldiers learned much of the difficulties of the march that was still before them and the state of the rebellion. Already their advance was having its effect. The rebels were fleeing; whole districts that had been pro-Boer were rapidly becoming British. "Before we came," says Mr. John Ewen, "we were told by the real loyalists of Carnarvon, rebel feeling was gaining headway, but the sight of these guns, with the husky fellows seated on the limbers, had a distinctly tonic effect."

The march had told on some of the men, and it was necessary to leave ten sick Canadians behind when the advance was continued. The Boers had hoped that the dry season would continue and that the progress of the column would be hampered by the drouth, but before it left Carnarvon sheet lightning filled the sky promising rain. Nor were the British disappointed; by the time they had reached Van Wyks Vlei the roads were running rivers of mud. It was necessary to halt for a day as the transport waggons were having a difficult time floundering through the ditches and streams; and although it was possible to get food for the men, forage was scarce. Shelter too could be obtained here and the officers had very comfortable (?) quarters in the cells of the jail.

The whole column was not so well off, however. D Squadron of the Mounted Rifles, under Captain Macdonell, and a section of D Battery with two guns, under Lieutenant McCrae, had pushed on north to De Naauwte Poort, and here they had to halt without covering or shelter.

Still no rebels were met. The Boers had been in

the little town a day or two before, looting the inhabitants, but the approaching guns of the Canadians had frightened them off. Van Wyks Vlei was, indeed, a very much deserted place; the loyal inhabitants in terror of their lives had gone to the Cape, while the rebels had joined commandos and were at the front, or had deserted their homes at the approach of Sir Charles Parson's column. It was said, however, that they were concentrating to resist the advance at a spot about twenty miles from Kenhart.

It looked as though they would have ample time to concentrate and entrench; the rain continued to come down in torrents, the road was a running river and the rivers were rushing cataracts. However Africa is a land of sudden extremes, and when the rain ceased the hot sun rapidly dried the soil and many of the streamlets made by the rain buried themselves in the thirsty ground.

The advance began once more and the guns and transports went bumping along over the deep ruts made by the storm and splashed their way through the swollen streams. As they went north a new incentive was given them for the work in hand. Into Van Wyks Vlei refugees flocked from the Kenhart district—loyal subjects of Britain who had been plundered and threatened with their lives by the marauders.

The advance continued through the torrid heat aud drenching rain until April 1, when Kenhart was reached. This district had been annexed by the Boers of the Orange Free State at the beginning of the war; it was now re-annexed to Cape Colony and Sir Charles Parsons raised the Union Jack once more over the public buildings.

OFFICERS OF STRATHCONA'S HORSE.

THE FLAG OF STRATHCONA'S HORSE.

The march had been in every way most successful; the demonstration had thoroughly quieted the country and the loyalists felt safe. No rebel in arms had been met, and not a shot had been fired. This was largely due to the guns of the Canadians. The lesson taught the Boers by the artillery practice of Major de Rougement and Captain Bell at Sunnyside three months before was still fresh in the minds of the rebels. They wished for no more shrapnel, and either quietly submitted or kept far out of range. The Canadians were the heroes of the march and the letters on the shoulder straps of the men of D and E Batteries were given a jocular significance. The R. C. F. A. (Royal Canadian Field Artillery) was interpreted by the loyalists to mean "Rebel Chasers From America."

After the re-annexing of Kenhart Colonel Drury in command of the Canadians received orders to report at De Aar on April 14. To accomplish this task it would be necessary to average over twenty miles a day. Leaving many rebels in prison at Carnarvon, among whom were some of the most notorious leaders, the Canadians set out from that place on April 8, and did their work so well that they were outside of De Aar nearly twenty-four hours before the required time.

This bit of forced marching was the hardest on the route. The men were on half or quarter rations part of the time, and the horses were short of fodder—yet they were forced forward. A horse would stagger as he tugged at the guns or stumble with shaking knees under his rider. He was promptly unhitched or unsaddled and to free him from his sufferings humanely shot, and his carcase left to the vultures. All along the route from

Carnarvon to De Aar the dead carcases of the splendid mounts of the batteries and the Mounted Rifles marked the rapid progress of the advance.

De Aar was reached on April 13, and bivouac was formed outside of the encampment. This had been the longest march made by any forces so far during the campaign. The Canadian Mounted Rifles had done in all about 500 miles and the artillery about 350; and that too through the worst district in South Africa—worse even than the region between Graspan and Bloemfontein. They had made it, too, without loss. It is true that one death had occurred at Van Wyks Vlei, but that was the accidental drowning of Private Bradley and might have occurred as easily by the banks of the St. Lawrence as in the South African pond. Of course the inevitable sickness followed this extraordinary exertion and exposure, and at Carnarvon on March 31 there were 24 sick men, and 50 at Van Wyks Vlei; but when De Aar was reached the men were hale and hearty and ready for more work.

They dreaded this encampment. It was the most important one on the line of communications and they feared that they might have the tiresome, inglorious, but very necessary work of spending their days and nights in guarding tracks and culverts and bridges. They had had five weeks of hard work without glory, they now wanted to smell the powder of their own guns and to listen to the booming of the enemy's fire. The night of the bivouac outside of De Aar was to still further try them. The rain came down in torrents and it was a thoroughly soaked and tired looking lot of men that marched into the great base camp on the following morning.

All who had come on the Laurentian and Pomeranian were once more encamped together with the exception of two guns of D Battery which had been left at Kenhart on garrison duty, and D squadron of the Canadian Mounted Rifles which was still on the road.

The Mounted Rifles had a pleasant surprise in store for them. At De Aar they were joined by Lieutenant Moodie with a part of C squadron which had come on the Milwaukee. B Squadron of the First Battalion, they learned, had been pushed forward to Springfontein in the southern part of the Orange Free State on the direct line to Kimberley. It was learned, too, that the entire force of the Mounted Rifles were to be brigaded under General Hutton, and that they were to move forward to Bloemfontein at once to take part in the forward movement on Pretoria for which Lord Roberts had been making preparations for nearly two months. So they rode out of camp on their jaded steeds, leaving D and E Battery behind cursing the fate that kept them tied down to dusty De Aar.

The batteries had to wait long for the action they coveted, but when it did come to a portion of them it came with a fury as fierce as any force suffered during the war. For the remainder of April and until the middle of May they stayed at this base camp doing outpost duty, sweltering by day and shivering by night, and devouring in their food and drink much sand.

Since the Sunnyside affair and the expedition of January the great central movement had left the rebels about Douglas very much to themselves, and they had once more become bold. A considerable force had collected among the kopjes in the region about Richmond, Rooi Pan and Douglas, and was persistently terrorizing the country. It was determined to put an end to their looting, and so a strong force under Sir Charles Warren of Tugela fame, now Governor of Griqualand West, was organized. It consisted of Imperial Yeomanry, Duke of Edinburgh's Own Volunteer Rifles, Paget's Horse, and a part of E Battery R. C. F. A., now known from their success in capturing rebels as the "Rebel Catchers From America," instead of the "Chasers."

The force left De Aar and marched to Belmont, where two guns were left under Lieutenant Good; then over the ground so often travelled by the First Contingent through Richmond to Rooi Pan. Here they halted for three days and on Sunday May 20 set out for Douglas, around which place the rebel Boers were said to be entrenched in very strong positions. Two guns were left behind at Rooi Pan under Lieutenant Ogilvie, the remaining two marched through the night with Sir Charles Warren's column till five in the morning when they bivouacked. In the early morning they advanced to within a couple miles of Douglas. That excellent intelligence officer Colonel Sam Hughes and his scouts had accurately located the Boer laager on the kopjes in front.

The guns of E Battery were ordered into action at once. The drivers at length had their wish—the pleasure of rushing their horses under fire, and they lost no time in gallopng to a good position. They took no round-about way, but galloped over stones and ant-hills and ruts with a recklessness that made it difficult for the men on the limbers to keep their seats. The next instant the guns were trained on the enemy's position, and the shells began to fall into the distant circle of the waggons. It was too much for the Boers and they fled in confusion, no doubt fearing a repetition of the fight at Sunnyside Kopje.

The force then entered Douglas, where Sir Charles Warren hoisted the Union Jack over the public buildings. The rest here, however, was but a short one; almost immediately after their entry it was reported that the enemy were coming back to their waggons, and the guns were again rushed into action, this time with drag-ropes; and the firing continued till some Boer women came forward with a white flag. The river was then crossed and the Boer laager taken possession of.

Although routed the Boers still hung about the column trying to pick off isolated parties, but a shell or two that killed several of their men, kept them for the future well out of range.

The guns that had been left behind came into Douglas about the middle of the week, and on Saturday, leaving Lieutenant Good's section to garrison the town, the remaining guns marched out with the rest of the column to Faber's Farm, eighteen miles distant. Here they were to have one of the most thrilling experiences of the war. The rebels were about in force, but seemed to dread the guns, and did not show themselves near the camp. They had, however, been very active, and had planned a movement, which if it had succeeded would have filled the war columns of the press with another instance of magnificent Boer strategy.

Their spies had given them detailed information with regard to the British camp. Every gun, every waggon, every tent had been located; and the officers' quarters had been specially marked. They knew, too, that the column had no thought that they would take the offensive; and that, with the exception of a few men, it was entirely composed of soldiers who had not yet experienced battle. The outposts they found to be new at their business. It would be easy to pass them; and they determined to capture the guns they dreaded, and add another disgrace to the British arms. Their plan was to creep up in the darkness and at dawn to pour a deadly fusilade into the camp. They had not only carefully marked the officers' tents, but had detailed their best shots to bring down the leaders; six of their best marksmen, it is said, were especially chosen to kill General Warren. The officers removed, a panic would spread through the raw soldiers, and the guns would be theirs. So they reasoned; and the attempt to carry out their plan all but succeeded. During the early hours of May 30 they successfully passed the outposts and completely surrounded the sleeping camp. That the soldiers expected no surprise was evident from the fact that they were undressed and cosily muffled up in their heavy, winter sleeping apparel. At the first streak of dawn, just as some of the lighter sleepers were opening their drowsy eyes expectant of the "rouse," a sharp fierce fire snapped from all sides of the camp. The enemy were apparently at their very line. The fire could not have been more than 75 yards distant! A rain of lead swept through their tents, and clattered against the guns. On the instant a calamity occurred that almost ended the fight. The horses of the Yeomanry and Paget's Horse stampeded with fright and rushed wildly from the camp, but the battery horses stood their ground. The men, however, were as cool as if they had been under fire a hundred times.

The Canadians went to their guns, moved what horses they could to a place of safety behind the farmhouse about which they were camped, and then lay down by their guns waiting the order to fire. After enduring the trying fusilade for nearly an hour the order came, and at the first shot at the close range the Boer fire slackened. The Maxim gun and the Colts were brought into action, but a deadly hail against the Colts smashed the shields, and no man dare stand near them. The rifles of the Yeomanry had since the first alarm been playing into the orchard where the unseen enemy were lying. The guns now dropped shells among them, and the Maxim searched their line. Their fire soon ceased, and leaving many dead behind them, and carrying off their wounded, they fled.

The battery had saved the day; the calm tenacity with which the Canadians stuck to their guns and brought them into action under the steady shower of lead turned the tide of battle. Off they then went after the terrified Boers and took up a position in magnificent style on a bit of rising ground from which they sent shell after shell into the disordered rabble that was fleeing out of range. If the mounted men had not lost their horses the whole force of the enemy would have been captured or cut to pieces.

This battle of Faber's Farm, although but little commented on, was one of the fiercest of the war; on the side of the British alone twenty were killed and nearly a hundred were wounded. The Canadians were peculiarly fortunate; on the four guns they lost only one man killed, Bombardier Latimer, and eight wounded. No. 1 gun suffered most having no fewer than six wounded.

Surgeon-Major Worthington had a heavy list of severe cases to attend to, but he did his work with a tenderness and sympathy that greatly endeared him to the men.

The Boers had paid dearly for their attempt to capture the guns. Thirteen dead bodies were found in the garden alone and a number more picked up in the track of the gun-fire.

In this fight one Canadian particularly distinguished himself. Colonel Sam Hughes was present with the column, and he and his scouts had daily been bringing in flocks of sheep and goats and other loot, together with an occasional bunch of rebels, and now and then a particularly noted Boer leader. On the morning of the fight he was in the camp, and at the sound of the rifles passed coolly along the Canadian battery encouraging the men. It was a miracle that he was not shot. One of the men seeing his danger called to him to lie down, but he replied: "Never mind me, boys; give them beans." As a fighting man during the entire time that he was actively engaged in South Africa he proved himself, as no less a paper than the London Times has said, "An ideal leader of irregular mounted forces."

After this fight the batteries continued in their good but inglorious work of capturing rebels and helping to keep the line of communication intact, while the comrades of their march to Kenhart were sweeping onward to Pretoria, clearing the way for Roberts' great army; and while the Canadian press was filled with the praises of the work C Battery had done at the relief of Mafeking.

MAJOR SAM HUGHES, M.P.

MAJOR JOHN STRATHEARN HENDRIE.

CHAPTER IV.

THE FIRST AND SECOND CONTINGENTS JOIN HANDS
AT BLOEMFONTEIN.

BLOEMFONTEIN was a blessed relief to the men of the First Contingent after the rapid marches they had endured to reach it. They were not sorry when they learned that it would be some little time before Roberts would be able to pursue the forces of the Boers who had retired towards Pretoria. Bloemfontein, however, was far from being a weary soldier's paradise. Food, although they now had plenty, was not too abundant; and if they wished any change from the dull monotony of the army bill of fare—and the daily contact with fine residents, well-filled shops, and beautiful gardens made them long for a change—they had to pay most extravagant prices for the simplest luxuries. Worse far than this, they were still forced to bivouac in the open. Clothing, blankets, and tents were slow in arriving and it was not until three weeks after they had reached Bloemfontein that they were able to get under canvas.

The name Africa is so suggestive of heat that the unthinking are not apt to consider it such a terrible hardship for the soldiers to have to spend their nights there with only the blue sky for a roof. At this time the winter was rapidly approaching, and although the days were hot the nights were intensely cold and frequently very wet. For three weeks after their entry into the Orange Free State capital they endured the same hardships that they had experienced in their bivouacs at Paardeberg and Osfontein, with the exception that they were not forced to exist on a couple of biscuits a day. The remainder of March was a succession of alternate scorching sun and pouring rain. Often they were not able to cook their meals as the torrents drenched their fires.

Meanwhile it was beginning to look as if the Orange Free State had ceased to take an interest in the war. Hundreds of burghers daily came in and surrendered their arms, and although Steyn was north of the Vet River issuing his orders as President from his moveable capitals, it was generally recognized that the Free Staters were out of the contest and that the Transvaalers were now the only factor to consider. So the troops in camp thought. A few days rest, a swift advance, and Johannesburg and Pretoria would be theirs, if the cowardly Boers, as they now considered them, had not surrendered before the River Vaal, the northern boundary of the Orange Free State, was reached.

But while the British were waiting, and thinking how rapidly the war would be brought to a termination, and the Canadians were writing about a speedy return to Canada, the Boers were exceedingly active. Cronje was captured, and on March 27 General Joubert who was esteemed by all men, died; and it seemed as if the enemy's forces were without a head. In the place of these men two brilliant military leaders, soldiers by instinct, began to take charge of affairs. Botha and DeWet were now to take the place of the veteran generals and with greatly reduced forces to prove themselves ideal men for South African warfare.

On April 1 England was startled by news of a disgraceful reverse. The mistakes of White, Warren, and Buller on the Natal border were still fresh, not even the capture of Cronje's army had made the British people forget them. Roberts, however, would make no such blunder. Suddenly the Water-works disaster awoke the War Office and the public out of their over-confidence. It looked for a moment as if the reputations of Roberts and Kitchener were about to find a place in the great "Grave of Reputations."

It was a terrible disgrace for England to bear; again outwitted, outmanœuvred by these despised and beaten Boers. There was one bright ray of sunshine in the gloom—the gallant conduct of the British soldiers. Generals might blunder, but the bravery of the men of England was beyond question.

In this fight the Canadians played their part, though a minor one. Colonel Otter was ordered to march his regiment from camp with the 9th Division at daylight on March 31. The Canadians advanced as rear guard of the Brigade to Waterworks Hill which they reached about noon. A part of the battalion was left about half way in the rear as escort to the supply column. That night was spent at Waterworks Hill. Next day the firing in their front told of a fierce struggle and soon they knew of the disaster to Colonel Broadwood's command. They had accomplished nothing when the order was given to retrace their steps to Bloemfontein at which place they arrived on April 3.

This time, although but half their original strength, they had gone forth eager for battle. The reverse to the British arms must be avenged; besides, if the Boers remained in possession of the Waterworks it would be a serious thing for the army of fifty thousand men in the vicinity of Bloemfontein. But even as they marched forth, stumbling through the darkness, news was coming in of another disaster to the British arms.

Gatacre had been advancing a body of Royal Irish Rifles and Northumberland Fusiliers, when on April 3 these regiments were surrounded by a force of Boers under that brilliant leader General De Wet and nearly 500 had been taken prisoners; not without a fierce struggle however.

Two sudden blows had been struck, and the wily enemy flushed with victory had retreated to cover. The 9th Division could not find them excepting in the (for the present) impregnable position at the Waterworks, and so after much weary marching through rain and sun, returned to Bloemfontein.

It was luxury to get into new clothes and to once more sleep under a tent. Fifty-three days lying in the open had been too much for even these men hardened by their long stay at Belmont. The end of the campaign, too, was now growing more and more remote, and they felt that they might need these tents for some weeks in their present camp. Roberts' line of communication was threatened; there was scarcity of water in Bloemfontein; the men were being stricken down by the score with fever; each day the Canadians laid some comrade to rest; and there was nothing for it but to wait, eating their hearts out, till the army could advance in force. Only overwhelming numbers could subdue this wily enemy fighting in a country every foot of which they knew perfectly. What the English needed most was an efficient body of scouts. The reverses of the Waterworks, or Sannahs Post, and Reddersburg could never have occurred in an army thoroughly equipped with these indispensable soldiers, particularly in modern warfare.

The men they needed were on the road to the front. That excellent body of western plainsmen familiar with the veldt and kopje of the North-West of Canada was hurrying towards Bloemfontein. B Squadron was at Stellenbosch remount camp with C Battery when news of Reddersburg reverse reached them. On April 8 they entrained for Norval's Pont where they detrained and marched towards Bloemfontein. On the 9th A Squadron followed in their track, and acted as escort to a convoy of provisions till on April 14, they reached Springfontein, where B Squadron then was. But B left them on the following morning and pushed on to Bloemfontein. A week later A was within three miles of the Orange Free State capital, and as they advanced they heard the boom of big guns and the crackling of rifles. They were too late to be in the fight, but they knew that the comrades of their voyage were receiving their baptism of fire.

When B reached Bloemfontein they quite expected to find the First Contingent still resting in that town; many were looking forward to renewing old friendships and having a comparative rest for a day or two before joining in the great northward march that had been planned. But the First Contingent was out to the east of the town helping in an important bit of work. Before the general advance could begin the Boers who were infesting the eastern side of Bloemfontein to a point within twenty miles, had to be cleared away. The 19th Brigade, now known as the "Fighting Nineteenth" had been sent to help in this task, and so B Squadron found only the Canadian sick in the hospitals, and the exhausted and footsore in the camp—and far too many they found. It was but a poor shadow of the regiment which marched to the Sardinian seven months before, amidst the shouting of ten thousand people, that now toiled along the road towards Thaba N'Chu where it was to win fresh laurels.

B Squadron was to have no rest. Almost on their arrival at Bloemfontein they received orders to advance at once towards the Waterworks. Out they went, and now the Royal Canadian Regiment of Infantry and the Canadian Mounted Rifles joined hands. Both were doing good work in the same great movement. The British had smarted under the disgrace of the Waterworks and Reddersburg disasters for three weeks; they were now going to do what they could to retrieve these disgraces. This time there would be no such blunders; they had studied the country, and they had a sufficient number of scouts with them to thoroughly investigate the districts through which they were advancing.

The Boers still held the Waterworks and the kopjes surrounding this important centre, and B Squadron was sent forward to assist as the scouts of General Pole-Carew's army to capture them or clear them from their strongholds. The Boers, however, made a very short stand. They saw that there was no trifling with the force that was sent against them this time, and so after a few hastily aimed shells evacuated their position which was promptly occupied by the British mounted infantry.

Shortly after this B Squadron scouted in advance of the victorious army that was moving forward towards Dewetsdorp. Major Williams was in command and on reaching a somewhat perilous and unfamiliar district, sent Lieutenant Straubenzie forward with twenty mounted men to examine the surroundings, to find out if the spruit at that place was fordable, and if there were any of the enemy in the farmhouse near the spruit. The buildings looked suspicious, and the reconnoitering party advanced cautiously, but when within 800 yards of the place the white flag was raised, Lieutenant Straubenzie and his men threw off all caution. They had heard of the use the Boers had been making of the white flag, but it is hard for an Anglo-Saxon to think any man capable of such depravity.

Scarcely had they begun their bold advance when the distant farm house sputtered with a rapid rifle fire. A rain of lead played about Lieutenant Straubenzie, his horse was instantly shot under him, and he himself had a narrow escape. It was B Squadron's first experience under fire, and the men behaved with great coolness. They dismounted at once, threw themselves on the ground, and while the bullets splashed the dust about them waited for reinforcements. It was impossible to retire, and Lieutenant Straubenzie sent back word to that effect to Major Williams. Assistance was hurried forward, with Lieutenant Young's troop in the firing-line, Lieutenant Turner's in support, and Lieutenant Borden's in reserve. They took up a position at 700 yards from the farmhouse and opened fire. Lieutenant Straubenzie as soon as the enemy's attention was engaged by Lieutenant Young's men commanded his soldiers to remount and gallop to cover.

An artillery duel went on between the British column and the treacherous Boers till darkness. At daybreak the British made preparations to drive the Boers from their position, but the farmhouse was silent. The Boers had slipped away during the night and taken with them their guns and camp supplies. However the house from which the base treachery was practised was properly looted and burnt to the ground. After this fight B Squadron returned to Fischer's Farm, and the 1st Battalion was once more united.

In the meantime A Squadron was resting very comfortably at this place, about six miles from Bloemfontein, relieving the Inniskillings of outpost duty. Herr Fischer was in Europe endeavoring to get some of the Powers to interfere on behalf of the Republics. He was evidently a man of very excellent taste, and the men of A Squadron after their forced marches and hard work with the convoy, thoroughly appreciated his breezy veranda, the tropical trees and plants, the orange and lemon trees, and the shrubbery of blooming roses that adorned his estate. They might have forgotten the warlike mission on which they had come, but occasionally the distant rattling explosions of the "pom-poms" and the boom of big guns spoke of battles that were being fought but a short distance away, and at night the continuous flashing of the searchlight on the surrounding hills told them how watchful the great army had to be.

On April 23 General Hutton, whose experience

GROUP OF OFFICERS.
Royal Canadian Mounted Rifles, in the Van of the Great Army marching to Pretoria.

and organizing ability had done so much towards successfully mobilizing the 3000 Canadians in Africa, inspected the Canadian Mounted Rifles at Fischer's Farm; and, a few days later, Lord Roberts, anxious to see the men who were to be the scouts of his army on its march to Pretoria, likewise held an inspection and was much pleased with their appearance.

C Squadron after a hard march of 120 miles from De Aar joined A and B at Bloemfontein, and the three awaited the advance on the Transvaal. C was far from being as fresh as the other two. In the last seven weeks the men had marched in all nearly 700 miles, without tents most of the time, with scant food for men and but little hay for the horses. Many of their mounts had been killed; they themselves were worn out with much privation, but a couple of days rest and the feeling that they were to be right in the van of the fighting freshened them up. D Squadron had not yet arrived; it was toiling through the sand and over the veldt, but in a few days it would be with them, and then the whole of the Canadian Mounted Rifles would be a unit for the first time.

Meanwhile a running fight was going on east of Bloemfontein; that sly fox De Wet was dodging the British, and keeping a considerable part of their forces engaged. For months this Will-o'-the-Wisp was to appear and disappear with astonishing rapidity; striking, and retiring before his enemy had time to recover from his well-directed blows. However, he was kept running, and both the First and Second Contingents did not a little to give wings to his heels.

CHAPTER V.

FIGHTING NORTHWARD.

WHILE the Canadian Mounted Rifles were enjoying the sweet odours of Mr. Fischer's garden, and waiting for the general advance in which they were to join, the Royal Canadians were in the middle of marches and engagements as severe as they had experienced in their rapid dash on Bloemfontein.

After the Boers had been driven from the Waterworks the "Fighting Nineteenth" followed them up, driving them before them. The Canadians seized a kopje about two or three miles from Sannahs Post and bivouacked for the night. All the surrounding kopjes had been seized by the British, and there was now no furthur danger of the Boers recovering possession of the important position they had held for the past three weeks. The morrow, the 25th of April, was to be one of the most important days in the history of the Canadian Regiment.

The Boers were discovered in the early morning in an easily defended position on a line of kopjes several miles in front. At half-past nine the 9th Division started forward to attempt to force them from their stronghold, and shortly before noon the first shot of what was to be an all day battle was fired. The Canadians halted for several hours while the mounted infantry skirted round the enemy's flanks and the artillery shelled the kopjes to beat down their rifle fire. At 3 o'clock the Canadians were ordered to advance on the kopjes, which they were to rush if they could do it without too great loss, but if they met a very determined resistance were to seek cover and wait till the mounted infantry and artillery had forced the enemy to evacuate their strongest positions.

The fight was one of the best planned in the campaign. While the frontal attack was being conducted by the Canadians, the mounted infantry were to surround the enemy on the right and left and the other infantry regiments were to execute a turning movement on the left threatening the Boers with the fate of Cronje at Paardeberg. At the same time the batteries posted in the rear of the advancing regiment were to keep up a steady shell fire over the heads of the Canadians.

Colonel Otter formed his men into four double companies. G Company on the right, H on the left in the firing-line, with E and F in support; C, D, B, and A were arranged in the same manner in the rear. It looked as though the battalion was about to experience another Paardeberg. Every precaution was therefore taken for safety. When the advance was begun the men were extended at intervals of fifteen paces, and the long line of earth-brown figures dotted the veldt for nearly a mile. Major Pelletier, who had been wounded at Cronje's Laager, but who now had rejoined the regiment, was in charge of the firing-line; with him was the commanding officer directing the movements of the entire battalion. Colonel Buchan commanded the rear lines. In this order the regiment advanced for about a mile, the earth occasionally being puffed about them by the singing bullets. At length a donga was reached affording excellent shelter, and as the bullets were dropping somewhat faster than at first the men would gladly have halted for a time, but they were ordered to continue the advance. When about fifty yards from this valley they came upon a wire fence; the wires were supported on stone posts that shone in the sun, making excellent targets.

The Boers had evidently had this position marked, and were reserving their fire, for scarcely had the advancing line reached the wire-entanglement when a deadly and continuous fusilade at a distance of about 700 yards was rained along the thinly extended line. To advance would have been as great folly as the Sunday charge at Paardeberg; to stay where they were on the unsheltered veldt would have been to court death. The order to retire was given. It was intended that the men should steal back quietly to cover, but the face once turned from the rifle-fire the heart weakened and the whole line began to rush in disorder to the rear. At such a time the metal of the officers was displayed. The captains of the companies boldly showed themselves and steadied their men as best they could, while Colonel Otter, as on former occasions, exposed himself to the rifle-fire while checking the disorder in the firing-line on the right; in this work he was ably seconded by his adjutant Lieutenant Ogilvy, who courageously came forward to assist in the dangerous work on the left.

Colonel Otter remained standing till the last man had got safely to cover. His commanding figure, evidently directing the movements of the soldiers, was observed by the Boers. They had his range to the yard, and after the usual custom when an officer was sighted poured a volley at him. He was just settling to cover when a storm of bullets whistled about him, one penetrating his neck within an inch of the jugular vein, and another cutting the badge on his shoulder. It was a close call. Despite the painful wound, however, he remained on the battle-field directing the battalions for the rest of the day, and at the end of the fight walked unsupported to the field-hospital.

For nearly an hour the men remained in their safe shelter listening to the guns sending shrapnel into the kopjes and hearing the steady rifle-fire of the remainder of the 19th on the left. The firing-line kept replying to the Mauser bullets that sang over their position, but as they could not see the enemy their fire had little or no effect. However the fire of the Boers slackened and the Canadians hoped yet to seize before darkness fell the kopje they had been sent out to take.

Captain Burstall, who has very frequently in the despatches been mentioned for bravery and judgment, noticed that a sheltering donga led towards the coveted kopje and gallantly volunteered to lead B Company through this towards the hill. Permission was granted him to make the attempt and under cover of the valley B advanced stealthily, with D nominally in support following so closely behind as to be practically a part of the advancing line. On all the surrounding kopjes the fight was being vigorously waged by artillery and mounted infantry and infantry; a continuous rattle and boom was going on, while this small force advanced to give the finishing touch to this day of fighting.

The Boers had begun to weaken; many of them were already trekking away for their lives, and when B Company emerged at about 500 yards coming at them on the double with bayonets fixed they fired a few wild parting shots and fled; and the victorious Canadians climbed to the summit of the hill, and the task they had been allotted to do was done, and done well. The Canadians were once more the first regiment in at the finish of a hard day's fighting.

The Boers were scattered and in flight towards the high hills some miles distant where yet another battle must be fought. The day's work done, the regiment bivouacked for the night, a tired and weakened force scarcely half the number with which they marched from Graspan. Despite the trying fire to which they had been exposed the casualties were small, but one man killed and three wounded, including Colonel Otter. This battle, generally known as Israel's Poort, but likewise called Yster Nek and Black Mountain, cost the entire British force engaged only some twenty in killed and wounded, notwithstanding that the army had been almost continuously engaged for nearly six hours. This fight cleared the way for the advance to the little village of Thaba N'Chu, and on the following day the column was marched into this place unopposed. Colonel Otter's wound was severer than he at first thought, and he was compelled to return the thirty-five miles to Bloemfontein where he was forced to remain for nearly a month.

The Boers who had been in force about Dewetsdorp

and engaged in besieging General Brabant at Wepener, were known to be trekking north, and an effort was made to ambush them as they passed Thaba N'Chu, so when the Canadians arrived at the foot of the great black mountain that rose 2000 feet above the plain and the surrounding kopjes they were posted in a donga expecting the Boers to fall into the snare. But De Wet and his men were taking no chances, and making a wide detour escaped to the north without coming in contact with General Ian Hamilton's division.

The next day was one of much needed rest, for the Canadians, but in the cool of the night two companies with the Gordons went out to help rescue a party of Kitchener's Horse who were reported to be in a dangerous position. All night long they stumbled over the plain, and when they got back to Thaba N'Chu next day they found they had been on a wildgoose chase; the Kitchener's were long since out of danger. In the meantime the rest of the battalion became alarmed for the safety of their comrades and went out to assist them and the Kitcheners if necessary; but probably while the men who had been tramping around all night were sleeping in the heat of the morning the others passed them by; and they too had much tramping to no purpose until midnight.

Next morning the "rouse" awoke the men at four o'clock and they made ready for a day's marching and fighting. Eden Kopje was their destination, and as they marched towards it they were subject to an occasional shot but no man was struck. This mountain, 1500 feet high, they ascended at five in the afternoon only to vacate it at once. It was a dangerous position and another

Spion Kop might of been the result of an attempt to hold it. It was dangerous, too, to march back to Thaba N'Chu by the road over which they had come, and so they made a wide detour through the darkness, tramping through thorn bushes, stumbling over ant-hills and rocks. It was midnight before they were able to roll themselves up in their blankets.

The morrow was Sunday: war is usually no respecter of the Sabbath, and even the pious Boer had been forced to fight on this sacred day; but the 19th was too much spent to look for fighting, and so they rested. In their camp they could hear on their left a brisk artillery duel going on, while in the little village below them the church bells were calling the burghers to prayer. The sounds mingled strangely; and as the soldiers looked out towards those gloomy kopjes that still had to be stormed, there was not a man but wished that the cruel war were at an end, and they could be back listening to the sound of church bells in their native town. But there was nothing to be gained by wishing. Next day, while the great spectacular march was going on from Bloemfontein, they were to be subjected to the severest shell-fire they had experienced during the war.

On April 30 they marched out as rear guard of the brigade, and as such did not anticipate very severe fighting; but no part of the "Fighting Nineteenth" was ever very long out of the thick of battle. The Boers retreated from ridge to ridge as the division advanced, making a determined stand on their entrenched positions of Taba Mountain and at Hout Nek. The enemy were here found to have a widely extended line; it would be hard indeed to

THE BRITISH COLUMBIA CONTINGENT.

THE DEPARTURE OF LORD STRATHCONA'S HORSE FROM OTTAWA.

Sir Wilfred Laurier bidding the Regiment farewell on Parliament Hill.

take these tall kopjes and turn the flanks of a force that had a front of over four miles. The Gordons were the first to attempt to force the stubborn enemy from Taba Mountain, but were repulsed after a dashing attempt. It was thought, too, that the enemy were making an effort to turn the British flank, and the Canadians were ordered to advance in support of the Gordons and to assist in preventing this turning movement.

Three companies moved forward with Captain Rogers, of Ottawa, directing the firing-line. Up to this time the Boer guns at Taba Mountain and Hout Nek had been giving their attention to the mounted infantry, but as they saw the Canadians coming into action they turned two heavy guns on them and swept their line. The soldiers had lost a good deal of respect for Boer riflemen, but they had now every reason to admire the foreign artillerists who were directing the Creusot and Krupp guns that were sending shell after shell with such accuracy into their line. Luck—we can call it by no other name—was with them again; indeed, when the work done by both the Canadian infantry and mounted rifles is considered, and the ridiculously small list of casualties, it would not be surprising if "The luck of the Canadians" would become proverbial in the army. Men were stunned, men were knocked down, in several cases they were actually tossed some feet into the air, but only one was killed. For the most part the shells did not explode; had they done so the regiment would undoubtedly have suffered heavily in killed and wounded. After a shell or two had fallen into the firing-line the men became as steady as if at drill on the barracks' square.

On this occasion the Boers were not using smokeless powder, and so the grey cloud on the hill several miles away told when the shell might be expected. Captain Rogers ordered his company to keep their eyes on him and double when he doubled. As soon as the smoke showed itself he rushed forward a few paces and the men lost no time in following his example. They advanced thus for about a quarter of a mile while the shells kept dropping, occasionally among them, but for the most part, owing no doubt to Captain Rogers' coolness, a few feet in their rear. On one occasion Harry Cotton, a son of Lieutenant-Colonel Cotton, lagged a little behind in the rush, and a well-directed Boer shell found him. It was one of the few that burst, and his comrades were, for the time being, forced to leave him where he fell. Rifle-fire the soldiers were by this time accustomed to, but this shell-fire was a comparatively new thing; however no man wavered and although there was a good deal of ducking heads as they rushed forward none threw themselves on the ground. The huge projectiles screeched through space, great columns of dust were dashed on high as they buried themselves in the ground or bounded over the plain, or a thousand spiteful hisses filled the air as the fragments of the occasional shell that burst fell about the advancing line. It needed nerve to keep from showing a white feather, but the fine example of the officers kept the men steady.

Despite the shell-fire and finally the rifle-fire, the Canadians succeeded in gaining a position at the base of the mountain, where as darkness fell they threw up stone shelters to protect themselves from the fire of the Boers who sniped away during the night.

It had been a most unsatisfactory days' marching and enduring fire with very little offensive fighting. The artillery practice was altogether on the part of the Boers, as their heavy pieces completely outranged the British 15-pounders, and the naval long range guns were still toiling in the rear. Nightfall was not unwelcome, and the Canadians tried to enjoy as best they could their thoroughly uncomfortable bivouac. They had no blankets and the night was piercingly cold; they had to maintain absolute silence for fear of attracting the enemy's fire, nor could they light fires for the same reason; and so they munched at the scant rations of hardtack they had with them and huddled together, shivering with cold waited for the morrow and more fighting.

When night had descended on hill and plain Captain Rogers and a party of Ottawa men went out in search of their comrade who had fallen in in the advance. They found him where he fell, his body mangled by the cruel shell ; and they buried him in a soldier's grave on the battlefield.

Early next morning the fight began once more. The crest of the hill had to be won, and the Canadians were there to win it. Hills can be stormed ; that was shown 19 years ago when the Boers wriggled their way up Majuba Hill and shattered Sir George Colley's force. The Canadians could not do better than follow their tactics, and so they began the ascent, grovelling along the ground, taking advantage of every bit of cover that presented itself. They were cold and hungry and exhausted from want of sleep, but the fever of battle is a powerful stimulus, and the men as they slowly crept up the steep mountain forgot all about their physical sufferings. They advanced and fired, fired and advanced, outdoing the Boers in their skill in keeping themselves invisible. They were at length exposed to the enemy and a terrific fire swept across the line. Several men were wounded, and to continue the advance would mean a heavy list of casualties, and so they were compelled to retreat to a sheltering valley.

Captain Burstall from his shelter observed a bit of rising ground that commanded a full view of the Boer's position. Private Rorison bravely volunteered to pass through the rifle-fire and examine this spot. He went boldly forward, but as he reached it he was wounded in the leg. A firing party had followed him up and they had an excellent point of vantage from which they could fire into the Boer lines; and the Canadians were absolutely safe in their cover.

In the meantime the naval guns had appeared on the scene, and the "Ocean Cavalry" began to drop shell after shell into the Boer trenches. Their rifle-fire slackened, the booming of their artillery was heard no more, and towards evening a general advance was ordered. The position was won with but little loss. In two days fighting, despite the heavy shell-fire and the thousands of Mauser bullets that had been showered among them, the Canadian regiment lost but one man killed and six wounded.

The British captured a few prisoners, among them some important commandants, but the main force was trekking rapidly north, hurrying to get beyond the Vet river before Roberts could reach that important point. They had made a stubborn stand, and although pressed back they had succeeded in carrying away their heavy guns.

The Boers were now in full retreat and the forward movement could go on with greater rapidity. The enemy on the east had been scattered and the plan of Lord Roberts became evident to all. A column under General Ian Hamilton was to be a part of the general advance on Pretoria, and was to proceed on the eastern flank of the army of fifty or sixty thousand men, through Winburg on to Kroonstad.

On the morrow they marched steadily forward to Isabellafontein and bivouacked at four in the afternoon. Here they were joined by three other infantry brigades. They were now a powerful army in themselves that no force of Boers left in arms would be able to resist. In all they must have numbered between fifteen and twenty thousand men with a host of infantry, a complete division of mounted men, and a thoroughly efficient artillery force. The Creusots and the Krupps of the enemy could no longer outrange them as they had attached to their artillery two powerful 5-inch siege guns.

The following day they once more came up with the enemy, and the 19th Brigade were placed in support and never came under fire or pulled a trigger. They had, however, the pleasure of witnessing a most interesting artillery battle which lasted during the entire morning; but the siege guns sending their fifty pound shells a distance of over six miles terrified the Boers who fled, and the advance began once more. Just as darkness was falling the Vet River was reached and here the army halted for the night. They expected to enter Winburg on the morrow, but they expected to have to fight their way in. The passes to the town were easily defended, and it was thought that the Boers who had retreated from Wepener, and who had been driven from Taba Mountain and Hout Nek, would concentrate their forces and make a hard fight. But Lord Roberts had already occupied Brandford; the vast army under him was irresistibly sweeping northward with a forty mile front. Delay might mean capture and so the commandos passed through Winburg without offering any resistance to General Hamilton's progress.

On the afternoon of the 5th this town, an important Boer base of supplies was entered. The white flag was flying over the market place, and not a shot was fired. As a reward for the excellent work they had done since leaving Bloemfontein the 19th Brigade had the place of honor in the march into Winburg. As they entered the town General Botha with some 500 Germans and Hollanders on fresh horses galloped out at the opposite side.

The Canadians expected a sorely needed rest of a couple of days here, but they were not to have it; swiftness of movement was what was needed now to speedily finish the war. The Boers were running; they must be kept running and given no time to concentrate their forces till Pretoria was reached. On the day the column entered Winburg, word was received from General Roberts praising them for the good work they had done; a march of over 100 miles in thirteen days, battling with the enemy on nine occasions, the capture of two important towns —this was not bad work. The Field-Marshal recognized all they had done, but desired them to endure still further, that release from marching and fighting and privations and death might come all the sooner.

Forward the Canadians had to go, and only twenty-four hours after entering the pretty little town of Winburg they were once more a part of the great river of men that was overflowing the land in its onward rush. As a regiment they were now greatly weakened, some seventy men sick with enteric and dysentery and unable to march from sore feet had to be left behind at Winburg. The strength of the battalion was now a bare five hundred. Fortunately the draft that had come on the Monterey and had toiled over the Orange Free State from Norval's Pont to Bloemfontein and from Bloemfontein in the wake of the Royal Canadians for the past thirteen days, joined them, and three officers and ninety-one men were thus added to their strength.

The unexpected now happened. They were halted nine miles from Winburg, and for two days they rested; then once more the order was, "On to Pretoria!"

CHAPTER VI.

THE SCOUTS OF AN ARMY.

It is no easy thing to move an army of 60,000 men. That means that the population of a good sized city would have to be provided for; and the food, clothing and blankets could not be kept in stores and warehouses, but in the lumbering convoys dragged in the wake of the army by oxen and mules, ever liable to collapse or to stick in the bridgeless rivers. Seven weeks were expended in getting the host ready to advance, and to make Bloemfontein a sure base for the moving city of men that were to press ever north till they could at last rest in Kruger's Capital.

The advance had indeed already begun. The 9th Division were hard at work fighting their way mile by mile; but it was reserved for May Day to see the magnificent spectacle of one of the largest armies of modern times moving forward on what was to be a victorious march.

On May 1 the army moved northward, and as the long line pressed forward on the road to Pretoria they saluted and cheered enthusiastically the Commander-in-Chief whose will they obeyed, and whom they were ready to follow in the most hazardous or trying enterprises with unquestioning faith.

Most conspicuous in this host were the Guards; Grenaders, Scots, and Coldstreams flowed **past in**

STRATHCONA'S HORSE PRESENTATION OF GUIDON'S AT OTTAWA.

STRATHCONA'S HORSE, OTTAWA.

their magnificent strength; regiments of fusiliers, infantry corps seemingly without end followed in their wake; after these trundled the artillery,—naval guns, field-batteries, siege guns, Maxims, Vickers-Maxims, Colts,—every conceivable heavy engine of war stirred up vast clouds of dust as they began the march through the towns of the Orange Free State and the Transvaal. The streets were packed with cavalry regiments and mounted infantry, and none showed up better than the three squadrons of mounted rifles from the Great Dominion. When the fighting men had passed, a moving city of transport waggons laden with supplies sufficient to feed this host for weeks creaked and groaned in the rear. The cracking of whips, the lowing and braying of countless oxen and mules, the angry yells of the Kaffir drivers made a hideous din. Last of all came the ambulance corps ready to pick up the sick and exhausted who might fall on the way, or in the hour of battle to march into the deadly firing-line to help the wounded.

The long line of soldiers was two days in getting out of Bloemfontein, and yet Bloemfontein was not deserted. An army was left at the base doing garrison duty, and attending to the other army of sick that lay in every public building and in the white tents that gleamed in the suburbs.

At the beginning of this great march D Squadron of the C. M. R. was absent. It had been making forced marches with jaded steeds to get to Bloemfontein in time, but only arrived after the other squadrons were out of the town. Many of the men were worn out, the vultures were feeding on the bodies of many of their horses that had fallen victims to the march, while many others were unable to bear their riders. There were plenty of horses in Bloemfontein, however, and with new mounts the squadron on the following day hurried forward to catch up to their comrades.

The Second Battalion had now a new commander. Lieutenant-Colonel Herchmer had been struck down with fever, and although by this time he was able once more to go to the front, General Hutton, knowing what terrible hardships the squadrons would have to endure on their northward march in the African winter, felt that it would be unwise to risk giving the command of this important battalion to a man who had just risen from a sick bed; and so for the rest of the campaign Lieutenant-Colonel Evans, a splendid soldier and very popular with the men, had command of C and D Squadrons. It was no doubt hard on such an excellant commander as Lieutenant-Colonel Herchmer.

When well out of Bloemfontein the Mounted Rifles became the very van of the army, scouting to the right and to the left, examining kopjes, and dongas, and stream beds. Behind them came a more compact body of cavalry ready to charge forward at the warning of the scouts or to fall back till the artillery and infantry could come up to keep the enemy engaged in front while they wheeled round their flanks.

While this march was thus proceeding along the line of railway, on the east the Winburg column was rapidly moving forward in an almost parallel line to its right flank, and on the far west north of Kimberley another column was pushing forward to Fourteen Streams on the boundary of the Free State and of the Transvaal. What was of more interest to the world at large was the news that at the same time a flying column under Colonel Mahon was despatched to the relief of brave little Mafeking where Colonel Baden-Powell and his heroic followers were still keeping a large body of Boers at bay.

For the first two days the advance was unopposed; occasionally in the distance a rifle would crack and a bullet sing over the heads of some of the scouts or bury itself in the veldt, but it was not until after Karree Siding was past that the main advance came in contact with the enemy. Houses were deserted, or if the owners had remained the suspicious white flag which had now taken the place of the flag of the Republic, begged the English to be merciful.

After leaving Karree Siding the Canadian Mounted Rifles were in advance of the column. The enemy were located in a spruit some miles to the front and two squadrons advanced to draw their rifle-fire or unmask their guns. As they marched along they commandeered sheep and cattle, and examined the farmhouses finding quantities of explosive and split-nose bullets and Mauser rifles which the Boers had left in their haste. Before noon the two squadrons came in contact with the rear-guard of the Boers who were trekking north as fast as their hardy little ponies could carry them, or as the long line of oxen could bear away their guns. The squadrons were in close range before they became aware of the enemy's presence and then it was by means of a fierce and steady rifle-fire. They had found the enemy and wheeling their horses about galloped back to the main body.

The horses were now sent to the rear and A

squadron, commanded by Major Forrester, with no better protection than the ubiquitous ant-hills, replied steadily to the well-directed rifle-fire in their front. The whole of the mounted infantry in this part of the column was soon engaged. Lieutenant Howard galloped his Colt gun hurriedly on the scene, and for a time Maxim, "pom-pom," artillery and rifles blended their notes in the chorus of a very interesting battle. After a time the fire grew too hot for the Boers. Their fire grew fainter and fainter and at last ceased, and when the British troops gained the position they had held they were already galloping away to join the main body of their retreating army.

While this brisk little fight was going on Lord Roberts and his staff were at Karree Siding, where they had come by train, waiting to hear that the column had forced its way into Brandford, the first important town on the northward road. They had not long to wait. After this first brush the whole column advanced seven miles to Brandford. The enemy had made preparations to resist the advance and had four or five big guns posted outside the town. The booming of the long range fire was heard for a time, but the wide front of the British threatening the flank of the Boers, and the vast army coming like a swarm of locusts from the South, thoroughly frightened the gunners holding the advance, and they limbered up once more and trekked as swiftly as they could in a mad endeavor to get beyond the River Vet. Meanwhile the Colonial mounted infantry corps drove their riflemen from the kopjes in front, and the army entered the small town unopposed, and the first important step on the road to Pretoria was taken. When the heliograph flashed the good news of the success of the movement back to Roberts at Karree Siding he knew that the waiting time at Bloemfontein had not been in vain.

For the mounted brigades under Hutton and French there was to be no rest. D Squadron joined the Canadian regiment shortly after Brandford had been entered, and the whole force under Lieutenant-Colonels Lessard and Evans, went forward in pursuit of the fleeing Boers. They soon came up with the rear guard; hoping to surround them they dashed ahead, but the Boers were conducting their retreat with excellent judgment. It was a retreat, but not one of wild confusion. They had their long range guns ready to stop the advance of the mounted men. On this occasion they came boldly into the open and shelled Hutton's men, who were forced to fall back out of the accurate fire to await the arrival of the main column, but before this happened the main body of the Boers were once more out of danger and the "Long-Toms" trekked rapidly after them, and so the Mounted Brigade again started in pursuit.

As the Canadian mounted rifles went forward widely extended, peering into the kopjes to right and left, suddenly a shell, like a bolt from the skies, burst in their midst. It was impossible to tell whence it came; the gun that hurled it might be one mile or six miles in front. A part of the mounted rifles were now given a duty to perform that must have tried the nerves of the boldest. They were ordered to advance and draw the enemy's fire; to make targets of themselves that the position of the Boers might be located and their guns unmasked. They moved forward, forward, expecting every moment to hear the boom of the big guns, the "putt-putt-putt" of the "pom-poms," or the crackling of the Mausers. For two miles they advanced until they reached a threatening kopje on their right when from it a shower of bullets rained about them. No one was hit, although they were but a little over two hundred yards from the Boer trenches. They had done the work they were sent forward to do, and wheeling their horses about galloped back to join their column under cover of the fire from a part of their regiment.

The Boers were evidently in force and in their easily protected kopjes had determined to make an effort to stem the onward march of the British. They were the body that the mounted rifles had scattered on the previous day, and were now much stronger in men and guns; but despite their additional big guns and "pom-poms," they could not withstand the heavy and accurate shell-fire of the British, and when they saw the mounted men galloping round their flanks they fled. A number of prisoners were captured, and large quantities of fodder and provisions were found in the position the Boers had deserted, but much to the chagrin of the mounted troops all the big guns and Maxims had been successfully trekked away.

Notwithstanding the fire to which they were exposed and the rapid marches they were compelled to make, the Canadian Mounted Rifles suffered less than might be expected. When the Canadian Infantry crossed from Graspan to Bloemfontein by forced marches the privations were even severer than the fighting and the marching; but the mounted men were much better off; in the saddle from early morning till late at night, it was hard on the horses and many fell by the wayside, but the men fared not so badly. Usually far in advance of the main army and their convoys they had to pick up their food as they went along, and when they could not purchase supplies they did not hesitate to "commandeer" a dinner.

So far the Mounted Rifles had been fortunate; although constantly under fire for the past two days they had to mourn the loss of no comrade. They could hardly hope for such luck on the morrow; to force their way across the Vet river they must needs face a destructive fire. This running fight was not to their taste; a battle requiring dash and daring was what these young soldiers desired.

Into the saddle at daylight, they began scouting once more on the flanks of the main advance, and while reconnoitring a high kopje caught sight of the vast army of Lord Roberts like a mighty serpent winding over the veldt. For miles the infantry and artillery toiled along, the former marked by low thick clouds of dust, the latter by high rolling broken masses. In the rear an endless line coming ever up over the horizon lumbered the huge transport waggons. It was a magnificent spectacle. At least 40,000 men were in the great body, and as they gazed upon it they felt a certain pride in themselves. They were the fighting force which was clearing a way for this great army which would probably not be needed till Kroonstad was reached or even the Vaal had to be crossed.

In the early afternoon they came within sight of the Vet, and found as they expected that the Boers were strongly entrenched. The kopjes on the north side were full of them, and their firemen were placed here and there along the river bank protected by a thick screen of bushes. The Boers were in no hurry to begin the fight and calmly held their fire hoping to entrap some part of the British force. Once more it became the duty of the Canadian Mounted Rifles to advance to the front to draw their fire. When they were within comparatively close range of the enemy's guns shells began to fall along their thinly extended line; and now they had to perform perhaps the hardest task of their South African experience. They were ordered to retire, but to retire at a walk, and so with shells dropping about them they obeyed the order. To hear the detonation of the big gun behind and the almost simultaneous screeching of the projectile through space with the back to the music, is apt to make even a veteran wish to put spurs to his horse.

This movement was the beginning of an interesting fight. The enemy were not only in a strong position, but were in great force, with no fewer than five guns, two of which were evidently 50-pounders, completely outranging the British guns at present on the field. Nothing daunted, General Hutton wheeled his brigade to the left and dashed against the enemy's right. Although subjected to a heavy fire his troops reached the Vet, galloped along the river bed, and cleared the riflemen from their entrenched position, forcing them to fall back to the protection of the northern kopje.

Those big guns that were keeping the main body of the English at bay had to be silenced; and three field batteries of the Royal Horse Artillery escorted by the Guards' Brigade courageously advanced to within range of the shell-fire and an interesting artillery duel went on. The gunners of the Boers

LIEUT. H. C. BORDEN,
Canadian Mounted Rifles, Son of Hon. Dr. Borden, Minister of Militia for Canada, Killed in South Africa, July 16.

CANADIANS LEAVING CAPETOWN FOR THE FRONT, DECEMBER 1st.

dropped shell after shell into the British firing-line, but fortunately their shells as usual did not burst.

While this shell-fire was going on between the opposing forces all along the widely extended front of the enemy, lively skirmishing was taking place, and several times small troops got into tight corners, but in every case extricated themselves without loss. To one small party fell the honors of the day. Lieutenants Turner and Borden were close to the river bank returning the rifle-fire of the Boers from the opposite shore. Their horses had been sent to the rear, and they continued popping away at any spot that looked suspicious. At length the officers, observing a bit of high ground across the river, thought that if they could once gain it they might be able to direct an accurate fire on the opposing riflemen. A call was made for volunteers, and the whole troop wanted to go; but some eight or ten men with the officers were chosen to make the hazardous attempt. They began to ford the river, but were soon beyond their depth, and had to swim for it. Holding their rifles above their heads, the water splashed about them by Mauser bullets, all succeeded in crossing safely, one trooper alone suffering the loss of his rifle. They scrambled up the opposite bank, sought cover and sent two men ahead to reconnoitre, but these men exposed themselves and drew a heavy fire on the little band. The Boers were in excellent shelter and outnumbered the Canadians ten to one, but what the Canadians lacked in number they made up in spirit, and replied to the angry Mausers with such an uninterrupted fire that the Boers dared not show themselves. After the fight had continued for what seemed to them several hours—it was in reality only twenty minutes—a terrific fusilade from their friends swept the Boer position; but so close were they that the bullets intended for the Boers began to spitefully spatter amongst them. There was nothing for it but to retire; this they did without the loss of a man; recrossed the river, found their horses awaiting them, and galloped out of the treacherous range with the loss of only a couple of horses.

The fight was dragging slowly on when two naval 4.7 guns that had been hurried to the front came into action. They were not long in getting the range of the enemy and soon gun after gun was silenced. Within two hours after their arrival the Boers were in flight. The Mounted Infantry dismounted, rushed kopje after kopje and for a radius of three miles the country was cleared of the enemy, while their main army was trekking rapidly towards the Zand River followed by the shells of the "Ocean Cavalry."

It was dark night before the action was finished, and the troopers returned to the camp to have a well-earned rest before beginning the great man hunt at break of day on the morrow.

CHAPTER VII.

CROSSING THE ZAND.

At daylight there was no trace of the Boers left. It was Sunday, but the word was, forward! no time for rest; if the troopers wished to worship they must do it in the saddle. About ninety men of the Rifles under Captain Macdonell had been in the saddle all night endeavoring to cut the Boer line of communication with Kroonstad, in the hope of capturing some of their rolling stock. As usual the mounted infantry scouted in advance on the flank of the column but no enemy was sighted till Smaldeel, a little junction village, was reached. The Boers had just left this place after trekking throughout the night, and as the officers scanned the distant kopjes with their glasses they could see the last of their convoy lumbering over them.

The main column halted, but the mounted men divested themselves of all necessary lumber and galloped on after the retreating enemy. They were to endeavor if possible to keep them from blowing up the railway leading to Kroonstad. They were, however, too late; and all day long they could hear the explosions ahead of them and see the clouds of smoke and showers of stone as culverts were destroyed and bridges wrecked. They had a brisk gallop, a part of them advancing close to the Boer guns which shelled them back, and they returned to camp to wait the arrival of the siege guns without which they would never be able to force a passage across the Zand.

So far the march had been conducted with comparatively little loss; the main army had never been in action, all the fighting had been left to the mounted men and the artillery. The infantry were nevertheless suffering. The mounted men were setting the pace, and the foot-soldiers in their efforts to keep np endured the inevitable hardships of a forced march. Choked with the dust, parched with the heat, shivering with the cold of the winter night—growing colder with each day's march to the high land of the interior—they plodded on sustained by the one word, "Pretoria." They knew they could sweep everything before them, and they would soon have rest and comfort in the very citadel of the enemy. Even if they had to lay siege to it they would be freed from the horror of the daily march.

The main column rested at Smaldeel while Hutton's and Frenches' brigades dashed on towards the Zand. They came up to the enemy and the screen of scouts pushed forward to the dry river bed; but the Boers were ready for them and they met a hot reception from eight or ten guns. Shells were showered into the approaching horsemen. One Creusot apparently mounted on a flat-car was particularly dangerous. It was necssary to retreat, and the mounted rifles went back several miles.

The Boers had now taken the offensive and for a time it looked as if the mounted men composing the advance would have a difficult task to extricate themselves from a perilous position. The most brilliant generals leading the Boers—Botha, De

Wet, and Blake—were pressing hard after them with thousands of men, endeavoring to surround the force, but before they could accomplish this the rest of the mounted infantry and cavalry with some artillery had come up and the Boers halted. When the enemy, dashing forward on the flanks of the British, got within range of the field batteries of the Royal Horse Artillery they were beaten back by an accurate shell-fire.

The next two days were spent in examining the country, picking up prisoners, and preparing for the inevitable fight at the Zand. The main column left Smaldeel at daybreak on the morning of the 9th, and marched to Welgelegen. A part of the mounted rifles were ahead of the Zand reconnoitring the Boer position. It was a strong one, the front of their line extended for many miles and on every important kopje big guns could be seen, while through the glasses solid masses of men in great number could be observed. It was impossible to accurately compute the number of the men, but the experienced scouts reported that there were not fewer than from ten to twenty thousand.

The Mounted Rifles approached to within a mile or two of the trenches when the shells from the kopjes on the north side of the river began to drop among them, and they turned their horses about and leisurely retreated. The main column would now be brought into action on the following day, and cavalry, infantry, and artillery anticipated the greatest battle of the war.

Meanwhile General Ian Hamilton's column which had so distinguished itself at Thaba N'Chu, and which had marched through Winburg on the 5th of the month unopposed was now with the main advance. After a rest of two days they had marched twelve miles to Bloemplaats. A portion of the enemy was located here and the mounted infantry and artillery went ahead and shelled them and chased them from their position and the column bivouacked on the ground won.

On the 9th they knew that a battle had been planned for the morrow; the Boers were sure to be forced back, and if they offered a too stubborn resistance would very probably suffer the fate of Cronje.

French and Hutton were to attack the right and left of the Boers, while the 9th Division in conjunction with the 7th was to press back their centre in an effort to gain Mazel Spruit through which the main force would have to march on its journey to Kroonstad. The 9th Division, in which was the Canadian regiment, was a strong one, consisting of the 19th and 21st Brigades in all over 10,000 men, with six batteries, 36 guns of field artillery, two 5-inch guns and several regiments of mounted men. The 19th Brigade was to lead the attack and the Royal Canadians were to have the honor of leading them into action.

If the Boers had been in equal force a terrific battle would have taken place on the morrow. That night before the Zand at least 45,000 men bivouacked. The Boers, however, had the advantage of natural position. The dry river-bed, the screen of bushes, the kopjes on which they could plant their guns—all were much in their favor; but the British numbers outweighed any of these natural advantages. Besides the English siege-guns were no longer outranged by the enemys' Creusots and Krupps, and their lyddite and shrapnel seldom failed to burst, whereas it was the exception for the

Boer shells, long stored for this war in the armouries of Pretoria, to explode.

The night preceding the battle was cold and hundreds of fires flickered through the darkness as the host lay at rest dreaming of the morrow, or nervously wondering what would be the result of the battle. While it was still dark and cold the "rouse" was sounded, and after a bracing cup of hot coffee and a hurried breakfast of hardtack the stir of preparation for battle spread through the army; neighing horses, trundling guns, the muffled thunder of moving regiments of foot soldiers, these sounds filled the air.

There had been an interesting long range artillery duel between the opposing forces on the previous afternoon, and during the night C and G Companies of the Royal Canadian Regiment had been supporting the guns, and when morning broke they returned to camp to rest. A and H were to escort a part of the artillery during the day so that it was a greatly diminished regiment that began to lead the Brigade into action. There were about 150 men in the firing-line, the remainder being held in reserve. They were, through their experiences at Paardeberg and Thaba N'Chu, veterans in Boer warfare. They knew just how to advance on the foe without exposing themselves, and in the dim dusk of the morning they stealthily moved forward until within 800 yards of the Boer trenches.

The battle began before it was full day by the British big guns sending their shells at the kopjes where the Boer artillery had been located. For a time there was an interchange from these monsters of war, and as the detonations grew more frequent and the whole field could be seen, the infantry were commanded to advance fifty yards and begin firing.

The Boërs had been watching the suspicious line of figures on the distant plain. Suddenly they saw them rise and dash forward at the double; on the instant they sent a shower of bullets amongst them, but the Canadians succeeded in reaching the position to which they were directed with only one casualty. As soon as they had gained cover they began to reply to the rifle-fire in their front.

Now the battle went on in earnest and far and near could be heard the sounds of the struggle; of the movements of the troops but little could be seen. The enemy were absolutely invisible, hidden in their trenches and the river-bed or behind the screen of bushes on the opposite bank. Puffs of smoke from the kopjes that served as a background to the Zand told where the enemy's guns were posted, and on one high kopje two leagues away that commanded the river for miles they could see one of the "Long Toms," a worthy opponent of the naval and siege guns.

The position of the Royal Canadians was as trying as in any of their fights at Paardeberg. Opposed to the 150 men were at least 800 Boers steadily sending bullets right into their lines. Sometimes the fire would slacken, and only an occasional crack would be heard from a deliberate rifleman, but if a Canadian raised his head or changed his position a shower of bullets fell about him. There seemed to be no abatement to the struggle; "pom-pom," Maxim, Howitzer, and field batteries banged away through the long morning, while screaming and bursting shells passed and repassed over their heads. But what they feared most was the spiteful crackle of the rifles in the

LIEUT.-COL. THOMAS PAGE BUTLER, D.C.L., Q.C.

LIEUT.-COL. ALPHONSE D. AUBRY, M.D.

river-bed, and when the volleys rang out they hugged the earth behind their ant-hills and "made themselves as small as possible." For hours this fight went on, but at last in the early afternoon the Boer fire slackened in the river-bed, then only an occasional bullet puffed a quick cloud of dust among the ant-hills.

The Boers had had enough; they could not dislodge the 19th that had so well kept their fire under during the thirsty hours since morning broke, and they were in danger of being themselves surrounded, so they left their trenches, crept up the hill slopes, and hurried away towards Kroonstad. The Canadians then crossed the river while the guns were sending shell after shell into the retreating Boers. Here they bivouacked for the night on the very ground occupied by their enemies during the day. Once more they slept on a field their prowess had helped to win.

Counting the cost of a battle is the saddest part of a soldier's life. Although for the Canadians this fight had been an all day affair, so well had they kept to cover that they had but three men wounded and one killed. Private F. G. W. Floyd was struck by a Mauser bullet and killed almost instantly. Like many another Canadian lad during the past six months, "His remains had to be laid away in a shallow grave, without winding sheet or coffin, by the hands of strangers, and that with but a hurried prayer." Besides these men of the regiment one other, who had suffered their privations and had been under fire with them as often perhaps as any man in the firing-line on that day, was wounded. Of his casualty the official report gives no account, but by his excellent letters and his reflections on the work done at the front and the criticisms of the conduct of the Royal Canadians he fully deserves a place in the honor roll of the Sons of the Dominion in this war. While the action was at its thickest Mr. Stanley M. Brown was hit, and had to be carried to the rear, but his wound was not severe enough to prevent him sending an excellent report of this battle to his paper.

While the infantry led by the Canadian Regiment had pressed back the main force of the Boers from their entrenched position on the Zand, the mounted infantry and cavalry had long since crossed the river far to the west, and were endeavoring to circle round the right flank of the enemy. When a battlefield is spoken about a comparatively limited space is apt to be considered as the area over which the fighting takes place; but with the big guns sending their projectiles for miles, with riflemen able to keep the enemy's fire under at a distance of a mile, with a large force of cavalry trying to break through the lines or surround the wings of the opposing army, the front of a modern battle is a very much extended affair. From east to west on the 10th of May along the Zand river the British occupied a space of probably between thirty and forty miles.

Hutton's and French's Brigades crossed the river in the early morning. The probable strength of the British mounted force was between 7000 and 8000 men; but an enemy is apt to overestimate or underestimate the opposing army in accordance with the state of his feelings. The success of the British in corraling Cronje, and the continued success of the troopers since they started on their march from Bloemfontein made one British horseman look like ten to the Boers. At any rate a report went abroad that not fewer than 20,000 men were working round on the right wing of their army. T. F. Millard, who acted with the Boer army as correspondent of the London Daily Mail, and was therefore in a good position to give an accurate account of the retreat of the Boers, tells the effect of this news of the north bank of the Zand.

"We did not know," he writes, "whether that flanking column was a reality or a mirage. It never got in sight or made its presence felt in any tangible way. But it was a better ally to Lord Roberts than a hundred thousand fresh troops. Whether it existed or not, it became a fixed and certain quantity in the minds of the Boers. From this vision of their imagination they fled, nor could the combined efforts of their Generals stop them."

Botha, Blake, and DeWet all tried to check the mad rush towards the Transvaal, but they might as well have tried to turn back Niagara. A portion of them, despite the overwhelming numbers that Lord Roberts had actually against them, did make a desperate stand, and by protecting the rear of the retreating army for so many hours probably saved a large portion of the fleeing Boers from being made prisoners, and, what was quite as important, their guns from falling into the hands of the British troops.

By this time the Boers were used to running and trekked away with a method even in the madness of this rush. As Mr. Millard says of the stampede: "Its progress was rapid, as retreats go, but deliberate. It drifted steadily along like the current of some turbid but powerful stream."

They had reason to flee; after them came in hot pursuit the cavalry and mounted rifles, Iniskillings and Scots and Natal Carbineers—all eager for slaughter, or to round up a goodly number of prisoners. The day was a hard one on the mounted rifles. They were in the saddle for nearly eighteen hours almost continuously, ever pursuing the foe that ever eluded them. In the early afternoon a party of them came upon a sight that spurred them on to take vengeance on the dastardly enemy in their front. As they rode along keeping careful watch ahead they came upon a number of khaki-clad figures lying at the foot of a kopje.

Some Iniskillings and other troopers had preceded them by but a short time. They had evidently not been scouting properly, believing that no Boers would risk remaining behind the main body. They came upon a Kaffir kraal where the white flag was flying; never doubting its significance they dismounted and were standing in groups holding their horses or advancing to meet the men who were about to surrender, when a shower of bullets swept them. Men fell in heaps, wounded men writhing in the agony of wounds made by the devilish explosive bullets were struck down by tens. The whole party was killed, wounded, or captured, and when the Canadians arrived on the scene they found that the dead and wounded had been robbed, and the latter left to save themselves or to die where they lay. As best they could they attended to those not yet past help and then Colonel Evans with C Squadron galloped on in the track of the brutal murderers. It is little wonder that after this the Canadians talked as coolly of bringing down Boers as they would have spoken of potting partridge.

CHAPTER VIII.

OCCUPYING KROONSTAD.

WHILE the Canadians were resting on the slopes of the Zand, the chase of the enemy still went on. The Boers prayed for night, but it was to give them but little relief. Behind them thundered cannon and over them burst lyddite shells filling the air with their sickening fumes; among them fell the spattering shrapnel, and if they lagged for a moment the ping-ping of the bullets played through their ranks. At last sudden darkness spread over the brown, withered, treeless veldt, and for a brief period the thick mantle of night made them feel safer. But the hunters of men were close behind, and soon the sharp rifle-fire made them urge their horses and veldt-ponies and oxen on still faster. On they went, a great huddle of men and beasts; bumping through ruts and over stones; waggons breaking down and strewing the plains with household goods, animals tumbling exhausted on the plains.

In their efforts to escape they fired the dry grass of the veldt, hoping to flee the easier under cover of the flames and smoke. The night was dark, the moon hidden behind the clouds, and the leaping, running flames added a tragic color to the tragic scene of flight and death.

Kroonstad was in the wildest confusion; burghers were bivouacking in the streets and the squares waiting till dawn to continue their flight. From nearly every house lights shone as the inhabitants packed up their valuables and made ready to go into exile. The Government officials were busy preparing to remove President Steyn's Capital to Lindley, but such an easily moved institution had its destination changed, and the state papers were forwarded to Heilbron.

Meanwhile Botha and De Wet had succeeded in getting some two or three thousand men under control, and when Steyn joined them later with what few men he could induce to stand by him, they were hopeful of being able to make a sufficiently long resistance at Bosch Rand to give those who wished time to get well out of danger. Bosch Rand is a high ridge towering above Kroonstad, giving an excellent natural position from which to oppose the enemy's advance. It had been strengthened by trenches, but when the Boers saw the wide flanks of the army with Generals Tucker and Hamilton on the right, and Generals Hutton and French on the left, sweeping down with a forty-mile front, threatening to surround them, it is not to be wondered at that they did not dare to attempt even from their well-protected ridge to face the huge army of Lord Roberts. There were a few daring spirits, however, in the Boer ranks, and inspired by such leaders as Botha, De Wet, and Colonel Blake of the Irish Brigade, they turned their faces to the British to protect as long as they could the disordered host that was hurrying through Kroonstad.

At noon an occasional shell began to drop along Bosch Rand, while to the east and west the cavalry and mounted infantry were hurrying forward to

OCCUPYING KROONSTAD.

turn the flank of the rear guard. Botha saw his danger. He might at any moment find himself cooped up as was Cronje at Paardeberg. Still he tenaciously held to his position almost till dark, but a dashing charge of the cavalry and lancers drove the Boers from their trenches; and the rear guard, too, put spurs to their horses and rushed to Kroonstad.

Before this happened Botha had seen that Bosch Rand could not long be held, and that the mounted men of the enemy were rapidly surrounding Kroonstad. He knew that an engine with a train of cars attached, the last left, was waiting word from him to steam out of the yards, and so he sent in a message that the enemy were within three miles of the town. On the instant the train that was standing waiting began slowly to roll northward.

While the train was still in the yards, flames began to burst from the station and warehouses, and soon the whole town was as bright as day through the light of the burning buildings. An English battery caught sight of the fugitive cars and trained its guns upon them. All resistance was brushed aside, and another capital of the Free State had fallen.

In that great trek out of Kroonstad there were at least ten thousand men and twenty guns, and this force Botha's strategy alone had saved. The men might have escaped; but for him their guns, ammunition, supplies and rolling-stock would surely have fallen into Roberts' hands.

French with the 1st and 3rd Cavalry Brigades had worked forward close to Kroonstad, and when the dawn broke had the place well surrounded.

The 17th Lancers claimed to be the first men to enter the town, but a part of A Squadron of the Canadian Mounted Rifles under Major Forrester seems to have been at the front too, and simultaneously entered, driving a party of Boers before them. The remainder of the Mounted Rifles had gone back some miles to surround a force of the enemy who had a position on a kopje, and did not have a share in the final rush on Kroonstad; but during the entire day after the Zand River fight they had been skirting round the flank of the Boers who kept well out of range.

The game was up; it was useless to resist: the few shells that had fallen into the town during the night made the authorities, as at Bloemfontein, fear that the appearance of their pretty little town would be sadly disfigured, and so they decided to promptly surrender. While the Field-Marshal was at the drift over the Valsch the Mayor of Kroonstad and a deputation of citizens came out for a conference. The surrender of Bloemfontein was to be repeated; they were ready to yield without firing an opposing shot. The landdrost, however, was the chief official, and with him alone would Lord Roberts confer; and so after considerable delay the landdrost and the entire council came out to him and humbly surrendered the keys of the town.

There was still further delay. The infantry division had not yet reached the Valsch, and the Commander-in-Chief waited till it came up; and then surrounded by his body-guard of Colonials and accompanied by his staff he marched in state into Kroonstad. There were a few Englishmen in the town; some Dutch who had never taken up arms; and many cowards who were now, in the hour

THE OCCUPATION OF KROONSTAD; LORD ROBERTS AND HIS COLONIAL BODYGUARD.

GREATER BRITAIN TO THE SUCCOUR OF THE MOTHER COUNTRY.

This represents our soldiers sleeping on the Veldt beneath the bright African Stars. The rigid sentry guards his sleeping comrades, and over and above him there

OCCUPYING KROONSTAD. 427

of their defeat, ultra-English,—and his advance to the broad market-place was a triumph. Waving of flags, shouting and cheering accompanied him at every step. To one unacquainted with the circumstances of this march it would have seemed that the General was entering an English town in holiday humour.

Not only was the town occupied but it was thoroughly invested as well. Five miles to the the north were Frenchs' troops; on the south-west rested Hutton's brigade; and about five miles to the south-east on the banks of the Valsch river were bivouacked the "Fighting Nineteenth."

That the British troops would win was a foregone conclusion, but the speed with which the work was done amazed even the war-critics of Europe, and actually won from the Germans words of praise. It was Roberts of Kandahar once more; even greater on this march, for he had forced forward an army of 50,000 men with the swiftness of a Cavalry Brigade. The march, too, had been made with but few casualties; some regiments, such as the Canadian Mounted Rifles which bore the brunt of the fighting, not losing a single man. No wonder "Bobs" was the idol of England; a general who can win almost bloodless battles could not but be dear to the anxious hearts across the ocean.

During the last two days the Royal Canadians had been having a good deal of work without much chance for glory. A and G Companies had gone forward some miles on the night of the 10th, as escort to the 5-inch guns. At daybreak on the following morning four companies marched from their bivouac to join them, while the remaining two C and D stayed behind at the drift over the Zand acting as rear-guard to the slow moving convoy of waggons. All day the regiment marched, anxious to catch up with the main army, and thoroughly tired out went into bivouac towards evening at Moorplats. The next day they started out again at dawn and tramped on till the Valsch was reached and they were within sight of Kroonstad, which for some hours had had the Union Jack waving over the landdrost's office.

These last two days had been particularly trying on the men and numbers fell out. The draft which had joined them only a few days before had suffered most. As the Herald correspondent has pointed out it was too bad that the men sent to Africa to fill the gaps in the regiment were not selected with better judgment. Raw youths for the most part; they had not the powers of endurance of men of maturer years.

The First Contingent was a weak looking skeleton of its former self, notwithstanding the draft of almost a hundred men which had been added to it six days before. Its strength was now only 480, and of 45 officers only 23 were left. Even if it had been possible to continue the advance at once the Royal Canadians would have had to rest for a day or two; and so they stayed until the 15th at Bosch Rand. The records of the regiment show, too, that it was not only the march that was playing havoc with its strength; from Kroonstad 30 sick men were sent back to Bloemfontein.

The Canadian Mounted Rifles had done their share of fighting. General Hutton and General French were as dashing mounted leaders as any men could desire, and they seemed to rival each other in taking all they could, and a little more, out

OCCUPYING KROONSTAD. 429

of both horses and men. It was therefore welcome tidings to the men of the Canadian Squadrons that they were to spend a quiet Sunday at Kroonstad. The strength of both battalions was greatly weakened and the horses needed the rest even more than the troopers. The 700 miles through Carnarvon, Prieska, Kenhart, De Aar and Bloemfontein would have told on horses of steel; and when the severe advancing and retreating, dashing over the rough veldt by night and day, ever miles in advance of the main column, fighting hot fights when even the sound of their guns could not reach the host that was marching steadily, steadily on Kroonstad—when this is considered the wonder is that they had a horse left—almost as great a wonder as that in all their skirmishes from Bloemfontein to Kroonstad not a man had been killed and only six were wounded.

While waiting at Kroonstad for the general advance to begin once more the Canadian Mounted Rifles had several interesting outings. The white flag trick had been practised on a small party of British troops, and three squadrons were sent out to a farmhouse at Jordan's Siding where the crime occurred to investigate. They found four British dead, and in their just anger burnt the house to the ground.

On the 15th at five o'clock in the afternoon just as night was beginning to settle down on the veldt, 50 men from each of the two battalions of mounted rifles and 100 men from the First Mounted Infantry were ordered to saddle up for a rapid night dash. The 200 men galloped through the long hours of darkness, searching farmhouses wherever they were likely to find any of the enemy. When close to a farmhouse the body of the troop halted, held itself in readiness while a dozen or so horsemen dashed forward with revolvers cocked ready to shoot down anyone who attempted to escape from the suspected dwelling. The man hunt was a most successful one; they captured no fewer than twenty-seven of the enemy, and among the prisoners were a commandant, several field cornets, and four members of the Johannesburg Mounted Police. For seventeen hours they advanced through the darkness without off-saddling, and when at last they halted for a brief four hours rest, they had covered in all sixty miles. Even General De Wet would have had difficulty in beating this performance. When they returned to camp it was with considerable pride that General Hutton heliographed the splendid feat to Lord Roberts.

On the 15th, too, the forward movement re-commenced. The Winburg column under General Ian Hamilton moved out from Kroonstad, marching almost due east, and as a part of this column the Royal Canadians left Bosch Rand. They had had a rest of nearly three days and they needed it much for the work that was before them. Although on this first day they covered but six miles, until they crossed the Vaal they were to endure the same exhausting marches, the same privations that they had endured up to Kroonstad, with the additional hardship of having to sleep in the open with chill autumn fogs rising from the ponds by which they bivouacked.

CHAPTER IX.

CROSSING THE VAAL.

FOR the first three days of the northward march the 19th Brigade encountered nothing of peculiar interest. On the 18th they had so far outstripped their convoy that they were forced to rest until it could catch up. On this day the first exciting incident of the march occurred. Some of the soldiers were approaching a farmhouse with a white flag floating over it, when from a concealed position near by, the sharp crackling of a number of Mausers was heard, followed by the singing of the bullets among them. They retreated, and then a body of soldiers went forward to loot and destroy the place, but they found only women and children in possession. These claimed that they had nothing to do with the treachery, and as the Canadian soldiers were not making war against women they were allowed to remain in possession of their farmhouse—no doubt very much to their surprise. It would not do, however, to let the offense go wholly unpunished, and so the soldiers took what food they could find without paying the fancy prices usually asked by the Boers.

Meanwhile the 21st Brigade trekked on to Lindley, and, without any opposition other than an occasional badly aimed bullet from a Boer sniper, almost completely surrounded the town.

Commandant Piet De Wet was in the vicinity, and as soon as the 21st got comfortably bivouacked in the wretched village which had so narrowly escaped being a Free State Capital, began to harass the English. He industriously sent small parties of troops hither and thither against the British lines, endeavoring to shoot or capture the outposts and patrols; and he was eminently successful in his work. A graver danger was, however, threatening this force. It was learned that an army of Boers was assembling on the south, and that just as soon as it was reinforced with big guns would advance on Lindley. Several of the commandos were likewise massed on the north-west. Lindley was becoming a very warm corner, and as there were in all over three thousand Boers with five or six long-range cannon about it, and as it was of no strategical importance, it was decided to move northward at once on Heilbron.

While the 21st was taking such risks in Lindley the 19th had passed by the village without entering it and gone forward to Quaggafontein. The general advance of the Winburg column on Heilbron, some forty miles to the north, began at once. They had got but seven miles from Lindley when De Wet engaged the rear guard. He did not risk coming to close quarters, but watched the mounted flanks, and at every opportunity threw forward small parties who did very effective work. Several troopers were shot, a number wounded, and a few taken prisoners. It was tantalizing to have him hanging about the rear, but it would not do to stop the advance to attempt to bring him to a general engagement. He simply had to be endured.

A more serious affair awaited them at Karroo

Spruit. A lofty ridge, easily protected, loomed up before the column, and as the mounted men stole cautiously forward examining the kopjes they were met by a heavy fire. The Boers were there in considerable numbers, and for a time had checked the British advance; but soon the dashing work of the Household Cavalry and the 10th Huzzars on the flanks of their position frightened them and they fled. When the troops mounted the ridge they could see their long line of waggons trekking north with all possible speed. The guns had not yet come up, and the escape was made without much loss. Had the artillery but kept pace with the cavalry the whole of the convoy might have been captured. It was not until they were well on their northward road that a 5-inch gun got to the summit of the ridge and sent shells after them over a distance of nearly six miles.

The way was clear and with the Boer snipers hanging like so many wasps on the flanks and rear the column bivouacked two miles north of Karroo Spruit. A nineteen miles march relieved by a brisk little fight; not a bad day's work. But there was to be no rest; at dawn next morning they started out again and reached Witpoort a short distance south of Heilbron, and early on the following day arrived at a ridge overlooking the prosperous little town. Opposition was expected; it was never thought that Steyn would desert the last capital he could ever expect to hold on this earth without making a vigorous stand. He had been in the town two days before; but had concluded that it would be useless to make further resistance in the Free State, and so had packed up his capital and had moved it with him across the

Vaal. For the future matters were somewhat simplified; one capital was to answer the purposes of both presidents.

Heilbron was entered at noon on the 22nd. Boers were seen, but seen running, as the General and his staff with flags flying and bands playing took possesssion of the last important town in the Free State. The 21st had had the honor of entering Lindley, it now fell to the lot of the 19th with the Royal Canadians leading to follow immediately behind the General into this substantial little town of about two thousand inhabitants.

Despite the hardships they were enduring the Canadians were buoyant in spirit: at every step they were nearing Pretoria and each day won from their commanders words of praise. They had long known the worth of their own officers and of their Brigade Commander Smith-Dorrien, and they had now learned to esteem General Ian Hamilton next to "Bobs."

The Boers were now fleeing in force and as their long train of waggons climbed the grassy ridges, withered and brown from the autumn frosts, an attempt was made to capture their entire convoy. While the Infantry took possession of the town, and the Canadians were being placed on guard at the principal buildings, the cavalry and artillery galloped in pursuit. The mounted men were shelled back, but the horse artillery thundered into range unlimbered and by brilliant work succeeded in capturing some fifteen of the enemy's heavily laden waggons: later in the day several more were added to the list. Not only had the Boers failed to stop the British advance, but had themselves been dealt a severe blow. No more loitering now in the

LIEUT.-COL. JULIEN BROSSEAU.

LIEUT.-COL. A. DENIS.

path of the English guns: on to the Vaal they fled for their lives.

The halt at Heilbron was to be a very short one. The occupation of neither Lindley nor Heilbron had been any real part of the forward movement. The Winburg column had been sent out to cut off commandos reported to be hurrying north from Senekal to Heilbron to the support of Steyn. It would be a waste of men to occupy Heilbron, and so on the 23rd the advance began again. A few sick men, however, were left behind, among them Captain-Surgeon Fiset, who was down with enteric.

The British now moved towards the west to join the main column in its advance on the Transvaal Capital, and as soon as they were out of Heilbron the Boer commandos, which had been hanging about the rear, entered the place, engaging their rear guard and succeeding in cutting off several of their waggons. The sick men were well treated by the Boers who learned from Captain-Surgeon Fiset what an excellent Government the French lived under in far Canada.

The following day was the Queen's Birthday, and on this occasion it was to be celebrated by a stiff march of from fifteen to twenty miles. It was dark before a halt was called and few of the soldiers had thoughts for anything save the meal they were forced to make out of commandeered flour. Through the darkness, however, the strains of the National Anthem welled forth, and the tired soldiers raised their voices in a mighty chorus; and then the fifteen thousand men of the column burst forth into one great cheer that shook the veldt.

The main column had now been three days on the road, and on the morrow as the Winburg column crossed the railway line at Prospect they saw in the distance a moving cloud of dust and above it floated a great war-balloon. Once more they became a part of the body of soldiers immediately under Lord Roberts. By mere mass this army of 50,000 men was pressing everything before them. Boers might hang about isolated brigades, or attack remote parts of the line of communication, or even face the squadrons that fought in advance of the army, but it was only at their strongest positions that they dare stand for a moment against this sweeping sea of men. No danger of further conflict till the Vaal was reached, but it was fully expected that a stubborn resistance would be made at the drifts and among the kopjes of that difficult river.

On the morrow as they were advancing on the Vaal they were gladdened by the tidings that Colonel Otter was approaching with the convoy. Colonel Buchan had been an ideal commander but to most of the men the regiment had seemed incomplete for the past month, without the brave and considerate leader who had watched over it during its hardest days. He had grown in his absence in the esteem of the men, despite the memory of his strict discipline, and the scar he carried, the badge of his courage, added to the affection in which he was held. His coming, too, was a boon to the soldiers. He brought with him in the face of the greatest difficulties and much opposition on the part of the commissariat department, warm serge jackets, good thick underclothing, caps and socks and boots. The Transvaal winter was descending upon them, they would now be able to face it with less fear.

CROSSING THE VAAL.

No rest, however, to enjoy these things: On to Pretoria! That afternoon the Vaal was reached, and the Canadians were the leading regiment. The scouts brought in word that the way was clear, the Boers had fled before the flanking troopers and though a small army might have checked a host at Wonderwater Drift, not even a sniper was among the kopjes to alarm the British. The Vaal was cold and deep; no bridge was near, and the Canadians plunged into the chilly water and led the army into Kruger's land. Shivering and wet they climbed the opposite bank, the first of Lord Roberts' infantry to set foot in the Transvaal. If their bodies were damp, their spirits were not; and as they realized that they were in the Transvaal, they gave a sturdy Canadian cheer. That night they dried themselves by the fires at the bivouac a short distance from the banks of the Vaal.

Still they pushed forward and on the 28th after two bitterly cold nights Syferfontein was reached. All day the sound of distant guns reached their ears. The enemy were at last making a stand. They had heard much of, "The act that would stagger humanity;" they had expected that an attempt would be made at the Vaal to fulfil the threat; from the heavy and continuous firing they began to think that perhaps this was the prelude to the act.

For the present they waited in arms ready to cut off the retreating Boers if they should be driven back by Hutton and French who were hotly engaging them along the Klip River.

The Royal Canadian Regiment of Infantry had been days on the march before the Canadian Mounted Rifles got orders to advance towards the

Vaal. It was not till the morning of the 20th that Hutton's Division saddled up for the dash that was to end only at Johannesburg. It was the most serious movement of the war, and before departing they attended a mounted church parade held by Father Sinnett of Montreal. There was a solemnity and picturesqueness about this religious service in the chill of the autumn morning that deeply impressed the men. After the service General Hutton warned them of the nature of the work they were proceeding on. They must expect the hardest march of their lives. They were to be followed by Lord Roberts' main army, and he would spare neither man nor beast in his efforts to clear the way for the advance on Pretoria—and he kept his word.

The days had now grown very short, and much of the marching had to be done through the darkness. But forward they went, shivering with the cold, their blankets and overcoats wholly inadequate to keep them warm. At times the veldt was so rough and rutty that it was a common thing for the troopers to find themselves sprawling on all fours, thrown from their stumbling horses. They expected to meet the Boers at Rhenoster's Spruit, but the frightened enemy had fled before their advance.

The hardest day they endured was the 24th of May. Between Hutton and French there seems to have been considerable rivalry and both were anxious to have the glory of first invading Transvaal territory. It became known that French would reach it on the Queen's Birthday, and so an effort was made to push the 9th Division across the Vaal on the same day. It would no doubt have

MAJOR DONALD CAMERON FORSTER BLISS.

MAJOR HIRAM BENDER.

been an excellent thing to do, but under the circumstances was a very foolish thing to attempt. The "rouse" sounded at 4.30 and after a hot cup of coffee to drive away the night's chills, and a breakfast of tough meat, the advance began while darkness was still struggling with day. The country was a rough one; on account of the convoy the march was slow, and when darkness fell in the late afternoon they were still some miles from the Vaal. Wisdom dictated a bivouac but sentiment said forward. On through the thick darkness they pressed, and the bumping, tumbling, creaking noisy transport waggons struggled to keep up. The troops far outstripped them and at length were forced to bivouac in sight of the Transvaal, without food and with but the bedding they carried on their saddles.

If the enemy had but have been on the alert they could have smashed the convoy and added another disaster to the British army; but both the troops and the transports remained unmolested till morning, and then crossed the Vaal at Lindeque Drift without even so much as a solitary Boer Rifleman to snipe at them as they advanced. General French had been doing effective work ahead, and the Boers were falling back with all possible speed on Johannesburg. So the British advance-guard gained a point almost within sight of the mines of the Gold City without having met with any opposition. However the Boers still hoped to keep the British out of Johannesburg, and a hard battle would have to be fought before the Union Jack would be raised over the city of the Uitlander.

CHAPTER X.

INTO THE GOLD CITY.

FIGHTING was imminent. On the 28th the Canadian Mounted Rifles crept up to the crest of the range of hills overlooking a broad valley through which wound a quiet stream, and a road to Johannesburg. Several miles away on the opposite side was another range. In these the Boers were posted. It was a strong position and effectually barred the way to the Gold City. At first this was not realized, and the advance was pushed over the little bridge at Olifants Vlei.

The British rushed their guns to the top of the ridge and began to throw shells across the valley, but the range was too great and they fell short, and so the troops advanced to the broad meadow skirting the winding river.

The enemy had several big guns in the Klipriversberg Range and among them one "Long Tom," which far outranged the Horse Artillery guns. It was necessary to get their location and before noon a troop of thirty men advanced towards the enemy's position. They succeeded in unmasking the enemy's guns, and met with a hot reception from shell, "pom-pom," and rifle; but succeeded in galloping to cover without losing a man. This shell-fire was to continue for the rest of the day. Troops and convoy alike came in for their share.

A part of the Mounted Rifles were now given a task that thoroughly tried the men. Two kopjes connected by a high ridge commanded a view of the bridge and the meadow. The range of these kopjes the enemy had to a foot; but for the purposes of the advance it was most important that they should be occupied. C and D Squadrons, some New Zealanders, and a battery of the Royal Horse Artillery were sent forward to seize and hold this position. It was a hot spot, where shells fell and with great accuracy; but fortunately for the most part failed to explode, angrily burying their copper noses in the ground. The troopers, too, found shelter, and took it so well that among the Canadians on this day only one man was wounded, and that but slightly.

So important were these kopjes that orders were sent to Colonel Evans in command of the squadrons to hold them during the night.

At dawn they looked towards the opposite hills; the "Bloomin' Door-Knocker" was silent; the "Long Tom" had apparently withdrawn, and not a crack of a Mauser was to be heard. The enemy, they began to think, had stolen away in the night as on former occasions, and in this thought they were enjoying a hastily prepared breakfast. Suddenly the "putt-putting" of the "pom-pom" fell on their ears and simultaneously a succession of spiteful little shells fell in their midst scattering their fires and sending pots and food in the air.

On the previous day the general had seen what folly it would be to try to force the Klipriversberg hills, and had determined to withdraw his army and continue turning the flank of the enemy on the left. Hutton was no doubt cogitating the words of the American military attache with Buller on the Tugela: "Well, now, was there no way round?"

There was a way round this time, but the little company on the kopjes had to bear the battle while the army that had advanced over the bridge retired to take that way. They had, moreover, to let the enemy see that they were holding the position, and so frequently during the day parties of them would gallop along the ridge in full view of the Boers, inviting their fire. And the invitation was never refused; big shells and little shells hurtled amongst them, and on one occasion they even drew the rifle-fire of the Boers.

Meanwhile the main army under shelter of the fire from the kopjes was withdrawing across the bridge. It took three hours to complete the hazardous work, but was successfully accomplished. Hutton's division had had a narrow escape. If the Boers could once have got possession—and it would have been no difficult task—of the kopjes held by the Canadian Mounted Rifles, they could have swept the British army with a destructive fire. The order to withdraw was pleasant news to the troops who had been for two days exposed to the heavy shell-fire; but they were so accustomed to the shells by this time that they made the withdrawal as if on parade.

A and B Squadrons under Colonel Lessard had had their share of work, and although not exposed to the same steady shelling as the Second Battalion they had had both "pom-poms" and big shells dropping at intervals amongst them during the day. B Squadron had been exposed to a particu-

INTO THE GOLD CITY.

larly severe shelling on two occasions when it passed from its position to the support of C and D, and when it was ordered back almost immediately to its original place. The "pom-poms" played viciously on the troopers, as John Ewan said, "They worked over time;" but then the "pom-pom" was never designed to kill.

The retirement had puzzled the enemy, and before they could recover from their surprise they found the column hammering away at their flank, and fearing being surrounded fell back towards Johannesburg, and the advance was continued for ten miles in a north-westerly direction.

On the night of the 29th they marched through the darkness over the rough and difficut region of Doornkop made famous by the ill-starred Jameson Raid, and when morning broke found themselves with practically a clear road to Johannesburg. In the distance the stamp-mills of the Gold City and the towering smoke-stacks loomed up before them, and they felt as if the city were theirs.

They saw more than distant Johannesburg; they caught sight of a Boer convoy trekking away as fast as the drivers could urge forward their beasts. The convoy was in charge of some fifty men, and Lieutenant Borden and thirteen troopers started in pursuit. When within rifle range, they dismounted and did such effective work that three of the waggons were unable to proceed and were left a prize to the venturesome Canadians.

While the Canadian Mounted Rifles were winning laurels at Klipriversberg their fellow-countrymen of the Royal Canadian Regiment of Infantry were doing good work among the ridges of Doornkop. At this place one of the severest struggles and most costly to the British arms in the South African war took place.

There was poetic justice in having one of the climactic struggles of the war take place among the kopjes where Jameson's raiders came to grief; just as there was poetic justice in having the first great Boer reverse, the capture of Cronje, the turning point of the war, take place on Majuba Day.

While the mounted infantry under Hutton had been fighting so effectively at Klipriversberg the 21st and 19th Brigades came in for their share of work in this Doornkop region. The Boers were discovered in force with heavy artillery, checking the advance on Roodepoort and Florida. They had between two and four thousand men, and not fewer than six guns together with a number of "pom-poms." The British had suddenly come upon a difficult position, but there was nothing to do but fight, and that under the most trying circumstances.

Once more the Royal Canadian Regiment of Infantry was to take part in a general engagement, and once more it was to share the honors of the day with the brave and dashing Highlanders. The Boers were in a strong position to oppose this well-planned attack, and with the shrewdness that had marked their tactics from the commencement of the war they had made it doubly strong. The khaki uniform of the British soldiers had in previous fights served as natural protection on the brown veldt. At long range it was almost impossible to catch sight of the thinly extended line of earth-colored figures, and they as often fired at ant-hills and rocks as at men. But they had resolved that on this occasion if the British did succeed in driving them from their trenches they would pay dearly for their success. For several miles along their front they had set fire to the veldt, dry with the autumn frosts, and the British as they moved forward saw before them rolling slopes of fire and smoke, ridges along which ran spurts of fire, and broad stretches black with a deadly blackness. The khaki uniforms which had protected them in the past stood out on this black background an excellent target for the sharp-shooters making a last determined effort to keep the " rooineks " from entering the Gold City.

The 19th advanced in extended order, the Canadians in four lines. As the infantry moved forward the 5-inch guns and two batteries began to send well-directed shells over their heads at the Boer position. The British force was still several miles from the enemy's lines when shells began to scream through the smoky air and bury their noses in the blackened plain, fortunately bursting but seldom. Still the advance continued; that distant ridge guarding the way to Johannesburg had to be won before nightfall. A mile was crossed under this shell-fire, and still another mile of blackened veldt intervened when sharp and deadly the shrill Mauser bullets began to sing among the advancing soldiers. Through clouds of smoke, through belts of fire, across broad black stretches, the men hurried, reserving their fire. At length a Kaffir hut surrounded by a stone kraal was reached. This spot afforded excellent shelter and over two hundred of the Canadian Regiment took cover in this safe position, and for the rest of the afternoon poured a most effective fire into the enemy's ranks.

The Boers made an attempt to flank the right of

the Brigade, but the Canadian Maxim gun was in a good position and foiled their attempt. So till darkness began to fall the Canadians poured volley after volley into the trenches where the enemy seemed thickest; so till darkness was approaching the shells from the big guns and the quick-fire guns screamed and roared across the grim battleground.

The Gordons, however, bore the brunt of the fight. Their position was the most difficult on the field; they had but little shelter and their men fell in great numbers. The men of Dargai, however, were worthy of their reputation, and when General Smith-Dorrien sent in word that the Boers must be cleared from the ridge by nightfall they fixed bayonets, and with wild, reckless dash moved forward on the enemy's main position and scattered them before their impetuous charge. But they paid dearly for their bravery; twenty gallant fellows in the regiment were killed and seventy wounded—almost a sixth of their entire force in the fight.

In this final charge the Canadians played their part. When the cheer loud and long told that the main position had been stormed by the Highlanders the Canadians were ordered to advance on the double and drive the Boers from the trenches immediately in front. At their approach the enemy fled, they dreaded the cold steel, and when the Canadians breasted the height through a belt of fire and smoke they found that the enemy were galloping away in confusion towards Johannesburg.

They thus brought to a close a hard day's fighting. Their loss had been small, only seven men wounded. It was once more the luck of the Canadians, and the extended order which had saved them; but for the thirty paces between the men and the one hundred and fifty between the

INTO THE GOLD CITY. 451

lines the heavy shell-fire to which they were exposed and the steady rifle-fire which they had to face as they climbed the slope towards the ridge, would have found many a victim.

At 4.30 next morning they were under arms and started for Florida five miles away, where they got meat and groceries, but as the convoy had not yet caught up they were without flour or biscuits. Starving, cold, ragged, but happy. They had helped clear the way into the Gold City, whose mines and public buildings, despite the many threats of the Boers, were intact.

On the following day, May 31, the city was surrendered and Lord Roberts made his triumphal entry. The streets towards the suburbs were largely deserted and the stores and houses barricaded for the most part; but as the troops marched towards the public buildings the crowds gathered.

Soon from many flag-staffs, from the principal buildings floated the Union Jack, and, as Barnes tersely puts it, "Johannesburg was English.

For the present but few of the soldiers of the Royal Canadian Regiment of Infantry or the Canaeian Mounted Rifles, who had fought so hard and endured so much to reach Johannesburg, were to enter it. But the few who did saw a strangely new city, a city that had risen from the plains in less than twenty years, a city of about one hundred and fifty thousand inhabitants, a city with tall chimneys and staring factories, with piles of refuse from which the gold had been crushed, a city without churches, a city of saloons. A wicked, greedy, worldly city; and for this city they had crossed seven thousand miles of ocean, and climbed another thousand miles of veldt and kopje.

CHAPTER XI.

ON TO PRETORIA.

AFTER the surrender of Johannesburg the Canadian troops rested in their bivouacs some miles from the city, and waited for what they deemed would be the last stage of the war, the march on Pretoria. They rested quietly until Sunday, the Royal Canadian Regiment of Infantry at Braemfontein, and the Canadian Mounted Rifles close to the dynamite factory at Sandfontein. The fighting, marching, and privations of the advance from Kroonstad had thoroughly exhausted the men of both regiments, and but few had energy enough to journey into the city of the Uitlander. Indeed they had lost interest in South Africa, and were now thinking only of helping in the final struggle of the war, and hoping for a swift return to Canada via England. They all wanted to see the heart of the Empire for which they had been fighting.

On account of lack of supplies the entire army of forty thousand men was forced to wait in the vicinity of Johannesburg until Sunday, June 3. On that day the last great march of the army began, and the whole world was expectant of "the deed that would stagger humanity." While Lord Roberts' main army advanced rapidly along the road leading to Pretoria the Royal Canadians with Ian Hamilton's column left their bivouac at

ON TO PRETORIA. 453

Braemfontein and marched in a north-west direction over a rough stretch of country. That same morning Hutton's Brigade left Sandfontein, and the Canadian Mounted Rifles were only a few miles ahead of the Royal Canadians and were proceeding on the left flank of their column.

There was an unnatural calm on that June Sabbath. The British troops were rapidly nearing the seat of Government of the Boers, and yet they toiled past kopje, over ridge, and through easily-guarded passes and no shot was fired to check their advance. The enemy were not going to waste their men, but were concentrating their forces in the forts and among the hills in the midst of which Pretoria nestled. So thought the advancing troops, and as they marched they remembered the stories that had come to them of the strength of the Transvaal capital, and braced themselves for a hard fight and a long one.

Hillegas' description of the strength of Pretoria has already been given, but as late as March a more terrifying account of the capital of the Transvaal "asleep back of mountain-walls and the frowning guns of seven modern forts" was going the rounds of the press and was familiar to many in the army now boldly advancing on this impregnable position.

All day Sunday the columns advanced without opposition and the soldiers had ample time to brood over the stories that had reached them about the hot reception they were to receive at Pretoria. On Monday the Canadian Mounted Rifles began to expect trouble; the advance grew more arduous, and the drifts and kopjes more dangerous. At one drift they spent an hour toiling across; waggons stuck in mid-stream, waggons broke down and were overturned; and when at last all were safely over, cavalry transport and mounted infantry transport were sadly mixed, but the word was, "On to Pretoria!"

French's force scented danger ahead, and in the afternoon came on the enemy strongly entrenched with big guns and "pom-poms" ready to check the advance, and for a moment the British thought that the deed that was to stagger humanity was about to begin. The cavalry had gone forward to unmask the guns, and so close did they approach the enemy that they came under a heavy musketry fire. The artillery were rushed into action; the big naval guns drawn by teams of twenty bullocks each presented an exceptionally fine spectacle as they moved forward to points of vantage. The guns were quickly unlimbered and a rapid shower of shells sent against the Boers to cover the advance of the cavalry; but French found the fire too hot and had to retire his force.

When the cavalry found themselves under the close fire from the enemy's Mausers and Martinis, French sent for the assistance of Hutton's Brigade, and the Second Battalion of Canadian Mounted Rifles under Colonel Evans had the honor of being sent forward to help clear the way into Pretoria.

A line of kopjes covered the road along which the army was advancing, and the enemy on these kopjes effectively stopped the forward movement. The Canadians were ordered to seize these kopjes, and so dismounting they sent their horses to the rear and extending, carefully advanced upon the difficult position. They were now adepts at Boer warfare, and from shelter to shelter they crept and rushed with the bullets falling about them, but hitting no man, till they reached the foot of the kopje. The fire was now hot and dangerous; it was impossible to advance farther, and so for over an hour they lay in their sheltered positions while Boer guns answered British guns from height to height. The fire slackened towards evening and a little after 4 o'clock the Canadians slowly began to wend their way up the principal kopje, and when darkness fell the height was theirs. But the wily Boers were trekking away to Pretoria to add their guns to the number already in the impregnable city. The early darkness of winter prevented the British from continuing the pursuit, and so cavalry and Mounted Infantry bivouacked for the night.

The 19th Brigade was likewise playing its part in this advance. The Gordons were extended and under fire, but the Royal Canadians remained behind guarding the baggage, and while on this duty they had the pleasure of witnessing the West Australian Mounted Infantry, the Australian Lancers, and Saxe's Mounted Infantry in hot pursuit of a large body of thoroughly terrified Boers.

To the disappointment of the troops, and the amazement of the world, it was learned on the morrow that there was to be no more fighting about Pretoria. All along the line of advance on the 4th a feeble resistance had been made by the Boers, but the artillery and dashing cavalry and mounted infantry had scattered the enemy and driven them back, chasing them within range of their awe-inspiring forts. The naval guns for a time sent shells against the cordon of f rs about the valley city, but these forts about nich so much had been said and written spoke not. Humanity was staggered at their unnatural silence. Millions of dollars had been expended on them; the military world was anxiously expectant of the resistance they would offer to the British guns, but the Boer had such a distaste for having his property destroyed that, as at Bloemfontein, Kroonstad, and Johannesburg, he was prepared to surrender practically without firing a shot.

During the night the Boers made ready to surrender to Lord Roberts, and early on the following morning the whole British force moved to within a couple of miles of the city and waited for the triumphal entry which was to take place at 2 o'clock in the afternoon. At the hour appointed the Field-Marshal took up his position in front of the Government buildings, and the silken flag that had floated over Bloemfontein, Kroonstad and Johannesburg was run up amidst the cheering of the troops and the wild shouting of the British officers freed that day from the "Bird Cage." As the long line of troops marched past with bayonets fixed the band of the Derby's struck up "The Boys of the Old Brigade," and the tired, hungry, footsore men forgot their suffering. The goal was reached; Pretoria was theirs; the end of the war at last; homeward on the morrow.

But they were to meet with disappointment. Commandant-General Botha's resistance in the hills south of Pretoria had been but to gain time to remove his guns from the city and to get the rolling stock from the railway yards. He had succeeded in taking everything of value with him, and the British found an orderly town, a comfortable, clean, pious town, with a few harmless Boers in the streets, with curious, unshapely women gazing from doors and windows, with many blacks in every quarter; but they had captured no prisoners, and the guns of the enemy were being hurried away to batter at the lines of communication, and from the fastnesses among the hills to assist in picking off unwary and isolated companies of British soldiers. Many of the troops now in Pretoria had seen shell-battered Kimberley; some had been at the relief of Ladysmith, and remembered the starved, fever-smitten heroes, who had beaten back the Boers for months; all had heard of the heroic resistance of Mafeking so lately relieved, and as they looked on this city, strong as Gibraltar, and yet deserted by its guardians, they rejoiced that they were Britons and not Boers.

The Canadian Mounted Rifles were not in the march-past,—indeed the majority of the Mounted Corps were doing duty outside of the city on June 5,—but on the following day they marched through the quiet and orderly streets and out to Silverton, where they were to have a brief rest and to wait for re-mounts (over forty cent. of their horses were unfit for service) before going in pursuit of Botha.

On June 5, when it was decided to break up the 19th Brigade, the following order, issued by the Major-General at Pretoria was read with pride by the different regiments.

"The 19th Brigade has achieved a record of which any infantry might be proud. Since the date it was formed, Feb. 12, 1900, it has marched 620 miles, often on half rations and seldom on full. It has taken part in the capture of ten towns, fought ten general actions and on 27 other days. In one period of thirty days it fought on 21 of them, and marched 327 miles.   Casualities between 400 and 500, defeats, nil."

The Royal Canadians had two days' rest in Pretoria, where it was very hard indeed to realize that they were in a conquered city. It seemed to many of them as it seemed to James Barnes that, " It could'nt be Pretoria—this quiet little town with its churches and public buildings, its open shops, its watering-carts spraying the dusty streets, its English signs, and tennis-courts and flower-gardens." But it was Pretoria, and they had only to look at their parade state to see what it had cost them to reach this quiet town. Of the splendid regiment that had landed in Cape Town only twenty-seven officers and 411 men were able to answer to roll call on June 7. From the Cape to Pretoria their comrades lay in hospital; from Orange River to Pretoria the gloomy mounds of stones surmounted by rude crosses dotting the veldt, told the price that the Canadian Regiment had paid to win its way to the city of the Boer.

CHAPTER XII.

WINDING UP THE WAR.

AFTER the men of C Battery arrived in South Africa they had a long waiting time in Cape Colony, but on Good Friday they received orders to embark for Beira from which place they were to hurry by forced marches to the relief of Mafeking.

Their guns, waggons, and horses were loaded on the steamer Columbian, and after an uneventful journey the "dirty sand beach" known as Beira was reached. From this place they journeyed through a most picturesque country in flat-cars to Marandellas in Mashona Land.

It was Roberts' plan to have them join their forces with Colonel Plumer's little army which had been in the vicinity of Mafeking for several months, and with Colonel Mahon's force which was hurrying forward from Fourteen Streams. When united a swift rush was to be made against the besieging commandoes. From Marandellas to Buluwayo the distance is about 300 miles, and this distance had to be made in eight days. General Sir F. Carrington had made the most complete arrangements to have the force coached across the fever-haunted region between Marandellas and Buluwayo, and at least a part of C Battery would be at Mafeking on scheduled time.

When departing from Marandellas Major Hudon

decided to leave two guns behind with the transport, while the remaining four were to hasten forward with the coaches. Mules took the place of horses, and then the long line of coaches and guns began their march towards Buluwayo. At Buluwayo they were delayed for twenty-four hours, and then southward they went by rail for three days, and once more detrained to begin the final stage of the march. The battery was directed towards the Molopo River, and on its route was to join with Colonel Plumer's men.

It was a welcome sight to the gallant colonel on the 14th of May, this small force of Canadians trekking towards his base camp. They were hot and tired after a trying march through bush and sand, and rested till the following day when they once more began their journey towards the Molopo to join Colonel Mahon's Southern Column. Mafeking was still holding out; they might yet be in time.

After a hard march of thirty miles the Molopo was reached, and at Jan Massipis they joined hands with Colonel Mahon. The final advance began at once. All the artillery was directed to make its way along the southern bank of the Molopo. At Sanis Village about ten miles from Mafeking they became aware of the presence of Boers in their front. They had had a trying march and a brief halt was called while the animals were watered and the men rested. It was but a short rest however. They had scarcely begun their noon-day meal when the scouts brought in news that decided Colonel Mahon to continue the advance. The column had moved forward only between two hundred and three hundred yards when the enemy's "pom-pom" spoke, and shells began to fall thick and fast. The convoy was an excellent mark and the Boers were soon hammering away at it with their big guns.

When the firing began Major Hudon at once ordered C Battery to prepare for action. His men doubled to their guns, the mules were unhitched, and the native drivers with loud cries and well-plied whips hurried them to the shelter of a hill in the rear. They had need to hasten, for their path was swept by a hail of bullets. The sixty-four men of C Battery then brought their guns into action by hand and took up their position in a mealie field. The ground was soft and yielding and the gun-wheels sank into the sand. As they advanced to the high ground facing the Boer trenches which were some two miles to their front a shell fell close to them, buried itself in the soft ground, but did no harm. The Canadian guns were quickly placed in position, but it was impossible to locate the enemy's guns; and the men of C Battery underwent the trying ordeal of remaining steady under a heavy fire while they waited for the command "commence firing." A white house was spied, and as the enemy were thought to be near it the guns were changed to half-right and at 2.30 p. m. the Canadians fired their first shot—a shot they had traveled ten thousand miles to fire—at the hidden foe.

The Boer artillerists had the range of C Battery and soon their shells were dropping about the four guns that were for the most part silent or speaking only at long intervals; for, though the shells came screaming across the wide plain from the Boer position and buried themselves in the soil, or went shrieking overhead it was impossible to accurately locate the weapons that hurled them, and Major Hudon did not feel like throwing good ammunition into space.

The battery after a time moved in echelon 1000 yards east of their first position, and as they advanced the Boers with "Long-Toms," "pom-poms" and rifles tried to check their progress; but no man was hit and the guns were soon playing on a stone laager 3350 yards away. A brisk duel then went on between the Boers and C Battery, but Major Hudon had accurately located some of their guns and his well-placed time-shrapnel silenced them in short order. But a fire from another direction kept the Canadian gunners "ducking" to avoid the wicked little 1-pounder shells from the "pom-poms" and hugging the earth as the big projectiles fell among them. Away to the right field-guns and Vickers-Maxims in a bush near the white house were directed against C Battery. They quickly changed front and vigorously replied to this fire, and in a few minutes the enemy's guns spoke no more from that quarter. Still shells buried themselves in the dust and fell dangerously near the guns, but the gunners remained invisible. The fire grew hotter and more dangerous and several shells burst among the gunners. Two men were wounded but not seriously, and both remained with their gun till the end of the battle. Major Hudon now determined to get still nearer the enemy, and so while shells were falling fast, rapidly advanced his battery to a position from which he could play on the white house to better advantage. The Canadians then began a furious fire. It was too much for the Boers and they gave up the fight and beat a hasty retreat. They fired their last shot at the Canadians at 5.35 p.m., and five minutes later C Battery's guns were silent too, as there was nothing left to fire at. At the same time all along the Molopo the fighting ceased.

About midnight the men of C Battery were ordered to make ready to march on Mafeking. It was now very dark and they groped their way over the rough ground, expecting each moment to hear the rending explosion of the enemy's "pompoms" or the vicious crackling of the Mausers. But not a shot was fired, and between three and four in the morning the battery entered the tranquilly sleeping little town that was rent and torn with the iron storm of seven months. When morning broke the Canadians and the Royal Horse Artillery were ordered out to clear away the Boers still entrenched at Game Tree Fort. But General Snyman had had enough, and in less than an hour not a Boer was left in sight of Mafeking.

When the batteries returned in triumph after scattering the last of the enemy, the people who had been smiling at death that had so long sat grimly on their ramparts, went wild. They shouted and cheered and sang and wept; and none of the troops came in for a greater share of enthusiasm than the Canadian battery with Major Hudon, a French-Canadian, in command.

For the remainder of the summer the Battery remained in the Transvaal doing excellent work at Zeerust and Rustenburg, at Warm Baths and elsewhere, winning the highest praise from every officer who witnessed their work, and particularly from the hero of Mafeking, Baden-Powell.

D and E Batteries, however, were not so fortunate. It was not until July that D Battery reached the front; but it, too, came under fire frequently and assisted ably in the pursuit of De Wet and Botha. E Battery remained longer in the Kimberley district, but when the maple leaves in Canada were beginning to turn to scarlet and gold, word came over the seas that they too were distinguishing themselves, and that the fine work that they had done at Faber's Farm was being repeated in the difficult Lydenburg region.

For six weary weeks after reaching Cape Town the Strathcona's drilled and cursed their fate. On the Queen's Birthday, however, A and C Squadrons left Cape Town for Durban, and three days later B Squadron was speeding northward through the blue ocean, towards Kosi Bay, fifty miles from Delagoa Bay. B Squadron had been sent to perform one of the most hazardous deeds of the war. So long as the Lourenzo Marques line was intact, so long would the enemy be able to get in supplies and even men. To the Strathcona's was given the important duty of cutting this line of communication between Pretoria and Delagoa Bay. They were to land in Tonga Land and by forced marches were to proceed to Komati Poort on the Portuguese border and destroy the railway bridge at that important pass.

In their undertaking they were to be disappointed. Scarcely had they landed among the wondering natives of Tonga Land when they learned that the Boers were fully aware of their expedition and ready to meet them. The troops, therefore once more embarked, and the steamers that brought them to Tonga Land were soon steaming rapidly Southward to Durban to get ready to proceed to the front to join General Buller's main

WINDING UP THE WAR. 465

army. B Squadron after its return to Durban joined their comrades at the Tugela and the whole force pushed forward to Eshowe, the Capital of Zulu Land.

It was learned that a force of 2000 Boers was on the Swazi Land border waiting to annihiliate the Strathcona's the moment they attempted to advance into Boer territory. An invasion of the Transvaal by way of Zulu Land was now out of the question, and after a brief rest the Strathcona's were ordered to return to Durban.

When Durban was reached the regiment entrained for Newcastle from which place they were to be pushed forward with all possible speed to Sand Spruit in the Transvaal where General Buller's army of 20,000 men was encamped.

The journey to Newcastle was one of exceptional interest. A year before the rivers and hills would have had little or no attractiveness, apart from their picturesqueness, to the traveller; but now almost every mile of the journey had some importance in history. As they passed Estcourt, Frere, Chieveley, Colenso, Ladysmith, Elands Laagte and Glencoe; as they saw the shattered houses, the kopjes torn with shell-fire, the deep lines of trenches and well-constructed earthworks here and there, the bullet-scarred stations, they recalled the fierce fighting that had taken place through this region, the struggle that had made England for a moment tremble for her position as a world power.

After a day's rest at Newcastle they began a forced march of two days to Volksrust on the border of Natal. Here they learned that they were to become a part of Lord Dundonald's Brigade. From this place they advanced over the hard veldt, dry and hard as a brick, till the wide region about Sand Spruit, dotted with the tents of Buller's army, was reached.

The general advance began with a short journey of fifteen miles to Paardekop and after a night's rest they once more proceeded on their way towards Standerton. As the little town was approached the columns formed into order of battle and advanced with a widely extended front, but the Boers had beaten a hasty retreat before a British shot could reach them.

Fighting for the Strathcona's began on July 1. Their work was to scout in advance of General Buller's army, and for four months their duty led them into many warm corners. On Dominion Day a small party of them, deceived by a white flag, fell into a Boer trap, and the first man in the regiment to fall was Private Jenkins, of Red Deer, who was shot through the heart. A brisk running fight followed in which the remainder of the party, with the exceptions of Captain Howard and Private Hobson who were taken prisoners, escaped.

For over a week as the column advanced from Standerton to Greylingstad, Boer patrols and British patrols came constantly into contact, and not a day passed without casualties in the Strathcona's. They were constantly under fire and frequently walked into Boer traps, but they soon learned to fight the enemy at their own kind of warfare, and became such adepts at leading Boers into ambush that the Imperial Officers christened them the "Scalp-Hunters."

On the 5th of July at Wolve Spruit one of the most daring feats of the war was performed by Sergeant A. H. L. Richardson.

WINDING UP THE WAR. 467

Alex. McArthur was wounded at close range, shot in the arm and thigh; his companions had been forced to retire. In his attempt to escape his horse was shot and fell upon him. Sergeant Richardson saw his plight, and although his horse was wounded and he himself had just risen from a sick-bed, gallantly rode back under a terrific cross-fire till within 300 yards of the Boers and rescued his wounded comrade. It was a brave deed and won for Canada the Victoria Cross.

Till the end of November the Strathcona's continued to distinguish themselves, winning the praises of the best generals in South Africa. But they paid dearly for their reputation. All along their line of march, from Standerton, from Greylingstad, from Blakfontein, from Middleburg, from Belfast, from Amesfoort, from Ermelo, from Carolina, from Machadodorp, and finally from the Lydenburg region, came tidings of men killed and wounded and fever-smitten, till less than half the regiment was left at the front.

With the capitulation of Pretoria, however, the war practically closed. It is true severe fighting was experienced, but no general engagements were fought, and throughout the Transvaal and the Orange River Colony guerilla warfare, trying and disastrous, alone prevailed.

After the triumphant entry into Pretoria the Royal Canadians rested in Springs, and in August what remained of them went in pursuit of "The Swooper," Christian De Wet, a General who has kept all the British military genius in South Africa taxed to its uttermost. They saw no further fighting, and after enduring much fatigue all excepting two companies left the seat of war and returned to

Canada on the Idaho. A few days after they reached Halifax on November 1, news came that the rest of the contingent had sailed for England on the Hawarden Castle.

But since the fall of Pretoria the Mounted Rifles have been mentioned more frequently than any other Canadian force at the front. News has reached Canada of fight after fight in which they have distinguished themselves, and of gallant fellow after gallant fellow who has heroically died in England's war. Time and again small outposts of the Canadian Mounted Rifles have held large bodies of Boers at bay for hours. The most noteworthy of these occasions was when the Cossack post at Horning Spruit on June 22 held a party of fifty Boers in check. The deed of the gallant Pincher Creek men on that day should live in Canadian history. Perhaps the loss sustained by the Canadian Mounted Rifles which most stirred Canada was on July 21 when Lieutenant H. L. Borden and Lieutenant J. E. Burch were killed. The brave son of the Minister of Militia and his gallant comrade died heroic deaths fighting against fearful odds.

A chronicle of the events after Pretoria would, however, be but a repetition of slight skirmishes with individual cases of great bravery.

Canada cannot but be proud of the men she sent to South Africa in the Empire's war. In the three great arms of the service—in infantry, in mounted rifles, and in artillery—Her Sons on Kopje and Veldt have proved themselves without superiors.

APPENDIX A.

OFFICIAL LIST OF THE OFFICERS AND MEN OF THE FIRST CANADIAN CONTINGENT IN SOUTH AFRICA.

The First Contingent was composed of eight Companies, recruited from various parts of the Dominion. The formation by Company and districts was as follows:
A Company, British Columbia and Manitoba.
B Company, London, Ontario.
C Company, Toronto, Ontario.
D Company, left half, Kingston and vicinity; right half, Ottawa, Ontario.
E Company, Montreal.
F Company, Quebec.
G Company, New Brunswick and Prince Edward Island.
H Company, Nova Scotia.

Each Company consisted of 125 men, which, with the staff and officers, brought the total force up to ten hundred and nineteen. The mobilization of the Contingent took place at Quebec, and on October 30th, the Sardinian of the Allan Line sailed on her voyage to Cape Town.

Lieut.-Col.
W. D. Otter

2nd in Command
L. Buchan

Major
O. C. C. Pelletier

Capts.
H. M. Arnold
W. A. Weeks
D. Stuart
S. M. Rogers
J. E. Peltier
H. B. Stairs
R. K. Barker
C. K. Fraser

Lieuts.
H. A. Panet
H. E. Burstall
A. H. Macdonnell
H. G. Blanchard
J. H. C. Ogilvy
W. T. Lawless
F. C. Jones
A. E. Hodgins
J. M. Ross
J. C. Mason
C. J. Armstrong
A. E. Swift
R. B. Willis
W. R. Marshall
J. H. Kaye
L. Leduc
C. S. Wilkie
A. C. Caldwell
S. P. Layborn
A. Laurie
E. A. Pelletier
R. G. Steward
F. D. Lafferty
J. C. Oland
R. H. M. Temple
C. W. W. McLean

M. Gun Sec.
Capt A. C. Bell

Adjutant
J. C. MacDougall

Q. Master
S. J. A. Denison

Med. Officers
C. W. Wilson
E. Fiset

Staff Duty
L. G. Drummond

Attached for Special Duty.
C. W. Drury
F. L. Lessard
R. Cartwright
W. Forester
C. M. Dobell

Medical Staff for General Service.

A. B. Osborne
Miss G. Pope
" S. Forbes
" M. Affleck
" E. Russel

Historical Recorder.

F. J. Dixon

Chaplains.

Rev. J. Almond
" T. F. Fullerton
" P. M. O'Leary

Representative of the Y. M. C. A.

Dr. H. G. Barrie

S.M., D. Borland
Q.M.S., G. Galloway
Q.M.S., E. Reading
O.R.C., T. D. Potter
S. Bug. Tresham
T.S., T. Leblond
S.A., A. J Hoad

"A" Company

C.S. Holmes, W H
Ser. Whimster, P
" Northcote, J
" Scott, W
" Ingram, L
" Vinnel, A J
Cor. Fowle, W F
" McHarg, W H
" Irvine, A B
" Moscrop, J
L.C. LeBar, V E
" Barlow, R H
Allan, H S
Alliston, B D
Adams, J
Anderton, J
Andrews, H
Armstrong, E
Barrett, R J
Beach, A C
Berthour. W H
Battson, A S
Bonner, H M
Boyce, A W
Brooking, W
Carnagie, J
Carter, A
Campbell, R B
Campbell, A
Chisholm, A
Clough, P
Collins, J
Cook, J
Corbould, G B
Cowan, H J
Cornwall, F J
Court, S T
Crook, M
Davies, J E
Dickinson, F
Dickson, J H
Dickson, W J G
Duncalfe, C W
Docherty, M
Edwards, H
Findley, T A
Foord, F N
Finch-Smiles, F
French, J P
Gamble, C W
Groves, C E
Greaves, P
Hammond, J L
Hanson, S S
Hicks, H P
Holyoke, G C F
Hughes, E N
Hutchings. G
Jackson, W
Johnson, H
Jones, S L
Jones, J W
Kelly, E
Kennedy, D
Lee, A S
Leeman, R W J
Leamy, C S
Liston, B
Livingstone, J
Lohman, A O
Martin, A
Mackie, A S
Matheson, K
Maundrill, A
Mills C A
Munro, A E
Moier, W J
Moodie, W H
McCalmont, R J
McIvor, D
McKeand, D L
McKenzie, H
Neibergall, H E
Neil, G
Nixon, F S
Nye, A J
O'Brien, S W
Odell, S H
Parker, H F
Patterson, W O
Patterson, C
Perry, J C
Rea, J R
Rumsay F
Rush, F
Rorke, F B
Robbins, A E
Roberts, S C
Roberts, C M
Sherlock, H
Sherris, J
Sinclair, J J S
Smethurst, H
Smith, J
Snider, C H
Soper, A C W
Somers, J H
Stewart, J
St. James, G
Stebbings, W H
Talbot, A
Thompson, C C
Thompson, T
Todd, J
Wallace, W
Wallace, G
Welch, W
Western, T
Whitley, W F
Wilkins, G H
Wilkie, O J
Wood, A M
Wyatt, H R
Ward, R

"B" Company

C. S. Davies, R
Ser. McBeth, G W
" Bowden, R B
" Sippi, G R B
" Gorman, F
Cor. Bethune, A
" Adams, S
" Phillips, G R S
" Smith, J
" Little, R H
L.C. Power, L
" Stevenson, W R
" Northwood, J
" Merrix, A E
Adams, W G
Adair, A
Anderson, A H
Andrews, E C
Atkinson, D H
Bredin, J
Bollard, H E
Barr, H B
Barrett, P
Baugh, E
Beers, F C
Berges, H
Biggs, J C
Burns, W J
Burrell, H
Burwell, A E
Campbell, F W
Chapman, W H

APPENDIX. 471

Charman, A
Coles, F J
Cole, A E
Corley, J B
Crockett, S
Craig, E D
Collins, W
Dalgleish, A D
Day, J
Donegan, J A
Dolman, E N
Donahue. H
Delmer, P
Duff, J B
Edward, A
Evans, F
Farley, J E
Finch, C E
Floyd, F G W
Fox, W H
Foote, W
Gorrie, W B
Graham, G
Greene, C
Green, W J
Hill, J C
Herrick, J
Hessell, F W
Hyman, W J
Hennessy, J T
Ingamells, P C
Irvine, R
Jell, A P
Jones, M L
Johnston, K G
Kingswell, D
Leonard, G W
Little, G B
Lane, H
Lundrigan, J
McBeth, G A
McLaren, C D
McLean, M
McCalla, J
McMahon, W H
McMillan, D C
McMurphy, A
Marshall, A
McLean, A R
Marentette, V F
Moore, D L
Mullins, E
Munro. G H
Nott, W
Odlum, V
Odlum, G
Padden, A E
Piper, T J
Pinel, G F
Pert, E W
Powell, F
Purcell, J J
Reed, W G
Reid, D A

Redge, C
Robinson, J B
Rae, A H
Rorison, C K
Scott, C R
Smith, R
Stanberry, F G
Sutherland, J
Taylor, E
Taylor, G
Thompson, H
Trolley, F H
Turner, F W
Tutt, T
Wardel, A E
Webb, A B
West, W
Westaway, H
Wells, J
Wheatcraft, A H
White, G
White, W
Wilson, A R
Wigham R D
Woodliffe, G W
Woodward, A W
Woodyatt, W H
Wilson, H R

"C" Company

C S Campbell, J S
Ser. Beattie, A
" Middleton, H J
" Ramage, J H
Cor. Dixon, H W A
" Freemantle,
  A H O
" Rutherford, F H
" McGee, K
" Hoskins, R W
L.C. Ramsay, J F
" Hodgins, E W
Allen, L
Anderson, F T
Baldwin. J
Banton, T H
Black, N D
Blair, F
Bird, B M
Bingham, H S
Blight, W S
Brettingham, W P R
Brunton, H G
Burkhart, F
Butler, W B
Calvert, F M
Callahan, H A
Christie, D H
Cassel, K J
Curtis, W R
Coggins, A E
Coggins. H
Cuthbert, F

Dangerfield, A
Davidson, J
Day, E C
Dunham, F H
Eakins, G
Ellis, G S
Fawcett, J N
Findlay, J H
Graham, T H
Grant, W H
Gray, N
Haines, W
Hector, F T D
Hendrie, M
Henderson, R H
Hewett, W H
Holland, W C S
Holland, J
Hopeson, C W
Hornibrook, J L
Inglestrom, F
Ironside, G M
Jones, N J
Jordan, J
Kennedy, J
Kidner, R
Long, J L
Lorsch, F D
Love, W M
Machin, H A
Manion, W T
Martin, G F
Morley, N L
Mitchell. J A
Morse. T
McCall, A
McCosh, P
McCuish, D
McGiverin, L
McHugh, E
McKenzie, L C
McLaughlin, R H
McNish, M
McPherson, D
Noble, D A
Page, F C
Parry, C E
Perry, S
Preston, D G
Pringle, R
Raspberry, J
Rae. F A
Ridway, E H
Robson, A
Rogers, W R
Rooke, W J
Rorke, J H
Seager, J
Seymour, C
Sherritt, A W
Simpson, G C M
Smith, J
Smith, G M
Solari, J

Spence, J D
Stewart, M M
Sutton, J H
Thompson, G
Thompson, W F
Tice, C
Tomlinson, C
Travers, W
Usher, J F
Vanderwater, W J
VanNorman, A F
Vicary, S
Vickers, J R
Wallace, T G
Warde, S M
Warren, W C
Warwick, W H
Watson, R G
Weir, F E
Wellar, E T
Wilson, J A
Wilson, N W
Williams, D F
Whitehead, J
Wright, D M
Young, H
Young, A

"D" Company

C. S. Thompson, C H
Ser. Chitty, L M
" Ross, A L
" Carruthers, B
" Eagleson, S H
Cor. Gilmour, W J
" Hulme, G G
" Thomas, J M
" Ellard, J F G
" Brady, W S
L.C. Johnston, W
" Southey, E C
" McNair, J
" Lyon, J R D
Auger, E
Ault, C E
Bugler Cawdron, A J
Bartlett, E D
Benbow, H A
Bennett, A
Bolster, H G
Bolyea, A W
Bradshaw, J L H
Bull, E W
Burns, O T
Burns, R
Cunnington, R
Cairns, J S
Chidlow, J
Clarke, C P
Clother, A
Cluff, N W H
Clunie, P
Cockburn, G G

Coleman, J D
Cotton, H
Cotterell, A
Cram, J A C
Craig, C E
Croft, F
Croft, P C
Cunningham, R J
Dalberg, R P
DesLauriers, E
Deuchars, G D
Dunlop, E
Donaldson, C A
Dunlop, J R
Eley, D M
Escobel, N
Flemming, A J
Foden, W J
Foster, P R
Frye, C E
Gallagher, J
Gibson, C A
Gilmour, A E
Graham, J D H
Haig, H G
Hatton, J
Hogan, J R
Hennessy, J
Holland, C
Hugall, P
Jackson, C E
Jones, H H
Laird, A
Lamothe, G
Latimer, W R
Large, A L
Lawrence, W R
Lewis, Z R E
Living, F J
Lynn, F
LeBean, L P
Macauley, A
Martin, W A
Martin, H
Mason, C P
Matthews, A J
Malloch, E
Major, J
Mills, W W
Mitchell, N
Morgans, E F
Morrison, W A
Morin, J
Morrison, E F
McCullough, C
MacRae, R A
McConnell, J F
McCormack, A J
MacKay, R
McDonald, F
McFadden, F
McLennan, J A
McCrea, J M
Padmore, G T

Parr, W B
Peters, A E
Phillips, G
Prior, A
Porteous, R W
Ritchie, W G
Ross, W J H
Rowley, J
Schwitzer, W C
Shillington, W J H
Small, H C
Smith, J F
Smith, W A
Spence, C T
Street, L J
Swan, N W D
Taylor, A H
Thomas, C T
Thompson, R R
Tiley, G
Turner R H
Turpin, T J
Wall, A
Walker, L C
Wendt, W G
Williamson, A T L
Wood, F H
Wright, H O

"E" Company

C. S. Young, A
Ser. Allan, J
" Adams, J A
" Shreeve, J
Cor. Baugh, T E
" Downey, G
" Gardner, J
" Goodfellow, R
" Moody, F
L.C. Frawley, W M
" Molyneux, C R
Allan, C E
Ackerman, F
Allmand, W W
Aspell, T J
Bach, R C
Bailey, J
Barry, C H
Bigelow, J **A**
Bolt, G H
Byford, R
Byers, R T
Carter, M
Campbell, C
Canty, R
Carter, W
Clarke, R C
Coates, H W
Cox, F
Crotty, P
Curry, ?
Corner, F G
Dawson, A

APPENDIX. 473

Delaney, M J
Doyle, T H M
Durkee, A A
Dynes, E J
Erskine, F
Fisher, H
Fisher, R L
Fowler, W
Fraser, H
Gamble. J
Gorman, J F
Graham, R
Greenlay, G
Gunn, R
Harding, E
Hill, J K
Hale, W J
Hampson, G
Hannaford, A
Hawkins, J
Hayes, R
Hayward, H
Home, F
Hynes, P
Irwin, F B
James, A
Jones, F
Jeffrey, W
Jeffrey, J W
Kealey, M
Kelly, E
Leconteur, R
Lee, F
Lewis, C E
Lester, C
Malin, J
Marjin, H
Martin, A
Meade, D
Middleton, F
Mitchell, H
Moore, T D
Murphy, D
Murray, W R
Murdoch, W A H
McDonald, A
McCann, J
McGill, D R
McGoldrick, J
McIver, W
McLean, R G
McLeod, N M
McQueen, A
Nash, T B
Nickle, C R
O'Brien, J
O'Meara, J
Philips, J
Platt, J
Pope, A
Porter, W
Prince. R H
Price, G
Robarts, G P

Rupert, E
Ryan, P
Richardson, F
Shaw, A C
Shaw, R N
Sheehan, M
Stanning, W
Swift, M
Sword, A
Sword, D C
Thomas. A P
Thomas, G W
Travers, H B
Tregett, J
Tulloch, A J
Turner, A J
Tweddell, W
Walters, J H
Walters, T A
Walker, H H
Wasdell, F
Wardle, G
White A
Wilkin, W
Wilkins, A W
Williams, H
Wright, P E
Wright, J
Yelland, J
Youngson, J S

"F" Company.

Ser. Bessette, W
" Peppeatt, W
" Polkinghorn, J
Cor. Peterson, C F
" Withey, B
" McDonald R D
" Warren, C
" Vallee, L C
L.C. Desjardins, J F
" Gratton. E
C.S. Lafleur, L E
Arnton, C S
Anthony, P
Atkinson, G
Barclay, C N
Bagot, A
Bamford, W
Baldwin, C
Beaupre, C
Brown, H I
Brown, H
Brooker, L
Bouck, L
Bower, J. W
Carbonneau, E
Casey, J E
Champagne, M
Chatel, A
Cloutier, W
Chisholm, A W
Cooper, W

Conley, F
Cowgill, H
Curphy, J
D'Amour, J
Demais, A
Dolbec, L
Donahue, F
Downing, W
Duhamel, J W
D'Orsonens. G
Duberger, A
Dixon, W
Eite, Wm
Fancy, J G
Forest, H
Gates, L H
Gifford, B
Gingras, J
Good, R
Grecia, J
Harrison, R
Harrison. Chas
Harvey, R
Hennessy, B
Hill, J
Hudon, J A
Hunter, W
Hubley, C
Irwin, W
Ivers, M
Jette, G
Jewell, T
Jobin, E
Larue, L
Lambkin, H J
Lamoureaux, E
Laverdure, E
Lefebre, P W
Lescarbeau, T
Lightbound, G R
Leveille, L
Lewis, O
Lemay, A
Macness, J
Matheson, O
Medhurst, J
Michaud, L C
Monteith, J
Montizambert, H
McEllhiney, J
McNeil, J D
McCollom, G H
McDonald, J E
McIntosh, W
MacTaggart, J W
McLaughlin, H P
McMillan, A
McMillan, E
Orman, G
Paquette, G
Plamondon, J
Proulx, H
Pullen, E
Rae, J P

474   APPENDIX.

Raymond, J W
Remy, J
Redmond, C
Robertson, J H
Roy, A
Roberts, J R
Scott, J A
Sievert, J
Soucy, A
Smith, L
Strong, F B
Sutton, G J
Sutherland, A D
Tapin, J
Tattersall, H C
Tessier, E
Theriault, A
Thompson, W B
Touchette, J
Utton, F W
Walsh, J
Warren, W
Wiseman, N
Woodward, F
Wylie, R R

"G" Company.

C.S. Charlton, Chas
Ser. Sheldon, A
 "   Russell, J
 "   Hessian, E
Cor. Morrison, J
 "   Pringle, J
 "   Withers, F
 "   Wallace, W V
 "   Coombs, F W
L.C. Ward, G
 "   Miller, H
Adams, G F
Addison, J
Aitken, J M
Anslow, C
Baker, W
Bishop, W
Boudreau, J
Bowness, E W
Burnside, J
Brace, N T
Brown, H H
Bryant, W
Campbell, G
Carney, J
Chapman, G
Chappell, M C
Cox, R W
Craig, E
Creighton, C
Dillon, A R
Donahue, W W
Doyle, A
Dorion, N
Durant, H E
Dutney, J

Dyas, F
Fabre, D J
Ferguson, D
Flewelling, E
Foley, R J
Foster, M
Fradsham, H
Furze, F C
Gaudet, L S
Globe, A R
Hallamore, W
Hammond, A
Harris, B
Harris, J A
Harris, L
Hartfield, A S
Haydon, A
Hine, C H
Hubley, R C
Irving, W H
Jenkins, C L
Johnson, J
Johnston, J M
Jones, S
Keddy, E
Keswick, G
Kirkpatrick, F A
Kitchen, W
Lane, W
Leavitt, H
Leslie, J P
Leston, J
Lord, R E
Lutz, E
Lutz, J
Matheson, J
McCain, F
McCarthy
McRae, F B
McCreary, P
McDiarmid, J
McFarlane, B E
McKinnon, H V
McLean, H L
McLeod, J
McMullan, W
Mellish, A J B
Morley, H A
Munroe, J R
O'Rielly, J
Pascoe, J B
Pelky, A
Penny, R
Perkins, J A
Pickles, J
Quinn, M J
Raymond, W J
Rawlings, J
Redden, H
Riggs, W A
Rodd, T A
Roberts, A
Schofield, A
Scott, J B

Scott, J
Singer, L M
Simpson, A
Simpson, P
Small, J E
Sprague, F W
Stanton, L
Stevenson, P S
Stewart, L
Strange, E. H
Swatridge, W O
Taylor, R D
Tower, B C
Turner, R M
Unkauf, W C
Walker, F G
Walker, J S
Wannamaker, H L
Ward, R
Wayne, J F
Williams, J
Williams, F
Wilson, J H

"H" Company.

C.S. Eustace, J D
Ser. Grimshaw
 "   Dooley, F
Cor. Baugh, B
 "   Ferguson, W R
 "   Lindon, H
 "   Pooley, C F
 "   Rolfe, J
L.C. Stevenson, J
 "   Watson, J
Anderson, J H N
Adams, W F
Atwater, J
Ackhurst, F W
Bennett, G B
Blaikie, W
Borton, C N
Burgess, M
Blair, S
Bent, E E
Brown, S
Buchanan, K
Bingay, L W
Conrad, W
Coons, F
Cleary, W
Carroll, J
Cameron, A A
Chapman, F
Daley, F
Drake, J
Duncan, J
Defoe, J
Dewers, F
Elliott, W
Embree, G
Ewing, J
Ewing, D H

APPENDIX.

Farrell, G P
Farrer, De B
Fillmore. W A
Fitzgerald, A E
Forsyth, A
Fraser, H H
Gallagher, J
Grant, J W
Hancock, C
Harrison, G
Hartnett, J W
Harris, J
Hart, W J
Halliday, J
Huestis, G J
Hire, J
Hunt, G
Hurly, J
Hoult, E
James, G
Jewers, F
Johnstone, G
Jones, H
Kelly, J
Kennedy, J
Keogh, P
Keefler, R T
Kilcup, E
Kirkpatrick, F
Lewis, M

Lenahan, J
Lindsay, A C
Lockwood, A
Lowry, T P
MacDonald, C
MacDonald, D C
MacLean, W J
McDonald, G
Miller, C
Miller, R
Munnis, M
Muir, F
Murray, N G
Murray, A
McAldin, R
McCallum, B
McCollum, G D
McDougall, H A
McLean, J
McNab, F
Neily, R L
O'Brien, E
Oxley, W
Oulton, H
Osborn, D
Parkes, F S
Patterson A,
Parker, A
Pollock, W J
Purcell, E S

Purcell, L A
Regan, W J
Rector, R
Roche, W
Rose, J E
Rose, F
Roue, J F L
Ross, R
Ross, W J
Robertson, A
Rudland, R
Reid, W
Ryan, D J
Simmons, W
Sloan, R
Swinyard, W
Stuart, G W
Taylor, F A E
Tester, S
Trider, A
Trueman, W E
Walker, W A
Walsh, T J
Ward, E
Ward, G
Walke, C W J
Woods, D
Wright, P
Zong, A E

APPENDIX B.

OFFICIAL LIST OF THE OFFICERS AND MEN OF THE SECOND CANADIAN CONTINGENT IN SOUTH AFRICA.

The Second Contingent was composed of two Battalions (four Squadrons), recruited principally from the North-West, and of C, D and E Field Batteries R.C.A. D and E Batteries left Halifax on January 21 and arrived at Cape Town on February 17; the 2nd Batt. C.M.R. left Halifax on the Pomeranian on January 27, and arrived at Cape Town on February 26; the 1st Batt. C. M. R. and C Battery left Halifax on February 21, and arrived at Cape Town on March 21.

Com. Officers

F. L. Lessard
Lt.-Col. Herchmer
T. D. B. Evans

Com. Squadrons

V. A. S. Williams
W. Forester
J. Howe
G. E. Sanders

Captains

A. E. R. Cuthbert
H. S. Greenwood
C. St. A. Pearse
A. C. Macdonell

Lieuts.

A. H. King
H. L. Borden
R. E. W. Turner
R. M. Van Luven
H. Z. C. Cockburn
C.T. Van Straubenzee
J. H. Elmsley
F. V. Young
J. Taylor
F. H. C. Sutton
H. J. A. Davidson
T. W. Chalmers
F. L. Cosby
D. Moodie

J. V. Begin
T. A. Wroughton
W. M. Inglis

Adjutants

C. M. Nelles
M. Baker

Machine Gun Section

D. C. F. Bliss
A. L. Howard

Qt.-Masters

J. A. Wynne
J. B. Allan

Med. Officers

H. R. Duff
J. A. Devine

Trspt. Officers

C. F. Harrison
R. W. B. Eustace

Vet. Officers

W. B. Hall
R. Riddell

Nurses

Miss D. Hercum
Miss M. Horne
Miss M. Macdonald

Miss M. P. Richardson

Chaplains

Rev. W. G. Lane
Rev. W. J. Cox
Rev. J. C. Sinnett

Attached for Special Duties

W. D. Gordon
T. L. Boulanger
J. E. Burch
J. L. Biggar
J. A. McDonald

Canada Commissioner British R. C. S.

G. S. Ryerson

Postal Corps

W. R. Eccleston
R. Johnston
J. Lallier
F. B. Beddell
K. A. Murray

Rep. Y.M.C.A.

T. F. Best

Regimental Staff

J. C. Page, R.S.M

APPENDIX.

J. Graham, Q.M.S.
G. J. Simpkins, Fr., Q.M.S.
P. Dalton, O.R.S.
L. J. Inglis, S.S.T.
D. J. Carroll, A.S.
A. R. Skinner, S.T.
J. F. Dunning, S.S.

2nd Battalion

Adams, D E
Aston, G H
Aspinall, A
Avery, W
Ayre, C
Aylesworth, J E
Bagshawe, M J
Baines, H H
Barker, J M
Barry, J
Baldwin, H Y
Ballantine, J A
Ball, J E
Bassett, P
Bell, W M
Bell, C
Beyts, S B
Beyts, W J
Biddell, P J
Birney, J A
Bird, A L
Bird, T A
Biscoe, V H
Blake, J A
Border, J W
Bourne, L E
Bolster, G
Bolt, H G
Bradley, A W
Bredin, H H
Bredin, A N
Brewster, J N
Brindle, H J
Brinkworth, G W
Brown, G A
Brown, H J
Brown, T
Brown, A H
Brown, V S
Brown, J H
Bruce, E F
Bryans, T
Burke, J A
Burke, P
Butler, A C
Burke, W H
Brennan, R J
Callaghan, T
Camies. E J
Campbell, A W
Carson, T E
Carter, W
Carter, J

Charlton, H L
Champion, A
Charles, A H
Church, F
Clarke, D
Clark, E D
Clendinnen, B W
Colbert, J A
Courtney, T J
Crawley, A W
Cudlip, A J
Cunningham, W P
Clements, H H
Davies, H P
Davis, J
Davy, G A
Davidson, F
Des Barres, H
DeRossiter, W W
Dewey, J
Dennis, O G
Dean, A
Dill, F B
Dickson, R T
Dodd, V
Donovan, D
Doolan, J T
Donnelly, J A
Dore, G L
Dowler, T
Drury, P S
Duxbury, T
Durrant, W F
Durie, J D
D'Easum, B C
Eaton, R B
Eddy, J H
Egan, P
Elkington, A J
Ellis, P
Ermatinger, C P
Erwin, M
Esson, C
Ferguson, G
Ferries, C H
Fisk, C E
Fisher, J
Fitzgerald, F J
Fletcher, J
Flynn, W B
Foran, C J
Forbes, L R
Fortune, A P
Foster, W W
Fotheringham, D H
French, F
French, J P
Frost, W
Galwey, R M
Geoghegan, J
Giles, W A
Gladwin, J!M
Glover, F S
Goodfellow, G

Gordon, G F
Goodman, T
Gould, G N
Gow, A M
Gray, W
Gray, J
Greenall, F
Green, H F
Green, G W
Green, A E C
Griesbach, W A
Groat, F
Gunn, H A
Haddock, A G
Hammond, W H
Hanna, W H
Harris, W J
Harley, T
Hayne, M H E
Head, H A
Healy, J M
Hendren, G G
Henry, W A
Herchmer, S
Hertzog, W
Hewetson, J S
Higinbotham, W B
Hilling, T J
Hilliam, E
Hobbins, S
Hodgkiss, S H
Houlgate, H L
Howden, G T
Huckell, B W
Hughes, T P
Hughes, L C
Hughey, J
Hutchinson, C E
Jackson, F A
Jameson, F C
Jarvis, A B
Jeffery, N
Jenkins, H
Johnson, N S
Johnston, D F
Johnstone, A
Kelly, P H
Kerrigan, M
Kerr, G
Kerr, R J
Kibby, A
King, R S
King, G
King, J E
Kirwan, H J
Knight, R S
Krag, C
Lane, H G
Laroque, J A
Lawe, A W
Laws, B
Leach, R
Leach, F E
Lee, H

478   APPENDIX.

Leggat, M.
Lett, H
Lett, R
Lindsay, J
Lloyd, B H
Long, J F
Long, A T
Long, J P
McArthur, J
McCallum, A D
McCall, W
McCallum, L
McCauley, A J H
McClelland, W
McCulloch, D, Fr.-Ser.
McDougall, D
Macdougall, H V
McGeachy, T
McKay, C T
McKen, W
Mackenna, R J
McKinley, A
McLaughlin, S
McLaughlin, S
McLaughlin, P J S
McLeod, W B
McLeod, R W
McMillan, C J
MacNeil, A C
McNeill, J
McNeil, M R
McNicol, J
McNicol, P H
Maloney, J D
Marchand, C H
Marshall, E
Martin, H J
Manson, J R
Mead, C G
Miller, H
Miles, T R
Miles, H V W
Millie, S B
Moloney, A C
Mongeon, J
Mooney, J
Morden, J F
Morrison, A S
Morrison, D
More, P J
Mullen, W J
Napier, W H
Near, B
Nettleton, T
Nevile, H S
Northway, R J
Nunneley, E
O'Grady, S C H
O'Kelly, A N
O'Kelly, G M
Oliver, W R
Olsen, J A
Ouimet, T O
Paling, E J

Parker, F E
Patterson, F D
Patterson, J A
Patteson, T E
Peebles, H W
Perry, F
Peters, C R
Petersen, C F
Pierson, A
Piper, S F
Pifer, W W
Pointon, F
Pope, H W
Porter, W T
Pratt, F E
Quinn, D G
Ramsay, T M
Randall, R C S
Raper, A C
Reeve, G H
Redpath, J R
Reichert, E
Reid, W A
Ritchie, J
Robertson, A I
Robertson, J
Robinson, C W
Rochfort, C F W
Rodgers, E H
Ross, A
Ross, G A
Rubbra, F H
Rubbra, T C
Ruck, L
Russell, J
Ruth, F C
Salmon, G F
Sargent, J B
Schell, J J
Scott, T
Sexton, F
Shobbrook, H
Sharp, L
Sharpe, S L
Sharpe, G G
Sheppard, W F
Sheppard, R H
Shunn, A
Simms, J
Stewart, J F
Skeet, R C S
Skinner, W P
Slack, C J
Smart, J
Smith, R
Smith, H D
Smith, J A
Smith, G G
Smith, O
Smith, W C
Soper, F P W
Soube, A
Spreadbury, A
Sprott, W

Stayner, R W
Stephens, R H
Stevens, R C H
Storey, A
Strong, H
Talbot, M S
Taylor, S
Taylor, J E
Taylor, F J
Taylor, J R
Thackwell, E H
Threadkell, F
Thevenet, M R
Tracey, A W
Travers, O
Tryon, C R
Tucker, H W
Unlacke, A G
Vernon, W G H
Villebrum, P
Waite, A S
Waldy, E F
Waller, P
Walsh, R G
Walters, P
Walton, J
Warene, H T
Weatherald, C E
Weaver, O J
Weir, R H
Westhead, C G
Wetzell, O
Whittaker, J
Wildman. G E
Wilkie, W
Wilson, M S
Wilson, T G
Wilson, G P
Wilson, J D
Windfield, H
Wood, W
Wood, P A
Woollcombe, J

"A" Squadron.

Widgery, J, S S M
Hunt, B, Q M S
Ser. Rhoades, W
" Fuller, H F
" Hudson, G
Harraden, C F, S F
Ser. Smith, W T
" Till, L A
" Steer, E A
" Purdon, E L
" Terrill, W H
Cor. O'Connell, M
" McDonald, A A
" Latremouille, S
" Bennett, J
" Cartwright, J W
" Price, P R
" Willoughby, A G

APPENDIX. 479

Cor. Callahan, M J
Lovegrove, A J,
      Cor. S S
Agassiz, R H G
Allen, E B
Allum, D
Anderson, C E
Anderson, C H
Anderson, W L
Anderson, W J
Ardiel, E
Baldwin, E
Bates, E
Baxter, J
Beaton, A
Beers, L M
Bishop, W G
Bragg, W Q
Brown, A W
Brown, F
Brown, J B
Bouchard, A
Bowman, N
Builder, V D
Burnett, S
Burritt, J W
Butler, A
Butterfield, W J
Campbell, G
Campbell, J E
Cameron, H P
Chambers, E
Clark, J
Clendenning, G M
Cline, S
Collins, G H A
Cook, C
Cooper, C
Cordingly, W E
Crowe, D J
DeLisle, C D
DeRochejocquelain, A
Dougall, W
Daoust, D
Duguid, J F
Dunsmore, R J
Eagleson, E
Elliott, W V
England, G
Evans, W L
Farrell, J
Filson, E A
Fitzgerald, E
Flemming, G E
Forbes, G A
Fraser, J E
Gifford, T A
Glover, W M
Gold, W S
Graham, G C
Gurnett, E
Hall, A J
Hampton, W J
Harbottle, F

Harman, J W
Hartman, F
Harper, J S
Hagen, J
Henry, A
Heron, J B
Hiam, H
Hillyard, A E
Hibbett, J
Hodgson, W
Hopkins, J A
Holland, E J
Horner, H
Hull, M A
Hubbard, J
Tpr. Hughes, N
Hullett, A
Inglis, A G
James, M
Jefferson, J
Jenkins, V
Johnson, I
Johnston, R G
Jordon, J
Keohler, C H
Kinsley, W A
Landels, A F
Loosemore, A J
Loosemore, H H
Lougheed, D
Low, J W
Lyon, H H
McCarthy, P
McCulla, J W
McCusker, F
McGahey, J W
McGee, C E
McIlroy, F
McIntosh
McIver, M
McKibben, D M
McRae, G A
Marsh, C S
Marshall, H W
Maycock, W R
Mayne, J
Metcalfe, F
Miles, F
Middleton, J
Mitchell, W
Moluskey, W E
Morrison, W J
Morrison, W T
Mulloy, L W R
Muir, W B
Munroe, J H
O'Brien, J J
Palmer, G D
Pearce, W
Pelton, R J
Peck, F C
Potts, J
Price, P. R
Purdon E L

Ratcliffe, A
Reynolds, R H
Richardson, A M
Robinson, R R
Robinson, R S
Roche, H E
Ross, A
Richardson, G
Richardson, J
See, D
Scott, C D
Semple, W G
Shaw, C E
Shipp, T P
Slater, N J
Smart, D
Sparks, J
Spence, D M
Spicer, R W E
Spink, W B
Smith, G
Smith, H
Stewart, M E
Stonor, A F
Sully, W P
Taylor, H J
Terrill, W H
Thornton, F
Thompson, E
Tilley, W
Tripp, E H
Townley, W J
Trusler, A
Turner, A W
Van Every, C P
Vine, J
Vizard, A H
Walker, J H
Wandley, E
Warren, D J
Wasson, P
Wheatley, W J
Wigle, M S
Wigle, L
Willoughby, A G
Winyard, W
Wyatt, F
Wright, W
Young, D D

"B" Squadron

McMillan, A, S S M
Sparks, J R, S Q M S
Ser. Dyer, W A
" McLeod, W
" Allison, H
" Bisset, W
" Hayward, G F
" Ryan, R H
" Arnold, R H
" Bradner, R
Ser.-Farr. Spencer, J S
Cor. Square, H

APPENDIX.

Cor. Whitlow, F
" Harriott, J
" Carter, A
" Holliday, W J
" Pope, H B
" Parks, J H
" Markham, R J
Warrian, J S, Cor. S S
Allen, C C
Arnold, A F
Armstrong, B R
Ault. A E
Baker, S C
Barton, P
Beckwith, B M
Bell, W H
Bellamy, G A
Bettle, F
Berg, F
Bing, A B
Boulton, D E
Brand, W E
Brown, J J
Carter, G St. L
Church, J
Clarkson, J S
Cope. E C
Cummings, H M
Currie, C V
Dean, J W
Danby, E S
Dawson, W
DeBalinghard, J C
Dill, C E
Dix, M H
Dixon, J A
Douglas, H S
Doyle, F L
Drought, T
Drummond, L
Elmhurst, F J
Findley, J
Fraser, J R
Fowler, J
George, J M
Gray, A W
Hagen, T
Harvey, J J
Hawkins, J F
Hayden, D
Head, W R
Hawkins, W J
Hilder, A E
Hobbs, B
Hood, A Y
Hoy, C N
Hubbard, F W
Hyry, P
Irvine, J H
Jay, W J
Kaven, J
Keiller, J
Kelly, W D
Key, W

Kingsley, A R
Lawson, F W
Leavitt, A
Linden, T E
Little, A
Lobbin, J M
Lockhart, J H
Lord, J W
Macafee, T R
MacCaffrey, J J
Mackay, J D
Mackintosh, A C
McMillan, L C
McCulley, J R
McIntosh, A L
McIntyre, R
McClintock, G
McGregor, S J
McKelvey, A
Merchant, E
Mallory, A P
Marriott, T H
Marshall, H N
Massie, J O
Metzler, H
Miller, L R
Moody, H D
Morrison, D A
Morrison, F T
Moorehouse, A H
Mortimore, E A
Newton, C R R
Nilant, J
Othern, C R
Owen, C C
Palmer, H
Pawsey, A J
Pickworth, A
Ramsay, D L
Rae, J G
Rea, L A
Reid, W J
Reid, G
Ridley, T
Roberts, A H
Roberts, P C F
Robinson, G M
Rodger, W D
Rose, E P
Russell, R
Ryan, J T
Ryan, B
Ryan, W C
Ryerson, C E
Sanford, E A
Shea, I
Simpson, J
Sinclair, J
Snyder, W H
Stevenson, H T
Stevens, C
Sterrett, J S
Thompson, J
Thompson, S H

Thompson, T A
Treadhill, J
Todt, T F
Turner, A
Tylor, M H
Venning, W E
Wallace, F W
Ward, W H
White, J N
White, H B
Wilkinson, T
Wood, J T
Woods, R A
Wurtele, G E

ROYAL CANADIAN ARTILLERY

Com. Officer

Lt.-Col. C. W. Drury

Majors

J. A. G. Hudon
W. G. Hurdman
G. H. Ogilvie

Captains

R. Costigan
H. A. Panet
D. I. V. Eaton

Lieuts.

L. E. W. Irving
W. C Good
W. B. King
T. W. Van Tuyl
J. McCrea
A. T. Ogilvie
E. W. B. Morrison
J. N. S. Leslie
W. P. Murray

At. For Duty

H. J. Mackie

Adjutant.

H. C. Thacker

Med. Officer.

A. N. Worthington,

Vet. Officer

J. Massie

Medical Staff for General Service

L. Vaux

APPENDIX. 481

"C" Field Batt.

Gimblett, W H B.S.M
Bramah, W, Q.S.M.
Ser. McCully, A
" Shipton, W J
" Graham, R W
Ser. Slater, S
" Kiely, W
Harper, S, F. S.
Cor. Wherry, M E
" Gray, E
" Hilton, A
" Aldcroft, G
" Higginson, J
Bdr. Barnard, W
" Boyle, R
" Hope, R S
" Tennant, W H
" Marling, B
" Williams, O V
Trptr. Robert, E
Allan, W
Anderson, A
Andress, B
Andrews, W
Armstrong, A
Barker, H A
Baird, G A
Bell, P
Bell, Wm
Bellamy, R E
Benson, W
Birch, C E
Black, J
Blackley, F
Blackeby, A E
Bond, J C
Bradford, A
Burton, W
Cavins, B
Chandler, G
Clarkson, L
Cobb, R
Coffey, G
Cosby, N W
Davenport, J
Derwent, F C
Derwent, W R
Eastwood, W
Evans, H C
Eby, F
Fuller, C B
Gare, E C
Garry, J
Glenn, M
Goodbrand, A
Genge, R
George, W
Gillen, J W
Gillespie, W
Gordon, H
Gowdie, B
Gray, J W

Grant, J A
Green, J F
Greenfield, J K
Guest, J W
Hamill, W
Hamilton,
Hammond, D B
Hanson, C
Harrison, E
Higginson, J
Holbrooke, G
Holmes, W
Hopson, E H
Hopkinson, W
Howe, G
Hudson, E A P
Hudson, H J
Hughes, C
Hughes, E
Irving, C H
Irwin, J F
Isbister, M L
Jackson, W
Johns, J C M
Johnson, A S
Johnson, E
Kenny, E L
Laird, G A
Laidlaw, W C
LaValle, J
Letten, J
Loosemore, R
Maulthouse, H
McCalla, G B
McCamis, H
McCullough, J A
McCollum, W
McCoy, A L
McDonald, W E
McDonald, A
Macdonald, W J
Macdonald, F C
McEachern, C E
McGregor, D J
McIntyre, W
McKnight, W I
McKenzie, K
McLean, J
McNabb, J A
McQuarrie, A
Marling, T W B
Marsden, A
Marshall, G
Martin, J
Martin, T
Mathias, C
Miller, J W
Moore, A
Moffatt, J N
Munsie, H S
Murray, H
Newdick, N
Newnham, T F
Newton, S

Norwebb, S H S
O'Neill, R
O'Reilly, J A
Paget, O E
Patton, W.
Peasnell, A
Porteous, W
Powell, G
Price, J R
Raynor, H
Richardson, J R
Robertson, W J
Robertson, W A
Robinson, A
Robinson, G F
Ryder, E
Schell, G
Seward, F W
Shaw, J
Shaw, E
Shaw, E
Shedd, F
Smith, T
Smith, W J
Smythe, G
Speck, F
Stallwood, R J
Straley, W
Stringer, H L
Stokes, J T
Sweeney, G R
Sweet, C E
Tennent, W H
Thompson, C W
Tibbs, J W
Tranter, W D
Trotman, D
Turnbll, J
Tupper, R R
Turvey, A E
Turner, T
Tyner, E L
Vanorman, G
Walker, J A
Wallis, G T
Watson, L
Williams, S T
Williamson, W J S
Williams, A
Wilson, R
Wilson, H
Winger, J C
Wood, A H

"D" Field Batt.

McIntyre, W, S M
Slade, J, Q M S
Ser. Henderson, G
" Somers, L
" Lett, K
" Barnhill, J
" Stinson, W J
" Wood, B S

482 APPENDIX.

Cor. Kenealy, jr
 " Berube, J F X
 " Curzon, J
 " Ross, M H
 " Colter, C F
Bdr. Smith, W
 " Wagar, F E
 " Brown, G
 " Beaven, L E
 " Mattries, E E
Tptr. Barker, W
Abbs, F
Alexander, H
Anderson, J C
Ballantine, J
Bancroft, G R
Barber, S W
Bargette, T E
Barrett, G A
Bapty, W
Belford, J A
Beaven, N W
Bennett, T P
Bolton, D
Bott, E S
Boyle, R
Bradley, R
Bradley, S W
Bramah, E J
Bramah, T
Brown, J A
Burnham, H L
Cameron, H H
Campbell, J A
Cornett, H C
Cartledge, W R
Cause, H
Chisholm, D
Clarke, S A
Crowe, A R
Coogan, R J
Cormack, J
Daley, M J
Davey, W H G
Davey, F
Davidson, T C
Darlington, G W
Decasse, G
Denmark, J C
Denges, H D
Dickson, W
Donaghy, J A
Elliott, L
Evatt, E
Farquharson, G H
Fennell, C W
Flannigan, A
Forrest, H
Gamble, R B
Garnett, C G
Gavan, W
Gervan, J E
Gillespie, J
Glenn, W

Glenister, J
Gokey, F W
Gould, W J
Graham, G
Greene, E W
Griffin, T M
Hall, V A
Hare, W A
Hare, W R
Henry, B
Hinch, J E
Hodson, G G
Hopkins, W
Howard, G V W
Howe, H
Hugall, P
Hume, A H
Hutchinson, E
Igglesden, E
Irish, V A
Jackson, J
James, G W
Keehler, H
Kerr, I
Kerr, P A
Kidd, C
King, C
Kitcheman, H
Lacoste, J
Lafloor, S
Lamkin, W L
Lane, E
Lawes, G
Leach, W D
Lee, F E
Lefroy, C J A
LeRoy, L C
Lewis, C
Lyon, A
Macdonald, D A
McDonald, J C
McCuaig, A P
McGibbon, D
McKenzie, H
Mason, F W
Miller, A
Mills, C E
Mintram, A M
Moffatt, J N
Mole, C E
Moore, W J
Nicholson, H
O'Connor, T P
Ough, C R
Outram, F H
Pape, J J
Parker, G
Partridge, W R
Philp, J
Picot, G
Pryke,
Quinney, J
Quirenbach, H
Rendell, J W

Ray, J
Read, H
Richmond, A S
Robinson, A
Russell, D H N
Russell, J M
Sandercock, J
Sargent, A
Scollie, F L
Shepherd, G K
Shore, E R
Skirving, V A
Smith, W F
Somers, L
Sparrow, J E
Street, C
Street, J D
Stephenson, B
Sullivan, W H
Sutherland, W
Sutton, E
Symmes. H C
Taylor, T
Taylor, W
Thomas, H N
Thorne, W R
Tucker, W F
Tunstead, R F
Wallace, J
Walters, H
Welch, W
Wideman, W E
Williams, F W
Williams, M S P
Whitten, D A
Woolsey, E C
Wright, H A

"E" Field Batt.

O'Grady, J, S M
Clifford, W, Q M S
Cunningham, J, S F
Ser. Lyndon, A
 " Hughes, A T
 " Kruger, W A
 " Small, J
 " Agus, W
 " Jago, J R
Cor. Crockett, L
 " Brown, H M
 " Biggs, R J
 " Latimer, W
 " Black, S
 " Macdonald, J H
 " Laflamme, J
Bdr. Richardson, M
 " Daniels, G
 " MacGillivray, D
 " MacCormick, E F
 " Macaskill, J
 " Evans, P H
Tpr. Roberts, A
 " Bradley, G W

APPENDIX.

S.S. Cameron, N
" Fletcher, T E
" Stewart, D G
Wlr. O'Donnell, W
" Pedley, W
C'mkr. Pierce, H
" Macdonald, D D
Boyce, A
Byrne, T
Bartlett,
Beauchamp,
Blair, C D
Blyth, R B
Buck, F
Browning, J H
Borden, M
Boone, M
Brewer, F C
Carroll, T
Chesley, F T
Creighton, J F
Creighton, J A
Crocker, W J
Coombs, F E S
Cornish, H
Cunard, C W
Campbell, D
Craig, T
Dalton, D
Dysart, H B
Duncan, J
Duval, G T
Eustace, M
Everett, F H
Ferguson, W
Ferguson, D
Fielders, G W
Finnamore, B
Fletcher, G F
Fletcher, J E
Fraser, W D
Fradette, J G
Gordon, W S
Gorham, F R
Galliah, J J
Gilmour, E F
Grace, M T
Grey, H
Glew,

Gosselin, E
Hayden, J A
Hacquoil, E
Hall, H
Hague, J H
Hamley, J
Harrison, R A
Howard, A G
Hibbs, H H
Hill, T J
Horsfall, H W
Hughes, R
Huot, R
Jackson, R C
Jay, J
Johnson, G H
Jones, H
Jones, R
Kane, J
Kennedy, W
King, M R
Kirk, G P
Leigton, W L
Lightstone, H
Longee, M M
Lynn, W P
Macdonald, D
Macdonald, D J
Macdonald, J J
McLean, H G
McLean, R
Mackenzie, W A
Mackenzie, C L
Mackenzie, A
MacLeod, W P
MacLeod, G F
MacLoughlin, M J
Mason, B
Miller, R
Michaud, D
Molson, E A
Morrison, D
Morrison, S J
Mottram, A E
Munsey, S W
Myra, W A
Neild, J
Nethersole, P R
O'Handley, D

O'Reilly,
Pagean, C
Parker, G G
Perrin, J
Phillips, H
Phillips, G H
Pittman, J
Price, W E
Porteous,
Pugh, S
Randell, J T
Rawlings,
Reynolds, W H
Reus, J H
Roberts, W
Ross, G H
Ross, J G
Russell, G
Rutter, C W
Ryan, R J
Scott, I M
Searle, G
Sinclair, E H
Smith, R
Smith, A A
Smith, J W
Smith, J
Squires, J
State, A J
Stone, J
Taite, H B
Tapp, W
Tibbitts, A
Tibbitts, J
Tooker, T W
Vincent, T
Walsh, P
Wells, S
Welch, R S
Welsh, G E
Wilson, J W
Wilson, T R
Withers, S J
Woollard, C
Woods, J B
Woodeau, W J
Young, W B

APPENDIX C.

OFFICIAL LIST OF THE OFFICERS AND MEN OF
THE STRATHCONA'S HORSE, AND OF THE
EXTRA MEN FOR FIRST CONTINGENT
AND FOR STRATHCONA'S HORSE

The Strathconas and 100 men for First Contingent sailed from Halifax on the Monterey, March 17, and arrived at Cape Town, April 11. The reinforcement of fifty men for the Strathconas left Montreal, May 1, for England.

STRATHCONA HORSE

Lt.-Col.
S. B. Steele

2nd in Com.
R Belcher

Majors
A. E. Snyder
A. M. Jarvis
R. C. Laurie

Captains
D. M. Howard
G. W. Cameron
F. L. Cartwright

Lieuts.
R. H. B. Magee
F. Harper
J. A. Benyon
E. F. Mackie
P. Fall
M. H. White-Fraser
H. D. B. Ketchen
J. F. Macdonald
J. E. Leckie
R. M. Courtney
T. E. Pooley
A. E. Christie
A. W. Strange
G. E. Laidlaw
G. H. Kirkpatrick
S. H. Tobin

Qt. Master
W. Parker

Trsp't Officer
I. R. Snider

Med. Officer
C. B. Keenan

Vet. Officer
G. T. Stevenson

"A" Squadron.
Elliott, F, R S M
Crafter, A G, Q M S
McMillan, A, F Q M S
Hooper, H C L, S S M
Albert, E
Anderson, E F
Archer, W
Arnold, F G
Baker, W G
Barker, M
Barker, W J
Barrett, J
Bastien, H
Beckitt, F W
Bennett, J
Bland, E M
Bourne, R
Bradbury, J
Bride, F
Brigham, J R
Brooks, W
Brown, A M
Bullough, J
Burton, A E
Campbell, M G
Carpenter, J
Carroll, P E
Carson, T L
Cassidy, H E
Clark, G
Clark, E H
Common, A
Cosens, F C
Currie, W E E
Cuthbert, W
Dandy, C R
Daykin, A U
Deacon, B L
Dingan, A
Dickson, J
Dodd, G S
Doherty, G H
Donnan, J W
Drever, A
Dunsford, H
Dunsmore, F C
Edwards, E H
Ewing, A
Evans, J
Farmer, J T
Fisher, C W D
Fletcher, R
Flotten, P
Fraser, R N
Gammond, C
Garner, A C
Gilroy, H
Glass, N
Goodburn, O
Gooding, J E P
Gordon, R

APPENDIX. 485

Gowler, A W
Gregory, T
Grestock, H
Griffith, J J
Gurney, W B L
Harley, J A
Harris, M R
Hathorne, W
Hazeldine, F R
Henderson, J J
Hogarth, W R
Hudson, W
Inkster, J
Irwin, H M
Irwin, F
Jackson, W P
Johnston, J D
Keeling, J H
Kempster, H
Kermode, J O
King, W J
Kirkpatrick, A
Lambert, J S
Lamont, B
Locke, C
Lorsch, A B
Lowe, A A R
Lyle H
Macdonnell, K C
Machen, S R
Martin, R W
Matthews, F A W
Maveety, J D
McAlonen, R
McArthur, J H
McGillvray, A
McLaren, G
McLean, G
McLeod, W R
McLoy, J
McNaught, J Y
Mills, T
Milligan, W
Moberley, G A
Morrison, J H
Munroe, H S
Murphy, W M
Neville, J F
Nicks, J
Norquay, A
Norris, F
Nyblett, R W
Orr, F W
Page, C F
Palmer, P S
Palmer, G S
Parker, H
Parker, J
Perkins, G
Powell, F N
Ramsay, D
Reid, J
Richardson, A H L
Robinson, A

Rooke, C W
Rooke, R P
Ross, J T
Rushe, M J
Sabine, H E
Sawyer, W L
Saxby, H B
Sayce, W
Scott, L B
Scott, W
Skirving, G M
Smith, R W
Sinnington, A
Stanier, C Y
Starke, T B
Steadman, C D
Stevenson, A T
Stocker, J R
Stuart, A W
Stutt, W
Sutherland, A
Terry, N F
Thompson, H C
Thorne, A
Thornton, E
Thomas, C F
Townsend, P H
Traill, W M
Treston, J
Trelevan, A
Van Stan, A
Wade, R
Ward, J
Watson, A
Webb, E
Webb, H
Wemyss, D N
Wilkins, H
Wyndham, H S
Zimmer, W J

"B" Squadron

Steele, S J, S S M
A'Court, A W H
Abbott, W R
Allison, D
Anderson, J L
Armstrong, J F
Armstrong, J E
Banks, E M
Bannes, P
Barton, M E
Beaumont, T E
Bentham, W
Beresford, W P
Bingham, H B
Bertram, C F
Blick, C A
Bradley, R H
Brothers, J
Brown, H S
Brown, A S
Bull, J V

Burdett, A H
Burgess, D
Callin, T A
Campbell, N M
Carson, W
Clayton, A
Condon, F B
Corbett, W
Cronyn, E S
Cross, J R
Crozier, J A
Cruikshank, C
Cumming, F
Dalglish, A
Deane, J
Dick, M F
Dickinson, D
Donaldson, A S
Douglas, F C A
Down, G
Dupen, A E
Dunn F J
Eastmead, —
Edmundson, T L
Edwards, A J
Edwards, R H
Fawcett, N
Fennell, —
Flintoff, W
Ford, J
Fortey, A
Freezer, J R
Gamsby, G
Ganesford, W F
Gillies, A
Gilmour, J F
Grobil, A C
Graham, C H
Grey, W
Hall, F A
Hardwick, M D K
Hardy, A
Hart, C A
Haylett, J
Hayes, R P
Hicks, R C
Hobson J
Inglis, R C
Irwin, H
Jackson, H
Jameson, T
Jenkins, A
Kerr, G T
Kindrew, C E
Lafferty, W
Laidlaw, C E
Lamb, A
Leder, B
Lee, H A
Lewis, T A
Lewis, F C
Lindsay, A P
Linton, R
Loney, M F

486   APPENDIX.

Lowry, W A
Lowe, S
Lynch, W G
Macdonald, J R
Macdonald, A D
Madge, F T
Mansell, M
Martin, H
Martin, L A
Matallal, A
McDonald, G A
McDonald, R S
McClay, R
McCormack, E
McMillan, T
McNichol, A
McNair, E W C
McNeil, F J
McRae, D
McElray, G E
McIntosh, E
McKeage, F O E
McKinley, M
McKugo, G
Miller, A
Milne, A
Mitchell. G
Moir, R H
Mulligan, F
Murphy, E D
Newman, F G
Niblock, B L
Nichol, H F
Nichol, D
Paul, J
Pearce, R G
Pearce, E J
Pearson, A
Pinder, E G J
Percy, H N
Perry, T
Peyto, E W
Phillips, J W
Pillans, R B
Playfair, W S
Poole, H
Poole, F
Purvis, A S
Quick, H H
Rackham, W
Reed, W E
Rice-Jones, I E C
Robson, J S
Rogers, H M
Ross, A M
Routh, G F
Saddington, W
Scott, H H
Scott, F W
Shuckburgh, W C
Sharples, W A
Shaw, C W
Shiles, T
Simpson, T

Skinner, A
Smiley, S
Smith, J
Somerton, W
Spratt, A
Stewart, J S
Stranger, B
Swanston, C
Sutherland, R
Thomas, G D
Thompson, F
Tegart, H
Townshend, N S
Tucker, P H
Vernon, A A
Waite, J T
Walker, J C
Walker, B G
Watts, C C M
Watts, A H
White, S A
Watson, A
Whiteley, F C
Whitehead, C A W
Wilby, A W R
Wilkin, W
Watson, B
Wilson, F
Wilson, D
Williams, T H A
Woods, W T
Woodward, W
Woodward, A J
Wragge, E C
Wright, T W H
Wright, H H
Wyse, D
Yemen, N W
Yule, B

"C" Squadron

Hynes, J, S S M
Abbott, J
Agar, G S
Albert, G
Allan, P K
Armstrong, J W
Bell, P W W
Bell, W H
Bolton, N T
Bonner, L A
Bousfield, J
Bowers. G A
Brent, W
Brixton, J
Broadbent, E R
Burke, B
Cameron, N C J
Castelaine, L
Chancellor, E V
Childers, H C
Clarke, W F
Cochrane, R L

Cook, W
Cotterill, C W
Cree, A H
Curtis, E F E
Custance, T F M
Daley, H M
D'Amour, A P
Dawson, W H N
Davis, R S
Deering, R
Duncan, C J
Dunn, F T
Dunn, T
Edwards, W
Elliott, J
Ellis, F W
Eyre, G
Fader, G J
Fall, C S
Fanning, W
Faulder, E R
Fernie, W L
Fernie, M
Fisher, J C
Foster, J M
Fraser, J A
Fraser, H
Fraser, W
Fuller, J W
Fuller, J
Halcro, A J
Hall, A
Hambly, G
Hammond, R B L
Harding, J E
Harper, W H
Harris, C C
Harris, C B
Hawes, H
Haynes, W T
Hazel, G
Hicks, H J
Hirsch, J
Hulbert, T
Humfrey, W H
Hunter, E T
Graham, W F
Griffin, J
Grogan, R N
Ingram, W H
Jackson, C F
Johnson, A W
Johnston, H R
Jones, A
Jones, E E
Kearney, J
Kelly, S A J
Kennedy, J
Kerr, F
Ledingham, G W
Lee, B H
Lefroy, L B
Lindsay, W E
Lockhart, F O

APPENDIX.

Logan, A E H
Malalne, J H
McAllister, D
McDonald, A
McDonald, G A
McDonnell, C R
McDuff, J
McKenzie, A W
McMullen, J H
McRae, D J
McCullough, R J
Melton, E J
Monteith, W E
Morgan, H E
Murray, E
Murray, J W
Nash, J F P
Nesbitt, J L
Nicholson, C J
Norton, F
Norton, C
Noury, H W
O'Brien, A W
Ogilby, W L
O'Hearn, W
Oldham, P
Orchard, E A
Palmer, R H
Parkes, F C
Pearson, A C
Peterson, C
Parham, H J
Pettigrew, J
Pinkerton, T A
Powell, C J
Press, A
Pym, T M L
Radwell, A
Rennie, C
Robson, W
Routh, P
Ryan, J
St. George, B A
Seymour, E
Shaw, R
Shaw, A J M
Stillingfleet, H C
Simon, A B J
Skene, J G
Simpson, P E
Spencer, J
Squires, C
Strickland, C S
Swift, T
Switzer, P
Simmill, J
Swinburn, A
Tennant, C
Thomas, I
Thomas, H
Tuson, J
Venner, R P
Warren, F F
West, W

Wiggins, H J
Wilkie, J H
Winearls, R A
Winkle, W C
Wright, S
Woodhouse, F W B

REINFORCEMENTS

To Replace Casualities in the Field.

Capt. Carpenter, A E
" Winter, C F
" Boyd, A J
Aitken, R C
Anderson, S
Arbuckle, G A
Ardagh, H V
Austin, E F
Bailey, P
Barnstead, F E
Beecher, A V
Boulter, J W
Brown, H G
Browne, H G
Burrett, G H
Butler, J
Cameron, R W
Cameron, A R H
Cowardine, W H
Convey, J
Cook, W C
Coombs, W E
Dare, E
Dodds, J H F
Doucet, R P
Drum, A
Dunlop, F W
Eaton, W
Edmondson, W A
Edwards, W
Evans, A
Evans, W J
Fairweather, P
Ford, J
Fraser, J A
Gerhardt, F
Geen, E D F
Gladwin, J S
Gurney, T F
Hall, A J
Harne, R
Harris, W M
Hodgins, H A
Holloway, H B
Hooper, W H
Horan, H J
Howe, J
Hulme, T H
Jackson, L F V
Jones, J
Kennedy, D R

Kirk, R J
Lake, F A
Lamden, J
Lillie, C W
Lucas, L W
Lutes, B
Macbeth, T L
Mackay, J D
Mackellar, A
McCarthy, V O
McCormick, A S
McDonald, N
McDonald, M
McEachern, W A
McKerrihan, J R D
McNaughton, F M
Miller, C J
Milliken, J B
Mills, T
Moodie, G H
Mudge, H
Munnis, C H
Nicholson, J D
Nixon, C J
Pardee, J
Pay, A
Pepper, J T
Phillips, H
Pigot, J A
Playfair, S B
Price, E H
Proud, W J
Puddifer, W
Rattray, E E
Robertson, D
Robertson, J M
Russell, P
Scott, H C
Scott, C C
Sinclair, A
Smith, C L
Tennant, J
Tierney, G V
Turnbull, D
Walters, M P
Wandless, J F
Watson, A H
Webber, M E
Webster, P G A
Welch, G H
Wilson, J J
Wolfe, P
Wright, T M

REINFORCEMENTS STRATHCONA'S HORSE.

Officer.

Lt. Adamson

Anderson, G
Andrews, A M

Bartram, W B
Blakmore, P H J
Bruce, G B
Buchanan, J J
Burnet, D
Campbell, T G
Campbell, W J
Clampitt, J H
Carey, S T St. George
Cooke, J T
Della-Torre, W J
Fowler, W R
Gilbertson, J E
Greaves, J B
Green-Armytage, H R
Grey, C

Griffith, W R
Hall, C L
Henderson, T A
Heron, R B
Heygate, W A N
Howell, T E
Hunt, W de Vere
Hutchison, W
Isbester, C J
Macdougall, J G
Malet, C C
Martin, J S
McArthur, A
McDougall. J B
McMillan, C W
Morris, C

Myers, L
Palmer, W
Paton, S C
Preston, A J
Robertson, D
Robinson, H L
Rose, D W
Ritchie, D V
Shuttleworth, P P
Slocock, E F
Smith, W
Sparkes, F D
Sparks, G A S
Stewart, D M
Stringer, A
Tucker, R

DATES OF SAILING OF TRANSPORTS.

Second S. S. Battalion Royal Canadian Regiment, sailed 30th October, 1899, from Quebec, by "Sardinian."

"D" and "E" Batteries, Brigade Division Royal Canadian Artillery and Brigade Staff, sailed 21st January, 1900, from Halifax, by "Laurentian."

Second Battalion Canadian Mounted Rifles, sailed 27th January, 1900, from Halifax, by "Pomeranian."

First Battalion Canadian Mounted Rifles, and "C" Battery Royal Canadian Artillery, and artificers, sailed 21st February, 1900, from Halifax, by "Milwaukee."

Strathcona's Horse and Reinforcements 2nd S. S. Battalion Royal Canadian Regiment, sailed 17th March, 1900, from Halifax, by "Monterey."

Reinforcements for Strathcona's Horse, sailed 1st May, 1900 from Montreal, by "Vancouver."

APPENDIX D.

CANADIAN ROLL OF HONOR.

Official List of the Officers and Men of the Canadian Contingents who have died for Queen and Empire in South Africa:—

KILLED IN ACTION.

Capt. H. M. Arnold
" T. W. Chalmers
Lieut. M. G. Blanchard
" H. L. Borden
" J. E. Burch
Sergt. J. Brothers
" A. E. H. Logan
" W. Scott
" N. D. Builder

Corpl. W. S. Brady
" R. Goodfellow
" J. F. Morden
" J. R. Taylor
" F. W. Withers
" B. Withey
" E. A. Filson
Lance-Corp. W. G. Anderson

PRIVATES.

Arnold, F. G.
Banks, E. M.
Barry, C. H.
Burns, O. T.
Cotton, H.
Cruikshank, C.
Defoe, J.
Donegan, J. A.
Findlay, J. H.
Floyd, F. G. W.
Frost, W.
Jackson, C. E. E.
Jackson, W.
Jenkins, A.
Johnstone, G.
Johnston, Jos.
Jones, A.
Kerr, R. J.
Latimer, W.
Lee, B. H.
Leonard, G. W.
Lester, C.
Lewis, Z. R. E.
Living, F. J.
McCreary, P.

McQueen, A.
Manion, W. T.
Maundrill, A.
Neild, J.
Norris, F.
Orman, G.
Page, F. C.
Radcliffe, A.
Riggs, W. A.
Roy, A.
Scott, J. B.
Sievert, J.
Smith, R.
Somers, J. H.
Spence, D. M.
Taylor, R. D.
Thomas, C. T.
Todd, J.
Wasdell, F.
West, W.
White, H. B.
White, W.
Winyard, W.
Wiggins, H. J.

490 + XXII = 512.   APPENDIX.

DIED OF DISEASE OR ACCIDENT.

Capt. C. St. A. Pearse
Lieut. C. F. Harrison
Qtr.-Mstr.-Sergt., B. Hunt
(R.S.M.) F. Elliott

Sergt. A. Beattie
" P. Clunie
L.-Corpl., A. F. VanNorman

PRIVATES.

Adams, W. G.
Adams, J.
Ball, J. E.
Barr, H.
Bing, A. P.
Blight, W. S.
Bolt, H.
Bradley, G. W.
Bradley, R.
Brand, W. E.
Chappell, M. C.
Clements, H H.
Cooper, J. (Artificer)
Cotterill, C. W.
Cowen, C.
Crone, D. J.
Curphy, J.
Davis, L. S.
Deslauriers, E.
Duhamel, J. W.
Farrell, G.
Farley, J. E.
Forest, H.
Haines, W.
Hampton, W. J.
Harrison, R.
Hull, W. A.
Hunt, W. De V.

Irwin, R.
Kingsley, A. R.
Larue, L.
Lecontier, R.
Lett, R.
Liston, B.
MacMillan, D.
   (Artificer)
McNicol, A.
Merchant, E.
Moore, D.
Moore, W. J.
Mullins, E.
O'Kelly, G. M.
O'Reilly, E. P.
Picot, E.
Price, W. E.
Purcell, E. S.
Purcell, J. J.
Ramsay, D. L.
Raspberry, Jas.
Ross, W. J. H.
Shipp, T. P.
Simmill, J.
Smith, O.
Whitley, W. E.
Wood, William,
Woolcombe, T.
Zong, A. E.

SECOND EDITION.
Addenda.

DIED OF DISEASE OR ACCIDENT.

Lieut. F. H. C. Sutton
Sergt. E. Evatt

Sergt. L. J. Inglis
Trooper N. Hughes

PRIVATES.

Cancellor, V.
Ingram, W. H.

Dandy, C. R.
St. George, R. A.

Dunsmore, P. J.
Scott, L. B.

www.ingramcontent.com/pod-product-compliance
Lightning Source LLC
Chambersburg PA
CBHW051030160426
43193CB00010B/894